RAWN

WIT

Order and Disorder

LUCY HUTCHINSON

Order and Disorder

Edited by
David Norbrook

BLACKWELL
Publishers

Copyright © David Norbrook 2001

First published 2001

2 4 6 8 10 9 7 5 3 1

Blackwell Publishers Ltd
108 Cowley Road
Oxford OX4 1JF
UK

Blackwell Publishers Inc.
350 Main Street
Malden, Massachusetts 02148
USA

British Library Cataloguing in Publication Data
A CIP catalogue record for this book is available from the British Library.

Library of Congress Cataloging-in-Publication Data

Hutchinson, Lucy, b. 1620.
    Order and disorder / Lucy Hutchinson ; edited by David Norbrook.
        p.   cm.
    Includes bibliographical references.
    ISBN 0-631-22060-7 (alk. paper) – ISBN 0-631-22061-5 (pbk.: alk. paper)
        1. Bible. O.T. Genesis–History of Biblical events–Poetry.   2. Religious poetry, English.   3. Epic poetry, English.   I. Norbrook, David, 1950–   II. Title.
    PR3517.H85 O74 2001
    821'.4–dc21

                                                                00-010378

Typeset in 10½ on 12½ pt Galliard by Ace Filmsetting Ltd, Frome, Somerset
Printed in Great Britain by MPG Books, Bodmin, Cornwall

Contents

Illustrations

Abbreviations and References

All references throughout the edition are keyed to the Bibliography, pp. 265–272. The following frequently recurring abbreviations are noted here.

1679	The 1679 edition of *Order and Disorder*
CPW	*The Complete Prose Works of John Milton*, ed. Don M. Wolfe et al., 8 vols in 10 (New Haven, 1953–82)
DWW	Guillaume de Saluste, Sieur du Bartas, *The Divine Weeks and Works . . . translated by Josuah Sylvester*, ed. Susan Snyder, 2 vols (Oxford, 1979)
ed.	editor's emendation
'Elegies'	Lucy Hutchinson, 'Elegies' (Nottinghamshire Archives DD/HU2), in David Norbrook, 'Lucy Hutchinson's "Elegies" and the Situation of the Republican Woman Writer', *English Literary Renaissance*, 27 (1997), 468–521 (487–521)
JH	John Hutchinson
LH	Lucy Hutchinson
L	*Lucy Hutchinson's Translation of Lucretius: De rerum natura*, ed. Hugh de Quehen (London, 1996)
M	Lucy Hutchinson, *Memoirs of the Life of Colonel Hutchinson*, ed. Neil Keeble (London, 1995)
MS	The Yale manuscript of 'Order and Disorder'
MSC	Correction (in one of several hands) in the Yale manuscript of 'Order and Disorder'
PL	John Milton, *Paradise Lost*, ed. Alastair Fowler, 2nd edition (London and New York, 1998)
R	Lucy Hutchinson, 'On the Principles of the Christian

Religion', in *On the Principles of the Christian Religion, Addressed to her Daughter; and On Theology* (London, 1817)

T Lucy Hutchinson, 'On Theology' (translation from John Owen, *Theologoumena Pantodapa*), in *On the Principles of the Christian Religion, Addressed to her Daughter; and On Theology* (London, 1817)

Chronology

(Lucy Hutchinson's writings are in bold type)

1615   John Hutchinson born
        Marriage of LH's parents, Sir Allen Apsley and Lucy St
        John
1620   Lucy Apsley born in Tower of London
1630   Death of Sir Allen Apsley, LH's father
1632?   Lucy Apsley's mother marries Sir Leventhorpe Francke; they
        soon separate; Lucy Apsley spends much time staying with
        various relatives
1637   Lucy Apsley has begun composing **songs**, which win admi-
        ration of court musician Charles Coleman
1638   Lucy Apsley marries JH in London
1639   LH bears twin sons, Thomas and Edward
1640   Charles I summons first Parliament since 1629; dissolves
        'Short Parliament'; under strong pressure summons 'Long
        Parliament', which meets November and will continue un-
        til Cromwell dissolves it in April 1653; Parliament reverses
        many of Charles's civil and religious policies
1641   JH and LH move to family estate, Owthorpe, Notting-
        hamshire; LH bears third son, John
1642   Charles I, seeking a military solution against Parliament,
        raises standard at Nottingham; JH slowly becomes drawn
        into Parliamentary side; LH bears first daughter
1643   JH appointed governor of Nottingham Castle
1644–5 **Narrative chronicling JH's role in civil war**
1646   Charles I surrenders
1649   Execution of Charles I; JH a signatory of death warrant

Margaret Cavendish, Duchess of Newcastle, *The Blazing World*

1667   War with Netherlands, begun in 1665, ends in humiliation
        Milton, *Paradise Lost* printed
        Margaret Cavendish, Duchess of Newcastle, *Life of the Duke of Newcastle*

1667–8 **Statements of religious belief; verse fragments**

1668–74? **Autobiography**

1668   Marriage of daughter Barbara

1670   Secret Treaty of Dover: Charles II offers to become a Catholic in return for financial help from Louis XIV
        Milton, *History of Britain* published; consults with Anglesey

1671   Milton, *Samson Agonistes* and *Paradise Regained*

1672   LH sells Owthorpe estate to JH's half-brother Charles Hutchinson

1673   LH attends Owen's conventicle in London

1673–? **Translation from Owen, *Theologoumena Pantodapa*; treatise on religion addressed to daughter Barbara ?Resumes/begins work on *Order and Disorder***

1674   Death of Milton

1675   **Dedicates Lucretius translation to Earl of Anglesey**

1676   Government suppresses publication of Milton's *Christian Doctrine*

1678   Growing calls to exclude Charles II's Catholic brother James, Duke of York, from succession to throne
        LH involved in legal dispute over sale of Owthorpe

1679   New Parliament elected; Sir Allen Apsley, LH's brother and a member of the Duke of York's household, loses seat
        ***Order and Disorder*, first five books, printed**

1680   Conversion and death of Earl of Rochester

1681   Burial of LH at Owthorpe, October

1682   Anti-Whig reaction; Anglesey dismissed as Lord Privy Seal

1683   Burning of republican books at Oxford – including Milton and Owen

1684   Death of Sir Allen Apsley

1691   Anthony Wood, *Athenae Oxonienses*, attributes *Order and Disorder* to Apsley

Order and Disorder:
—— The Poem and its ——
Contexts

The poem here published in full for the first time has many claims to our interest. It is one of the first long poems by an English woman writer. As a poem in which a woman tackles the most controversial themes of the book of Genesis, it forms part of a debate in which current feminist critics and theologians are much involved. It throws new light on Milton's *Paradise Lost*. It opens up a neglected area of political and cultural history, providing a particularly strong corrective to the conventional view that literature after 1660 became firmly royalist. Quite apart from these considerations, it rises at its best to exciting poetry that deserves to be heard.

The author of *Order and Disorder*, Lucy Hutchinson (1620–81), has long been familiar to students of seventeenth-century history. Her biography of her husband, Colonel John Hutchinson, has become a standard point of reference. What has not been recognized is that her major, lifelong interest as a writer was in poetry. The prose *Memoirs* represented a diversion, however personally necessary, from that commitment. In her earlier years she composed the first complete English translation of a major classical epic, Lucretius's *The Nature of the Universe* (*De rerum natura*); in *Order and Disorder* she turned to a Biblical epic as ambitious as *Paradise Lost*.

Order and Disorder is not quite unknown to literary history. Its first five cantos were published, anonymously, in 1679. The poem was ascribed by the antiquarian Anthony Wood to Sir Allen Apsley, Lucy Hutchinson's brother. Wood's information was often unreliable, however, and there is a large amount of internal and external evidence to establish as the real author not the royalist Apsley, but his fiercely

Puritan sister. Briefly, part of the poem was amongst the manuscripts of Lucy Hutchinson in the care of the family in the 1730s; there are close parallels with passages from her Lucretius translation, her treatise on religion, and other verse fragments; a comparison with a database of twenty-five Restoration poets finds very strong parallels between *Order and Disorder* and known writings of Hutchinson, and equally strong divergences from the other authors; and the poem's political and theological outlook matches Hutchinson precisely (Norbrook 1999b, 2000a; Burrows and Craig). The 'Elegy' printed in the Appendix, which is undoubtedly Hutchinson's, is strikingly close in theme and style to *Order and Disorder*.

If this identification has not forced itself on readers, it is because Hutchinson was not a writer to place her own personality to the fore. Where her contemporary Margaret Cavendish, Duchess of Newcastle, constantly drew attention to herself and presented her own writings as incitements to changes in women's position, Hutchinson was much more guarded. Writings like Cavendish's are easy to assimilate with some common modern assumptions about gender and writing: that women's writing will be personal, emotional, self-expressive. Hutchinson was very far from the qualities often associated with 'feminine' writing. She tended to see individuals in terms of abstract constitutional theories; she vigorously defended one of the most abstract, impersonal and punitive theologies ever devised; though she does write sympathetically about the concerns of her female characters, these are subordinated to an ideological framework that privileges the male. Hutchinson's writings are in a fundamental sense passionately personal, but the passion was informed by a complex and coherent set of political and religious ideas, and this introduction will try to show how they drive the poem forward.

The lack of an assertive female voice may nevertheless be seen as part of the poem's politics: Hutchinson is readier than some of her contemporaries to accept, and defend, a position of female subordination. That is part of the truth; which is why it has been possible for a critic assuming Apsley's authorship to attack the 1679 poem as far more patriarchal than *Paradise Lost* (Wittreich). In the context of national politics, however, insisting on the poem's conservatism is highly misleading. Why, when the poem was printed in 1679, did she not put her name proudly on the title-page, like her contemporaries Aphra Behn, Margaret Cavendish and Katherine Philips? All those women repeatedly affirmed their loyalty to Charles II and celebrated his 'happy return' in 1660,

after years of revolution, as a great turning-point in politics and in literary culture. Conservative readers who disliked seeing women in print
were thus reassured that their writings were not going to shake the
foundations of society. These women's political views were sincerely
held (Barash ch. 2), but they did also serve as a counterweight to fears
of female unruliness. For Hutchinson, such a course would have been
unthinkable. At considerable personal risk, she remained loyal to the
values of the Puritan Revolution and committed to paper her belief that
the regime of Charles II was utterly illegitimate and would probably
bring down divine retribution. She declared that her husband had been
absolutely justified in signing the death warrant of Charles I. Such writings made her liable to the death penalty and their circulation had to be
carefully guarded; they belonged to a republican 'underground' which
has yet to be fully explored. The five cantos she did print, though less
outspoken than the manuscript portions of *Order and Disorder*, still
hint at her views. Had they appeared under the signature of a regicide's
wife, she would have provoked the kind of public scrutiny, and perhaps
searches of her papers, that she was anxious to avoid. She did not lack
courage, but nor did she court martyrdom. She believed that her political time would come again; in the meantime, she lived in the shadows.
As her third 'Elegy' reveals, however (see Appendix), she never acknowl-
edged the legitimacy of the regal sun who had confined her to those
shadows.

For the blind Milton, of course, the darkness of the Restoration world
was literal enough, and his political views were close to Hutchinson's.
Milton is often today seen as the arch-masculinist, identifying Eve's
responsibility for the Fall with a general female propensity to irrational-
ity in politics and religion. What would such a writer have made of a
woman poet who took it on herself to write an epic on the same subject? The two had their theological and political differences, but they
shared basic common principles and political aims. They had a mutual
friend, the Earl of Anglesey, to whom each of them entrusted sensitive
manuscripts. Whatever the precise chronological relationship between
Order and Disorder and *Paradise Lost*, it is fascinating to set these two
poems in dialogue. Does *Paradise Lost* reflect a Puritan disillusion with
politics, a retreat into the private world after 1660? The last two books
in particular are often seen as marking a weary quietism. Close comparison with *Order and Disorder*, which covers the same events at greater
length, gives a new perspective on that question. Does Milton's epic
express unorthodox views about the Trinity, and strongly anti-Calvinist

views about predestination? How can his views about divine kingship be squared with his republicanism? These questions, hotly debated in recent criticism, can be illuminated by comparison with this militantly Trinitarian and Calvinist epic. Does Milton overbalance the poem by the degree of imaginative investment in his Satan? Hutchinson's very different treatment of Satan offers a striking contrast. Is Milton unusually dismissive of women in his portrayal of Eve? Such issues have often been addressed by setting Milton's poetry against the discursive writings of the time; *Order and Disorder* offers the unique case of a woman poet who shared Milton's passionate engagement with the same concerns, and was ready to explore them in verse.

Lucy Hutchinson

Lucy Hutchinson's later life was darkened by personal and political crises. During the 1640s and 1650s, England had been convulsed by a civil war that toppled the monarchy, followed by a decade of uncertainty as differing Puritan factions struggled for control. For many contemporaries, then, 1660, when Charles II returned to England, was a welcome return of civil order. For Lucy Hutchinson, it was the prelude to disaster. On a national level, she and her husband had been committed to a godly republic, where the old state church, corrupted in their view by ritual and idolatry, would give way to freely tolerated voluntary Protestant congregations, while political corruption was kept at bay by strict limitations on personal power. With the old royalist county oligarchy in eclipse, the Hutchinsons had gained considerable status in their county, and their estate at Owthorpe in Nottinghamshire became a significant centre. The portrait by Robert Walker, dating from the late 1640s or early 1650s, shows Lucy Hutchinson with a laurel wreath, emblem of poetic achievement, in her lap. It was paired with a portrait of her husband in armour: her pen and his sword had worked in concert. Though her husband's hostility to Oliver Cromwell led him to withdraw from Parliament during the Protectorate, the couple enjoyed a life of relative opulence.

The restoration of Charles II brought with it the return of a persecuting state church and a return – though within limits that were yet to be fully defined – to the pre-war monarchical system. The change came home painfully on a personal level. Her husband had joined the small band who signed Charles I's death warrant in 1649. In 1660, that act placed his own life in peril. Many of the regicides were executed, and Milton's fate for a time hung in the balance. Lucy Hutchinson was confronted with agonizing choices. She intervened to try to save her husband's life, but faced his anger and guilt at having agreed to compromise his principles. In signing an undertaking to abstain from political action, he became deeply suspect to republicans without gaining the trust of royalists. For three years after his recantation, he lived in deep retirement, devoting himself to beautifying his estate and to intense study of the Scripture, which confirmed his belief in the justice of the Puritan 'good old cause'. It is possible that Lucy Hutchinson began *Order and Disorder* at this time. After her husband's death, she wrote nostalgically of Owthorpe as a kind of Eden ('Elegies' 7 and 12). The date on the only surviving manuscript of the poem is 1664. In the 1730s an excerpt from the poem with that date was circulating in the family, and Julius Hutchinson assumed that Eve's complaint after the Fall (5.401–42) was a personal lament by Lucy Hutchinson about her husband's imprisonment in the Tower.

If 1664 is the date of the entire poem, Hutchinson must have written very quickly, for she was probably working on Lucretius up until the late 1650s, and was busy bringing up her children; the last of the seven who survived was born in1662. In 1663 John Hutchinson was arrested for alleged involvement in an armed rising against Charles II. Having dishonoured himself, in his own eyes, by his submission, he now suffered the consequences facing those who had been active. Though never formally tried, he was detained and died in prison. For the next few years, Lucy Hutchinson dedicated herself to writing a memoir that would safeguard his memory against such charges. *Memoirs of the Life of Colonel Hutchinson* is particularly remarkable given the agonizing circumstances under which it was written. With a characteristic intellectual toughness, Lucy Hutchinson produced not just a personal testimonial to the head of her family but a sociological analysis, which placed his life in a larger pattern of social change and providential intervention. She channelled her more personal responses into a series of impassioned elegies – though here again her own grief is never separated for long from her anger against, and fiery denunciations of, the Restoration regime.

Her life did not end with the *Memoirs,* however. Even as she faced the growing burden of her husband's debts, selling off one estate after another, she also prepared the way for a new life as a writer. In 1667–8 she engaged in a detailed study of Calvin's *Institutes,* to which she added a statement of her own religious beliefs. The same manuscript contains fragments of verse which are very close in theme and wording to *Order and Disorder*. A treatise which she wrote after her daughter's marriage in 1668 contains close parallels with the poem (see note to 1.61–76 and elsewhere). Many other aspects of the poem seem to belong to a context considerably later than the early 1660s. There are several apparent parallels with *Paradise Lost*, implying a date after 1667, unless one writer had access to the other's manuscript – which, given their mutual friendship with Anglesey, is not wholly implausible. It is possible that the 1664 date on the manuscript has some other explanation, and that Eve's lament had been associated with 1664 because it was being read in isolation from the rest of the poem. *Order and Disorder* certainly reads like an entry into a new phase of writing, a dedication to a more explicitly Christian muse at a time when she was actively engaging herself in Biblical study.

Such study, of course, was hardly new to her. It was a normal feature of her household, and she had helped her husband's studies in his final imprisonment by bringing him commentaries on the Bible. Her own creative writings, however, had not been directly religious. As a young girl she had gained a reputation for love-songs (*M* 47). During the civil war she composed a vindication of her husband's political activities, which centred on struggles for power in Nottinghamshire. She had written a bitterly personal invective against the Cromwellian poet Edmund Waller (Hutchinson, Waller). Her translation of Lucretius had been a remarkable project for a Puritan, for she was bringing into the language a strongly atheistic or at least anti-superstitious text. Lucretius was being taken up by royalist exiles who admired his hostility to religious fanaticism (Barbour 1994). Hutchinson may in part have been motivated by a sense of emulation of a fellow-woman writer. Margaret Cavendish, Duchess of Newcastle, was a member of those royalist circles and was attracting attention with her atheistical, or at least highly sceptical, writings; her husband had been John Hutchinson's main royalist opponent during the civil war (Norbrook, forthcoming).

The preface to *Order and Disorder* strongly recants the Lucretius translation, self-consciously dedicating her to a new vocation as a divine poet. The preface is in itself a reworking of the dedication to Anglesey with which she had headed a new manuscript of her Lucretius translation in 1675. In both prefaces she laments having spent her earlier years in translating pagan poetry, and expresses her fears that if her Lucretius translation circulates further it will be guilty of corrupting her generation. She has written *Order and Disorder* as an antidote, to 'wash out all ugly impressions' of the fancies that had 'filled my brain'. Even without the modern associations of brainwashing, this is powerful language, and there is no doubting its sincerity. This does not necessarily mean, however, that it lacks a conventional element. Hutchinson situates herself in the long Christian tradition in which poets apologize for earlier, sinful works – a tradition that always had the effect of reminding readers of how powerful those earlier writings must have been for their ill effects to occasion such penitence. Such language was required of those who joined a Dissenting congregation; recognition and hatred of sin was itself a sign of regeneracy. In so actively repudiating her Lucretius – which she was, after all, further circulating even as she disparaged such circulation – she was also affirming her regeneration both as a Christian and as a writer. Though the poem was published anonymously, the language of the preface implies that she is confident a number of readers in her circle will recognize her identity.

What was that circle? Not a wide one, certainly. Given the subversiveness of her opinions, Lucy Hutchinson had to be very guarded about those with whom she shared them. But she had a small number of friends she knew and trusted. Her family was mainly royalist in sentiment – after the Restoration she was, in effect, the republican black sheep. Her brother, Sir Allen Apsley, was treasurer to the Duke of York, the king's brother, who was hated and feared by Puritans because he was a Catholic and also, in the absence of a legitimate heir, the successor to the throne. However, Apsley's cousin – and, some gossip had it, his mistress – Anne Wilmot, Countess of Rochester, was in Hutchinson's confidence, and possessed a manuscript of the poem. (Wilmot's more public friendship with Apsley probably explains why the poem became ascribed to him.) Though herself a continuing aspirant to courtly favour, the Countess was responsive to strong religious views, and deeply disturbed by her son's involvement in the licentious world of royal favourites. Lucy Hutchinson, republicanism apart, was a valuable counterweight to such tendencies.

We can more clearly understand Hutchinson's ambivalence about her Lucretius translation when we remember that Rochester himself was something of a disciple of Lucretius, and was encouraging his young niece, Anne Wharton, to voice sceptical views in her verse (Wharton). Hutchinson's parody of atheistic views in *Order and Disorder* could be a version of the kind of thing Rochester said:

Boasting they had attainèd to be wise
When they with manly courage could despise
Fictions of God and Hell that did control
A vulgar, weak, deluded, pious soul. (7.133–6)

Religion, on that view, was an instrument of social control; but for Hutchinson, such cynicism in fact colluded with tyranny, by undermining the major source of appeal against corrupt power. Losing sight of fixed, eternal principles, courtly atheists became playthings of fortune. They also, in Hutchinson's view, became liable to moral degeneracy, in which category she would have included Rochester's bisexuality; her account of the destruction of Sodom implies a bitter condemnation of love between men. When Rochester fell ill in 1680 and turned to religion, he became part of an ideological struggle in which opponents of the court eagerly claimed his recantation in their cause. His mother was in the forefront of those pressing him for a conversion. *Order and Disorder*, with its attacks on atheism and drunkenness, was the kind of weapon she might have deployed. The *Order and Disorder* preface hits at those who 'profess they think no poem can be good that shuts out drunkenness, and lasciviousness, and libelling satire, the themes of all their celebrated songs' – certainly the themes of Rochester's.

Another close friend of Hutchinson's was Arthur Annesley, Earl of Anglesey. Like the Countess, he did not share Hutchinson's political radicalism but respected her moral integrity and her dislike for many aspects of the Restoration regime. In his office as Lord Privy Seal, he tried to use his influence on behalf of the godly. An amateur historian himself, he is likely to have been confided with the *Memoirs*; presenting him with the Lucretius manuscript was itself a gesture of great trust, given her own strong ambivalence about the poem. Milton had consulted Anglesey over the publication of his *History of Britain*.

Anglesey's wife was a member of the congregation of the Congregationalist divine John Owen, and there is evidence that Hutchinson was close to Owen and attended his conventicle in London. This was something of a centre for Puritans nostalgic for the 'good old cause'. Owen had supported the regicide, and though he refrained from overt opposition to the Stuart monarchy, he devoted himself to challenging views that seemed likely to become its ideological foundations. In 1661 Owen published a stringent onslaught on the idea of a 'natural theology' that might provide a common ground for belief outside either Scripture or the traditions of the church. Such ideas appealed to the

'Latitudinarian' divines who were trying to effect some kind of compromise between different Protestant traditions; Owen was uncompromising in defending a high Calvinist position. Lucy Hutchinson translated
part of this work from Latin, and the view of early Hebrew history in
Order and Disorder is very close indeed to that presented by Owen. We
do not need to see her as a disciple of Owen: everything in her writings
makes it clear that she liked to think things out for herself – as she insists
in the preface to *Order and Disorder*, 'I have not studied to utter anything that I have not really taken in'. Owen did, however, represent for
her an admirable consistency, holding clearly through many political
vicissitudes to a set of principles she could endorse.

Hutchinson published the first five cantos of *Order and Disorder* in
1679, at a time when cautious figures like Owen and Anglesey were
finding themselves caught up in a large-scale movement of political
opposition. The crisis which erupted in 1678, and was still in process at
her death in October 1681, is normally described as the 'Exclusion
Crisis' because the immediate issue was a campaign to exclude the Duke
of York from the succession. Many of the key issues, however, revived
those of the 1640s (Scott). The 'Cavalier Parliament', which had stag-
gered on from 1661, was finally dissolved, and in 1679 the old censor-
ship restrictions lapsed, permitting a new opening of the press. Anglesey
and Owen became active in the coalition fighting York's succession.
For the more radical republicans, it might seem that the 'last gasps of
expiring monarchy' (*M* 61) were indeed at hand.

The family campaign to reform the Earl of Rochester formed part of
this ideological revival. Under these new circumstances – and the pressure of illness – the young ironist may have been readier to respond
sympathetically to the heavy moralism of his aunt's cousin. Lucy Hutchinson's voice was that of a generation whose experiences had been to-
tally different, and in her post-Restoration writings she expresses her
sense of alienation from this new world. She thought of herself as a
spirit speaking from beyond the grave in her own lifetime: 'the evil I
feared I now feel, if there be any sense in the dead; for however I appear
alive in my actions I would not have you believe it possible I could
survive your late fellow prisoner' (*M* 337). She records that after John
Hutchinson's death the prison where he had been detained was haunted
by 'a gentlewoman in mourning in such a habit as Mrs Hutchinson
used to wear there' (*M* 336). Lucy Hutchinson was writing in her lifetime about her own ghost. She looked back to her youth as to a time of
light and hope, thanking God that she was born

not in the midnight of popery, nor in the dawn of the gospel's restored
day, when light and shades were blended and almost undistinguished,
but when the Sun of truth was exalted in his progress and hastening
towards a meridian glory. (*M* 7)

By the time she wrote *Order and Disorder*, she was living in an era
of much more uncertain light, which she evoked in the transitional
passage between cantos 5 and 6, between unfallen and fallen worlds:

> When midnight is the blackest, day then breaks;
> But then the infant dawning's pleasant streaks,
> Charging through night's host, seem again put out
> In the tumultuous flying shadows' rout,
> Often pierced through with the encroaching light
> While shades and it maintain a doubtful fight. (6.1–6)

Were the shadows of her own time those of dusk and dawn? For all her
sense of belatedness, the political situation at the time of her death may
have led her to hope, at times at least, for a new dawn. Until recently it
has been thought that after completing the *Memoirs* Hutchinson lapsed
into despairing obscurity. *Order and Disorder* presents a very different
picture of the trajectory of her career, and more generally of the fortunes of republicanism after the Restoration.

Reading the Bible

We have seen that Hutchinson could be deeply suspicious of the powers of poetry to corrupt. Had that been all, it would have been surprising to find her continuing to write. Her preface helps to explain why
she nevertheless persevered: 'a great part of the Scripture was originally
written in verse'. This was an aspect of the Bible that had been obscured by the medieval church's use of a standard Latin translation in
prose. The Protestant Biblical scholarship which the Hutchinsons studied so intensely drew on humanist techniques of literary analysis. Early
modern educationalists disparaged the abstract, logic-based educational
system of the medieval universities and urged a heightened attention to
the arts of language. When this approach was transferred from pagan to
Scriptural texts, there were important consequences. Where medieval
commentary often looked behind the words for more general, allegorical meanings, Protestant commentary emphasized the literal sense,

assuming that behind each text was a specific author with the aim of influencing an audience as strongly as possible. John Hutchinson returned again and again to the Psalms, the pre-eminently poetic book of the Bible. He also loved Paul's letters, especially the epistle to the Romans, the centre of Calvinist predestinarian faith. They move from a colloquial idiom to rich and knotty imagery, with abrupt shifts of tone and theme, and are in some ways closer to poetry than to straightforward discursive prose. Lucy Hutchinson tells us that her husband's means of overcoming the difficulty of interpretation was to try to catch a consistent voice and occasion behind the text: he would 'read an epistle entirely at once, or as near together as he could, and he advised us also to do so; for he said the coherence and connexion of the parts, one with another . . . gave great light to the understanding of the soul' (*M* 328).

The book of Genesis exercises a more directly poetic fascination. Early modern scholars did not fully understand how much of the book was interspersed with passages of Hebrew verse, but they responded to the remarkable range of its styles, from the concrete and grotesque to the ceremonial and abstract. Modern scholars ascribe this variety to the fact that the five books, the Pentateuch, traditionally ascribed to Moses, in fact combined narratives by very different authors from different periods. In the first strands to be isolated, two different names for the deity are used, Yahweh and Elohim, giving rise to the labels 'J' and 'E' for their hypothetical authors. Later scholarship located a Priestly (P) and Deuteronomist (D) version, and a further author-figure, the Redactor (R), who brought the materials into their final order. In the P version of the creation, man and woman are created together, while in the J version Eve is created from Adam's rib. There are three very similar stories in which first Abraham and then Isaac pretends that his wife is his sister. Sarah's expulsion of Hagar is recounted twice. God's promises to Abraham are repeated several times, and there are many other minor discrepancies. To modern commentators the earthy, sometimes sardonic, style of the J version (for a striking modern rendition, see Bloom) is obviously very different from the repetitive, hieratic discourse of the P narrative.

If humanists were so interested in specific authorial voices, why did they not notice such discrepancies? In fact, recent textual work is reacting against the confidence of the earlier process of disintegration. Harold Bloom notes a vein of 'idealist anti-Semitism' in the assumption that the more concrete aspects of the narrative belong to a primitive strain which was later refined to bring it closer to a Christian narrative of progress from flesh to spirit (Bloom 21). Other scholars point out that the attempt to isolate so many distinct voices rests on nineteenth-century assumptions about literary realism and individualism that may not have held good for older forms of writing and interpretation; more subtle forms of unity can be found behind many alleged discrepancies (Fokkelman). Renaissance humanists, for all their interest in individual voices, were acutely aware of the need to change style and register for different rhetorical purposes, and they had less difficulty than the nineteenth century with the idea that Moses might have varied his styles in this way. In any period, indeed, literary scholars determined to prove that a given text is unified have been able to rise to the challenge.

It remains true, however, that in Hutchinson's own time there were early stirrings of a movement towards a historicist fragmentation of the Pentateuch. Hobbes's *Leviathan* (1651) had raised questions about Moses's authorship. In 1655 Isaac de la Peyrère had noted the discrepancy between the Priestly and Yahwist accounts of the creation and suggested that there were humans before Adam and Eve; he was also struck by incongruities over Sarah and Rebecca (Lods 30). Such questionings had reached Hutchinson's relatives; the Earl of Rochester was struck by the 'Incoherence of Style in the Scriptures, the odd Transitions, the seeming Contradictions' (Farley-Hills 65). Such an analysis was in accord with humanist principles of textual criticism which had long been applied to the transmission of classical texts, and with which Hutchinson had had to grapple in her own work on Lucretius. The problem for Hutchinson would have been that it was urged most vigorously by Catholic polemicists who wished to undermine the authority of Scripture as a ground for faith. Her associate John Owen, who was formidably learned in Hebrew and contemporary Biblical scholarship, vigorously defended that authority and attacked the new textual criticism (Bennett and Mandelbrote 182–3). For Owen and for Hutchinson, the book of Genesis was the work of one author, Moses.

An important qualification could be made, however: Moses had been inspired by the Holy Spirit, who had placed elements in the text which prophesied future events beyond his own awareness. Christians always had a strong investment in pushing away from a wholly literal reading of the Old Testament, since they wished to superimpose on that narrative a systematic foreshadowing of the story of Jesus: the historical events were also types of the future (15.227; cf. Bunyan xxxviii–xli). Puritans were especially fond of allegorizations of the love-poetry of the Song of Songs as foreshadowing Christ's love for the true church. *Order and*

Disorder is informed by such typological readings (e.g. 3.467–502).
Hutchinson often describes types as 'emblems', referring to the contemporary literary genre in which visual images were accompanied by
verbal explanations. She strongly believed that the 'covenant of grace',
given by God at Genesis 3.14–15, concealed in types the full core of the
Christian message, the coming of Christ whose grace alone could redeem humanity from the old 'covenant of works' (*R* 38, 52–5). There
was, then, no clear-cut distinction between Old and New Testaments:
the events of Genesis were quite as relevant for the believer as those of
the time of Christ.

Allegorization, however, for Hutchinson could only be pushed so
far. Owen saw himself as engaged in a twofold struggle: against Catho-
lics who claimed that the Scripture's truth was not self-evident because
of textual corruption and therefore needed the authority of the church,
and also against the more radical Protestant sects like the Quakers, who
claimed that the truth of Scripture was open to all through the impulse
of the Holy Spirit. Religious radicals engaged in more and more subjec-
tive allegorizations and interpretations of Scripture. Though Owen re-
sisted tendencies towards a rational religion, by the standards of
mid-century Puritanism he was himself a strongly rationalistic figure,
resistant to outbursts of enthusiasm. He tried with some difficulty to
steer the line between his own Independent belief in the Spirit and a
belief that some kind of objective consensus on interpretation was possible (Nuttall 10–14). Hutchinson often steers a similar course to Owen.
She reads certain key events typologically, as foreshadowing the apoca-
lyptic events she believes to be about to take place in her own time. At
other points, however, she tries to follow the literal sense closely and to
provide explanations of the human motivation of her characters. She
rationalizes the repeated events, such as the disguised wives. She shows
a sharp interest in the political implications of the events she narrates,
offering a kind of moralizing sociological history in her account of the
growing complexity of courtly societies and the struggles of the godly
to return to simplicity. For modern readers, the interest will lie as much
in the difficulties she has in reconciling discordant texts as in the means
by which she resolves them. Hutchinson was writing at a time when the
meaning and even the divine authority of Genesis could by no means
be taken for granted; defending her own version of the text was part of
a political as well as a religious struggle.

Biblical Verse

Hutchinson subtitled the first cantos of her poem 'Meditations upon the Creation and Fall, as it is recorded in the beginning of Genesis'. 'Meditations' implies a secondary form of writing, one whose main aim is not to tell a story but to summarize it and suspend the action to discourse on its meaning. Meditative poetry would normally adopt a plain, conversational idiom, and in her preface Hutchinson baldly declares that the poem lacks fancy and elevation of style. 'Fancy' is a word she normally uses with suspicion: fancy had led pagan poets and idolatrous Christians to confuse images with reality, signs with what they signified. Her guilt over her translation of Lucretius, and her decision to translate Owen's attacks on the pagan poets' corruption of pagan truth, testify to her genuine anxieties about the imagination. The most such a radical suspicion of the 'fancy' might seem to sanction is a bald paraphrase or stock moralizing.

Hutchinson's humility before her text, however, was not absolute. She trembled 'to think of turning Scripture into a romance', and attacked other divine poets who added to the text. She may have been hitting at Milton; the first critic to have commented on *Order and Disorder* regarded the poem as 'both an imitation of *Paradise Lost* and a veiled rebuke of Milton' (Moore 321; cf. Shawcross 251, Wittreich). For all her criticisms of 'invention', however, the preface dismissed with equal force those who attacked poetry altogether as partial witnesses, 'their genius not lying that way'. She made it clear that she thought her own genius did lie that way, and that such a genius was consonant with the Bible. Whether or not she began composing after *Paradise Lost*, she had ample precedents for composing divine poetry, and even for using pagan poetry in doing so. The creation was the greatest of all subjects, and Renaissance poets found it appropriate to adapt some of the devices pagan poets had used in their highest kind of poetry, the epic. There was a long tradition of poetic narratives of the six days of creation (hexameral epic). The most celebrated example was the *Divine Weeks and Works* (1578–84) of the French Protestant poet Guillaume de Saluste, Sieur du Bartas, whose translation by Josuah Sylvester became immensely popular in England, and was certainly read by Milton and Hutchinson. Sylvester's 'Second Week' includes all the Genesis material covered by Hutchinson. Du Bartas's highly mannered style adapted the elaborate verbal patterning of courtly verse-forms for a sacred subject.

Hutchinson is closer to Du Bartas than to the more allusive Milton in the degree of her reference to classical genres. Her extensive classical reading can, however, be traced in *Order and Disorder*. She imitated a passage from Virgil (10.71–8). She had shown especial interest in pagan poems whose subject-matter was in some ways closest to the creation story: Ovid's *Metamorphoses* and, of course, Lucretius's *De rerum natura*. She carries over some Latinisms, such as 'fragor' and 'congression', from Lucretius to *Order and Disorder*; though her style is less Latinate than Milton's, it has somewhat more 'elevations of style' than she claims in the preface. At 14.47–85 she recycles a lengthy passage from her own translation of Ovid, where the classical conventions are very conspicuous. The poem's recurrent visions of the world's final doom draw in equal measure on Biblical apocalypse and on Lucretius's descriptions of the destruction of the world. When she encounters a military episode in canto 11, she writes a mini-epic with a series of extended similes; and epic similes become increasingly common in the later parts of the poem. In dealing with the courtship of Jacob and Rachel, she turns to the conventions of pastoral.

Despite such classicizing touches, however, Scripture is at the core of the poem. Even the apparently secondary role of a commentary would have seemed much more positive in circles where knowledge of the Bible was second nature. Protestant Biblicism ultimately undermined the distinction between primary text and secondary commentary. The thorough – and often politicized – annotations of the Geneva Bible (1560), the Puritans' favourite English version, were a main factor for its popularity. Today the differences between Geneva and the 1611 Authorized Version are assessed in terms of relative literary merit, but in this period less attention was often paid to which version was used than to the annotations (Norton I.213; Hutchinson's wording seems to be closer to the Authorized Version, but she may have used one of the mid-century editions which included the Geneva annotations). During the 1640s and 1650s plans were made for a wholly new Bible translation that would come closer to the Hebrew wording, though the project lapsed (Bennett and Mandelbrote 174). In such a milieu, it is not surprising that the prophetess Anna Trapnel, a woman of humble background and education, was able to discourse for hours at a time, rendering her own meditations and paraphrases of Scripture in verse. Hutchinson's approach to prophecy is much more guarded, but she relies on a readership who will pick up her allusions.

The richness of the effect emerges in a very small sample from the

first few lines of the poem. The first gloss, denouncing man for rebel-
ling against God's will, may seem a politically conservative statement.
The gloss, however, refers us to Isaiah 10.5–7, where God, having lamented the injustice of rulers, denounces the idolatrous King
Sennacherib and declares that he will be cut down. Throughout the
poem, the word 'rebellion' will apply to the defenders of kingly power.
The next gloss refers us to Ecclesiastes 6.10: 'That which hath been is
named already, and it is known that it is man: neither may he contend
with him that is mightier than he'. We can thus recognize Hutchinson's 'They must be broken who with power contend' as a direct reworking of the text, reminding us that all humans, from kings to the
humblest, are small in the sight of God. We then return to Isaiah (27.4),
with another declaration of the immense power God may, even if he
does not, deploy: 'Fury is not in me: who would set the briers and
thorns against me in battle? I would go through them, I would burn
them together.' We are then referred to Genesis 45.4–5, where Jacob
reproaches his brothers for selling him into Egypt. Hutchinson's circle
would have recognized the Egyptian captivity as a standard parallel to
the return of Charles II. We then turn to the New Testament, to Acts
2.23: 'Him, being delivered by the determinate counsel and foreknowl-
edge of God, ye have taken, and by wicked hands have crucified and
slain'. This comes from the gathering of the apostles shortly after Christ's
death, when the Holy Spirit rushes on them and they are able miraculously to speak in all languages. Peter is delivering the central message
of the crucifixion; in stressing that it was predetermined, he is also offering support for those, like Hutchinson, who affirmed the doctrine of
predestination. To round off this group of citations we return to Genesis and to its final chapter (50.20), where Joseph receives and acts on
Jacob's dying command that he forgive his brothers the wrong they did
him: 'ye thought evil against me; but God meant it unto good'.

These annotations comment on a long verse paragraph where
Hutchinson stresses that man rebels against God but that all such attempts are ultimately futile and serve the divine end. The annotations
form a series of counterpoints. They give a sharp political resonance to
the more abstract generalizations of the verse; here as often throughout
the printed text, Hutchinson introduces subversive elements in the
margins. The annotations also bring home the recurrent theme of predestination. The second Genesis quotation balances the beginning of
this Genesis poem by looking forward to the end; and it hints at an
attitude to the unregenerate royalists that is conciliatory but at the same

time contemptuous, implying that in the long term their attempts to imprison the godly will never prevail. The Acts quotation introduces the theme of Pentecost, of language and prophecy, at the moment where the poet is expressing her own desire to prophesy:

> my weak sense with the too glorious rays
> Is struck with such confusion that I find
> Only the world's first Chaos in my mind,
> Where light and beauty lie wrapped up in seed
> And cannot be from the dark prison freed
> Except that Power by whom the world was made
> My soul in her imperfect strugglings aid,
> Her rude conceptions into forms dispose,
> And words impart which may those forms disclose. (1.22–30)

It thus becomes hard to separate the text from the margin, what is inside the poem from what is outside: Hutchinson has internalized Scripture so deeply that in one sense all that she writes is quotation, while in another sense she shows herself well aware that quotation is a pointed, deliberate art. Despite the humility expected of an invocation, the fact that the poem continues indicates her belief that the Spirit has indeed touched her, has enabled her to interpret Scripture and to communicate its power in language. The parallel between spiritual order and what we would today term aesthetic qualities recurs again and again in the first five cantos. In the description of the Trinity, the Holy Spirit is associated with 'universal Beauty' (1.122). Owen recalled that the Greek word for the world was *kósmos*, an adorned thing, and associated the Holy Spirit with the process of adorning that completed the world (2.72 and note). The poem's title thus indicates an aspiration to evoke the divine order through beauty of form.

The idea that nature is God's art, that there is a harmony between the natural universe and artistic creation, was a Renaissance commonplace. Given her acute awareness of the corruptions and distortions of the Fall, however, Hutchinson is much less confident that such a harmony has been maintained. Beyond Scripture, it is in the natural world that she finds the clearest images of the divine order, and *Order and Disorder* frequently vindicates nature against art:

> Scorn, princes, your embroidered canopies
> And painted roofs: the poor whom you despise
> With far more ravishing delight are fed

> While various clouds sail o'er th'unhousèd head,
> And their heaved eyes with nobler scenes present
> Than your poetic courtiers can invent. (2.21–6)

The extravagant masques of the Stuart court had regularly culminated in scenes where the courtiers descended on cloud-machines from a painted heaven. Hutchinson prefers real clouds. The

> peacock's gaudy train
> More beautifully is by nature dressed
> Than art can make it on the gallant's crest. (2.312–14)

Such sharp antitheses, however, simplify the issues: Hutchinson's poem is far from artless, and it benefits from her long training in writing verse. Even when she declares in the preface that 'I would rather breathe forth grace cordially than words artificially', she shows herself able to parody the style she rejects, using a careful antithesis capped by the figure of homoioteleuton (rhyme). It remains true that like Milton and some other mid-century Puritan republicans (Norbrook 1999a), she does favour a poetics of the sublime, of the open and various, as opposed to a fixed beauty that is associated with the court. Milton had brought out the political connotations of this sublimity by declaring that his blank verse had freed English poetry from the bondage of rhyme. He thus gave an ideological charge to his resistance to the metrical form that was becoming dominant in the mid-century, the closed iambic pentameter couplet, with each two-line unit offering a single idea or syntactic unit. Hutchinson does use pentameter couplets, but they tend not to be closed. Her metre is a little more irregular than was becoming the norm, with a number of shorter, tetrameter lines; some of the corrections made in the manuscript were rather fussy attempts to make the verse flow more smoothly. There are indications that Hutchinson, like Milton, could give political resonances to metre: her line-by-line parody of Waller's panegyric to Cromwell associates his smooth verse with political servility and calls for the English to resist the 'paper Crowne' (Hutchinson, Waller 85). 'Wit', a quality that was increasingly associated with the play of the heroic couplet, is condemned again and again in the poem. *Order and Disorder* does not have quite the openness of Milton's long verse paragraphs, but Hutchinson often aims at comparable effects. She is fond of anaphora, the repetition of a phrase at the beginning of a line or couplet, to allow her to carry on a theme over many clauses. Her syntax can seem very loose, though normally the long sentences do find a syntactic closure.

Against this pressure to openness, however, Hutchinson's verse does show a countervailing interest in epigrammatic concision. (Though perhaps these qualities are not so different when seen as developing different aspects of parallelism in Biblical style; see Kugel.) In *Order and Disorder*, as in the *Memoirs*, she reveals a gift for the sharp satirical maxim. Such distilled malice was common in the period's verse, where wit was increasingly identified as the gift of expressing sharp contrasts through skilful deployment of balance in the couplet. In Hutchinson's case, however, the verbal skill is invested with such confidence in echoing a divine judgement that it can be disconcerting. Both tendencies can be found in such set-pieces as her description of the Flood. Here Hutchinson is at once appalled and energized by the vision of a complete dissolution of form, a reversion to a primal chaos: 'Thought cannot reach this universal rack' (7.485); 'All turned to sea, sea bounded with no shore' (7.510). The long panoramas of formlessness alternate with moments of epigrammatic compression which come to imply a strong, predestined divine pattern behind the apparent chaos: 'They that bore all else down kept up that boat' (7.440); 'With spirits sinking as the waters swelled' (7.446). The waters 'At once both death and sepulture bestow' (7.452). The sinners become locked in their closed minds; God does not so much impose an external punishment as allow them to rush into claustrophobic confinement of their own making:

> Some unto Heaven would have raised their cries
> But only Hell and Death rolled in their eyes. (7.469–70)

In this harsh presentation of divine wrath, Hutchinson reserves compassion for the animals:

> The wet birds flew about but no rest found,
> Their food, their groves, their nests, their perches
>   drowned. (7.481–2)

Here the rhetorical figure of zeugma brings home their remorselessly narrowing options. Another version of the same figure moves us back from pathos to judgement:

> The gallants' scarves and feathers, soldiers' tents,
> The poor man's rags and princes' ornaments,

> The silken curtains and the women's veils,
> Themselves too borne up with light robes like sails,
> Bandied in sport awhile, at last did all
> Equally lost into the hazard fall. (7.491–6)

The delayed main verb springs the trap waiting for vanity. In this destructive moment the birds' feathers are no more useful than the gallants', but as at many points in the poem, the contrast between birds' simplicity and humans' vainglory retains force, here as the contrast between pathos and bathos.

Yet human artifice can be redeemed. The moment when the floodwaters recede prompts one of the poem's most remarkable similes:

> As women, with their proud fantastic care
> Ne'er satisfied, set and unset their hair
> A thousand times ere they themselves can please:
> So played the soft gales on the varied seas,
> Now crisped, now marbled the successive streams,
> Now weaved them into bredes with glittering beams
> Whose penetrations changed their sullen hue
> While gold appeared through the transparent blue.
>   What will full Restoration be, if this
> But the first daybreak of God's favour is? (8.19–28)

Here female cosmetics form part of the divine *kósmos*, the process of restoring the lost image of God. Redeemed only in part, as 'proud fantastic' reminds us; but the movement of the poetry brings us away from that stock moralism. The hair-setting becomes an image of redemption insofar as it is a process, not a static product; it thus images the divine sublimity that transcends a merely vainglorious or courtly beauty.

The Divine Narrative

Hutchinson finds in Genesis a story of

> Infinite wisdom plotting with free grace,
> Even by man's fall, th'advance of human race. (5.71–2)

God's repeated interventions in history always look forward to the future, insisting that however unclear it may seem, it will follow a coherent pattern. The poem may prefer the open air to the closed rooms of palaces, but its title reveals a deep longing for a coherent order in the universe. To this extent the poem is a conscious reversal of what she found in Lucretius. In the dedication to her translation Hutchinson repeatedly counterposes the divine order to the oscillations she found in contemporary philosophy, where the absence of a governing divine principle left a Nature reduced either to a blindly regular mechanism or to sheer randomness:

> They that make the incorruptible God part of a corruptible world, and chaine up his absolute freedome of will to a fatall Necessity; That make nature, which only is the Order God hath sett in his workes, to be God himselfe . . . deniing that determinate wise Councell and Order of things they could not dive into . . . reviving the foppish casuall dance of attoms, and deniing the Soveraigne Wisedome of God in the greate Designe of the whole Universe and every creature in it, and his eternall Omnipotence, exerting it selfe in the production of all things, according to his most wise and fixed purpose, and his most gratious, ever active Providence, upholding, ordering and governing the whole Creation, and conducting all that appeares most casuall to us and our narrow comprehensions, to the accomplishment of those just ends for which they were made. (*L* 24)

It is very important for Hutchinson that 'Whatever doth to mortal men befall / Not casual is' (5.676–7), that God 'orders all our human accidents' (8.404, cf. 12.295–6).

For Hutchinson, a crucial part of that order is the Calvinist doctrine of double predestination. In his preference for the reprobate Esau, Isaac,

> governed by a partial blind affection,
> Stuck to that choice which was not God's election,
> Who in their birth, without a reason shown,
> To make his boundless will and free grace known,
> Declared love to the one, to th'other hate;
> Well pleased in this, makes that a reprobate;
> Before the children had done good or ill
> Reveals the intent of his free-moving will,
> And manifests his great prerogative
> O'er all the creatures who their being derive
> From his vast power which, bounded by no laws,
> Acts freely without any second cause[.] (18.77–88)

This formulation is so uncompromising that it may remind some readers of Robert Burns's *reductio ad absurdum* of Calvinism in 'Holy Willie's Prayer'. Calvin had used the story of Jacob and Esau in precisely this way. On this view, God's covenant of grace, proclaimed at Genesis 3.15, made a sharp distinction: the seed of the woman, the elect, would be saved; the seed of the serpent, the reprobate, would be damned.

That doctrine did indeed offer reassurance against a world of complete accident. It was also, for Protestants hostile to the traditional rituals and church hierarchies, a bedrock of certainty against merely human traditions, a point from which they could be contested. The price was a heavy one, however. If, as Milton put it, God was the 'author' of the universe (*PL* 3.374), in Calvinist terms the divine narrative was one with a clear plot but lacking any clear connection between plot and character. In his *Christian Doctrine* (*CPW* VI.168–202) Milton challenged the Calvinist reading of Jacob and Esau, questioning the justice of a God who could act so arbitrarily. The Calvinist God resembled an absolutist king, acting out of pure, arbitrary will, choosing his favourites without any apparent reference to their qualities of character. The God of Hutchinson's poem certainly lives up to that paradigm (cf. *Order and Disorder* 1.249, 3.241, 4.148, 5.391, 18.252). Her 'They must be broken who with power contend' (1.17) places God's power before his goodness. To justify God's goodness, Milton structures his narrative in *Paradise Lost* to show an enormously complex series of connections between human actions and divine judgement. Given that the Fall is the central explanation of why humanity becomes blinded and closed to divine grace, it is striking how little attention Hutchinson pays to its process: it is narrated in a few lines, and attention passes to the minority who thereafter are chosen to find their way beyond the limitations it imposes on human understanding and will. Hutchinson insists again and again that fallen humanity is blinded, and lays stress on the physical blinding of Lot's assailants and on the failing eyesight of Isaac. God, it may seem, has blinded humanity and blamed them for their blindness. The blind Milton, struggling with his concerns about divine justice, was less ready to use the metaphor of blindness in such a wholly negative way (cf. *PL* 3.35).

Yet Hutchinson's divine narrative offers its own, distinct interest. Genesis was an intriguing text for a Calvinist imagination precisely because of its instabilities in characterization. The differing processes of composition outlined above had left its leading figures as perplexing enigmas, raising more questions about the connections between their actions and their divine favour than the text clearly answered. Hutchinson is fascinated by the way characters' Hebrew names prophesy their destiny, but often in an unexpected or ironic manner. It is at the point where Milton reduces his Genesis narration to condensed summary, in Book 11, that Hutchinson becomes most closely involved in the story. In the end, even if we 'can but make a wild uncertain guess' about motivations (5.261), Hutchinson is convinced that God's actions can be justified. Her characters come at moments of truth to a recognition, however imperfect, of a link between their own nature and divine judgement. The Flood's victims reach a painful flash of self-knowledge; the elect, like the animals entering the ark,

> Are wholly led by God yet unconstrained;
> Nor wrought like stocks, by his sure fixed decree,
> But by his free grace set at liberty
> From Hell's mists, which benight the natural mind,
> And lust's strong fetters, which the free will bind,
> And are, as here, by soft impulses led . . . (7.350–5)

The consolation offered here is a limited one: the will is free only because God allows it to become so, and the comparison with animals – even in a poem as sympathetic to the animal world as *Order and Disorder* – is not particularly good for human self-esteem. Hutchinson's focus here, as so often, is on the consequences not for humanity but for the understanding of God. He is both fixed and boundless, offering at once a sublime openness and an utter certainty. The poem finds an imaginative power in God's remoteness. Where Milton allows the reader to soar beyond human confines and see the cosmos from the divine point of view, Hutchinson remains on the ground and is fascinated by the rare moments when the mists part, when the monochrome world of the fallen vision is touched by the divine image.

These contrasts between the two poets may not have been so evident in their time as they are today. Hutchinson would probably not have known of Milton's *Christian Doctrine*, which remained in manuscript. There he attacked traditional doctrines of the Trinity, which Hutchinson was so keen to uphold that she extended discussion in revision (1.85–122). In *Paradise Lost*, however, a particular position on the Trinity and on predestination is harder to pin down with complete certainty, and recent scholars have raised some questions about his authorship of *Christian Doctrine*. The question can be put in a new light by setting the discussion of predestation by Milton's God (*PL* 3.80–343) against comparable passages in Hutchinson. It is hard to imagine Hutchinson's

God suggesting even in a subordinate phrase that his predestination could not overrule man's will (*PL* 3.114–15). But Milton may have been at least partly drawn towards the idea of a predestined elect by its power to offer the confidence and assurance of belonging to a spiritual elite (Fallon). For Hutchinson, holding on to predestination was to hold on to one of the central platforms of the original Puritan coalition that had led the struggle against Charles I (Tyacke). Hutchinson would have hoped herself to earn the comment made by a royalist after the Restoration that her husband was 'the most unchanged person of the party' (*M* 289, 299, 312), and her theology was a powerful support. With the same political defiance, whatever the differences in theological emphasis, Milton declared that 'I sing . . . unchanged' (*PL* 7.24).

Politics and Religion

The title, *Order and Disorder*, may arouse expectations of a strongly conservative politics. We should remember that it may not have been Hutchinson's preferred title for the poem as a whole. The 1679 subtitle is *Or, the World made and Undone. Being Meditations upon the Creation and the Fall, as it is recorded in the beginning of Genesis*. The manuscript, which takes the story long beyond the Fall, is headed merely 'Genesis Chap. 1st. Canto 1st.', and we cannot be sure that Hutchinson would have retained *Order and Disorder* as the overall title. It is, however, appropriate on many different levels. As has been seen, it evokes the activity of the Spirit in creating the universe. In more philosophical terms, it takes up the concerns of the Lucretius dedication, stressing that nature is God's order in his works. That order, however, is by no means easy to detect: men and women have been created in the image of God, but the Fall has darkened the image. Hutchinson uses a series of characteristic terms – masks, veils, shadows – to indicate her belief that true knowledge has been lost. The universe, once a mirror of divine order, had become a distorting mirror; fallen humanity turned the reflections into idols and lost sight of what they reflected. Hutchinson firmly rejected the natural theologians' view that true religion could be derived from rational knowledge of the universe: while the natural world did reveal enough of God to make idolatry and atheism 'unexcusable' (*R* 11; cf. Romans 1.20), divine grace alone produced salvation. In the treatise she translated, Owen traced the fall and restoration of theology from Adam through Cain to Noah, Abraham and Moses, consistently

stressing the human propensity to idolatry unless divine grace inter-
venes (*T*; Owen, *Works* XVI).

Hutchinson's emphasis on the blindness of fallen humanity gives her
poem its political bite. Again and again she suggests that the existing
political order is very far from reflecting the divine order. On the contrary, God works in history by breaking down the idols of false orders
and elevating the humble who seem to their enemies to be themselves
forces of disorder. The poem was printed, as has been seen, in a period
of intensifying ideological conflict, and the title may perhaps have reassured the licenser, the fiercely conservative Sir Roger L'Estrange, that
the poem was on the right side. Even in the more guarded first part,
however, there are clear indications that all is not well with the existing
social order. Already in line 11 a note is sounded that will recur throughout the poem: God condemns rebellion, but, as will emerge more and
more strongly, the true rebels are not the republicans and Dissenters
with whom figures like L'Estrange would have identified the word, but
the royalists and churchmen who are persecuting them. The Sabbath
was ordained

> That kings, hence taught, might in their realms maintain
> Fair order, serving those whom they command
> As guardians, not as owners of the land,
> Not being set there to pluck up and destroy
> Those plants whose culture should their cares employ. (3.634–8)

The sentiments here are parallel to the treatise to her daughter:

> Who gave him these lands, these ancestors, but God the greate proprie-
> tor of heaven and earth, and all things in them? Shall he, then, lift up
> himselfe before the Lord, usurping to himselfe a propriety in what God
> hath only committed to his stewardship . . .? (*R* 106)

After the Fall, in a strikingly provocative phrase, 'Hell's gloomy princes'
are 'the World's rulers made' (5.101); amongst the glosses is Psalm 2,
in which the kings of the earth set themselves against the heavenly king.
Such corrupt kings are the puppets of the fallen angels, of whom at least
it can be said that 'An order too there is in their dire state', that they
seek a 'common interest . . . Lest civil wars should make their empire
fall' (4.85–94). The emphasis on 'common interest' is characteristically
republican: Lucy Hutchinson believed that the 'prouder great ones'
despised 'the common interest', whose triumph would ultimately lead

to a 'free commonwealth' (*M* 33, 61). The sentiment here is very close
to Milton's

> Oh shame to men! Devil with devil damned
> Firm concord hold, men only disagree
> Of creatures rational . . . (*PL* 2.496–8)

   Milton presents the fallen angels as becoming more and more king-
like; but he also repeatedly describes God and the Son as kings, and this
has generated much debate about the possible incongruities with his
republican ideology. Milton, strongly distinguishing his God from a
Calvinist deity whom he associates with absolutism, tries to make him
give the reasons for his actions as clearly as possible. Hutchinson's God
is a more mysterious and remote figure; this may make his actions seem
more arbitrary, but it also lessens concrete associations with worldly
rulers. Hutchinson lays the emphasis on God's following constitutional
forms. Before he creates Adam he calls a 'sacred council' in himself
(3.4), to magnify the event but also with the implication that constitutional forms are important. Before he passes judgement he refuses to
punish sinners without hearing them, as an example to future rulers
(5.7–12). Adam is God's 'viceroy'; he is termed a king, but only in
relation to his domination over other creatures, not over humans, and
he is accountable when he exercises his charge badly.
   For Hutchinson, God's unfailing will is not a worrying parallel with
absolutism but a source of strength in her criticism of corrupt secular
orders. If everything were subject to chance, there would be nowhere
to appeal to against tyranny; but she writes with an unshakeable faith in
a God whose transcendence can question any secular power. Again and
again God's predestination is set in opposition to expected successions
in a worldly hierarchy. History is a drama of salvation and damnation in
which those who gain power and glory in the short term may very well
be those marked for the deepest damnation. Hutchinson's use of Genesis parallels here is very close to her republican contemporary Edmund
Ludlow, who invoked figures like Cain, Hagar and Esau as prefiguring
the evils of the Restoration regime (Ludlow 1193, 1205, 1214–15).
   Cain's murder of Abel is the first of a series of events which establish
a sharp discrepancy between human and divine orders. Eve, promised
that her seed will redeem the Fall, hopes that her first-born son will be
the redeemer and names him accordingly. On the contrary, her son will
in fact be the first great human enemy of redemption. The first-born

son slays his younger brother, in an episode that Hutchinson associates with the predatory domination of the nobles over the commons:

> alas, from whence
> Doth vain nobility raise its pretence[.] (6.61–2)

His arrogance is also associated with religious ritualism: Cain's 'pompous hecatombs' are emptily 'formal', while Abel's simpler observance is sincere. Cain becomes an image of the 'formal hypocrite' who dominates in today's church (6.331). The split between external form and inner truth has become extreme: Cain has been exiled by God, but in his own terms he flourishes, and establishes the first great city, the capital of the Worldly State. Adam begets a new son, Seth, who founds a rival Holy State. It is notable that at this early stage of history, when there are no magistrates (6.246), there is no clear distinction between church and state: the antithesis between Worldly State and Holy State is also that between 'The little Church and the World's larger State' (5.89). Religious observances take place with no formal organization or place of worship, and the visible church is effectively made up of the followers of the leading patriarchs.

Despite the poem's suspicion of ecclesiastical organizations, a notable difference from Milton is the recurrent interest in the godly as a church. Hutchinson, though opposed to a coercive state church, was more sympathetic than Milton to worship in existing public congregations. She sees all such groupings, however, as vulnerable once they grow in worldly glory: the Holy State remains pure only so long as it shuns cities, arts and sensual pleasures (6.443), and is steadily corrupted by Satan. That corruption manifests itself in increased atheism: even though God sustains the natural order, a constant reminder of his providence, the atheists 'miscalled his high help accident' (7.154). Only a tiny number remain immune: Enoch, who is elevated directly to heaven, and Noah and his family, who survive the Flood with which God punishes the rest of the world.

Even when the Flood recedes and the poem has a moment of relish for the beauties of the natural world, the political edge remains. The poem looks forward to the final restoration of God's image at the millennium, the return of a true vision of the cosmic order as the blindness of sin is banished to Hell and the elect are redeemed:

> What will full Restoration be, if this
> But the first daybreak of God's favour is? (8.27–8)

Hutchinson lyrically evokes the beauty of this restoration; but her Calvinist sense of damnation is never absent:

> But while you think his threatened day far off,
> Like the old world you these predictions scoff,
> With blindness cursed; not to recover sight
> Till your own dreadful flames be your first light. (8.59–62)

The mountains showing first from the waters are compared to princes and noblemen, and in a provocative challenge to the Restoration political order, she warns that 'Your new-restorèd glory shall expire' unless they rule well (8.51). Here Hutchinson plays on different senses of 'restoration'. For royalists, of course, the word mainly referred to Charles II's return in 1660; but Puritan republicans appealed to Isaiah 1.26, 'I will restore thy judges as at the first', as well as to Machiavelli's more secular theory, to present reform as an act of restoration, a return to first principles. Hence the provocative inscription on the republic's Great Seal: 'In the First Year of Freedom by God's Blessing Restored'. Lucy Hutchinson declared that her husband had worn his sword 'not to destroy but to restore' ('Elegies' 4.10). Those who aspire to regal and aristocratic glory are ultimately doomed. The poem then moves to the church, with an extended allegory of the church-ark as infested by hypocrites, the creatures of Cain's Worldly State, punishing the godly saints – a clear reference to the treatment of Dissenters in the Restoration world. To the raven is counterposed the peaceful dove of the Gospel. It is at this pivotal moment of the poem, where the references to divine and political 'restoration' are clustered most closely (see also 8.108, 249, 401), that the narrator's voice comes to the fore again for a moment in an address to the dove (8.189–94). As long as rebels defy God's order, however, harsher tones than the dove's are needed, and the canto ends with sharp defiance against the powers that be: those

> whom God did institute to curb
> The world's disorders, did the world disturb,
> To murder and to slaughter led whole hosts
> Till searèd conscience made their crimes their boast[.] (8.321–4)

The ensuing canto challenges one of the mainsprings of monarchist ideology. Noah's survival as sole source of political authority after the Flood had been taken by the absolutist Sir Robert Filmer as evidence that God approved kingship above all other forms of government (Filmer

7–8). The episode in which Ham laughed at his drunkenness, and was punished with a curse on his descendants, was normally taken as a warning against irreverent subjects who pried into the mysteries of state. The embarrassing fact that the royal paragon had laid himself open to this treatment was normally glossed over. Hutchinson begins her narration as if she were in line with royalist traditions, with an extended praise of the good effects of wine that might be expected to extenuate Noah's intemperance; but this adds to the shocking effect when she proceeds to attack excessive drinking in terms that link it with the general ideological deformities she found in Restoration culture, notably atheism (9.163–4), and graphically declares that 'Noah, the new world's monarch, here lies drunk' (9.187). The curse of Ham is, then, not primarily an attack on democracy – though, like Milton, she does open the way to reading it as a curse of peoples considered inferior, a potential validation of slavery (Jablonski).

In discussing Noah's judgement of Ham, Hutchinson draws a parallel with David's treatment of his son Absalom, who had killed his half-brother Amnon for murdering his sister, was indulged by his father and subsequently rebelled against him (2 Samuel 13–19). This comparison, rather indirect in relation to Noah, applied closely to Charles II. His illegitimate son James, Duke of Monmouth, was involved in a murderous debauch in 1671 and escaped punishment, his father having prepared a remarkable document pardoning him from 'all Murders, Homicides, & Felonyes, whatsoever' (Fea 49); Dryden compared this event to the murder of Amnon in his *Absalom and Achitophel* (1681). It is instructive to compare Hutchinson's ideological stance with Dryden's (though she would almost certainly have been writing before the publication of his satire). Dryden, defending Charles, suggests that the blame resides with the son for ingratitude to paternal indulgence. Hutchinson takes a much harsher line: a debauched sovereign must punish a sinful child to avoid favouritism; yet in the end he must take the main responsibility for setting such a bad example: 'Who sentences his sons his own sins dooms' (9.236). Though rebellion against kings is here condemned, no credit redounds on the monarch.

The onslaught on monarchy continues in canto 10, where we are forcefully reminded that

> the first mighty monarchs of the earth
> From Noah's graceless son derived their birth. (10.19–20)

Nimrod, the first tyrant, was descended from Ham. Still more than Noah in his drunkenness, he was an embarrassing figure for royalists, and republicans often invoked him as typifying the real spirit of monarchy. Milton denounced him for ending 'fair equality, fraternal state' (*PL* 12.26), leading a contemporary reader to conclude that he 'holds to his old [republican] Principle' (Norbrook 1999a 467); Hutchinson's portrayal is more explicit, though not without subtlety in its reworking of a Virgilian simile (10.71–8). Though Hutchinson is faithful enough to Genesis to admit the occasional figure of a virtuous monarch, kingship is normally associated with the corrupt rule of the Worldly State, which receives its due punishment in the spectacular episode of the destruction of Sodom (canto 13).

To such tyrants the poem counterposes the figure of Abraham, the divinely appointed ancestor of Christ. He shows his allegiance to the Holy State by his lack of pomp and ceremony. Filmer claimed that Abraham was a king, noting that he had led troops in battle (Genesis 14). Republicans retorted that he had fought not as a political leader but as a leader of volunteers, and noted that he treated his nephew Lot as an equal rather than a subject (Sidney 24–5, Locke 236–40, Ludlow 1194). *Order and Disorder* fully accords with that interpretation. Though Abraham's military exploits are related, the poem emphasizes that he fought only to help his kinsman Lot (11.359–62), and relishes the lack of pretension in those early days (12.239–42). The contrast between holy simplicity and worldly artifice recurs in Abraham's religion. He establishes not a temple but a simple grove as a place of worship. There was a contemporary parallel: the Restoration anti-Dissenting legislation had forced unauthorized religious meetings to take place in the open air. Hutchinson contrasts such simplicity with the idolatrous pomp that tries to confine the boundless God in local places (15.27–38). This will one day be the site of the great temple at Jerusalem; Hutchinson looks forward less to its days of glory than to its destruction (15.197–200). Once Christ's sacrifice has been made, the truest temples will be in believers' hearts. Once again the concept of divine restoration is played against the ethos of the English Restoration: God had no need to 're-store' the physical temple (15.261). In making this the point of the poem where Christ is most explicitly foreseen, Hutchinson emphasizes how God's order may cut violently across the dynastic order of succession and primogeniture: 'religion changes styles of things' (15.131).

Such a challenge to primogeniture follows in the story of Jacob and Esau. In the revolutionary period some radicals challenged the traditional priority of the eldest son in English inheritance, claiming equal treatment for sons (though not for daughters); they often invoked the divine preference for Jacob over Esau (Hill 1993 203–15). As in the Cain-Abel story, it is the younger brother who is righteous. Hutchinson develops the political and religious aspects of this story well beyond the commentaries. Esau aligns himself with the Worldly State, falling in love with a woman from an idolatrous court. Though the Biblical Esau smells pungently of the fields, Hutchinson gives him a more aristocratic perfume. His speech in which he insists on his right to love freely (17.484–500) might have come from one of the Restoration heroic plays in which libertines attacked social convention (his loved one's name, Aholibamah, happens to have the polysyllabic ring beloved of heroic dramatists). Esau's courtships of idolators – and his hypocritical attempts to nullify their effects by marrying a saint – manifest his pre-destined reprobation, which cuts right across his father's expectations of the lawful inheritance. Hutchinson uses an epic simile drawn from civil war to describe his emotions when he finds that he has blessed the younger son (18.111–21). The war between the elect and the reprobate is an eternal civil war, running right through families as well as states, and the right side may not be the obvious one. Though Jacob will have the inheritance, however, he sets off with no material goods and will earn his living, and his marriages, by menial labours; such simplicity is superior to the troubles of princes (19.9–12), whose blindness is contrasted with his 'penetrating sight' (19.71). The poem breaks off before Jacob's full story can be told.

Order and Disorder, then, shows a continued disrespect for monarchical order; it shares in the radical inheritance of the English Revolution. Hutchinson's is in many ways a levelling imagination, undercutting human hierarchies. Her sympathy for the oppressed extends to animals. The early modern period saw a new emphasis on humanity's role as steward of the natural order, which led to a more humanitarian view of relations with animals, and a suspicion of hawking and hunting (Thomas 154–62). In line with these developments, Hutchinson insists that God's providence extends to animals as well as man (7.541–2), presents hunting as a mark of the Fall, and takes a lead in attacking cock-fighting (variant at 5.346) – a sport which had been banned in 1654 but was reintroduced at the Restoration. The topic of birds always tempts her into digression.

The human victims of the Flood, however, receive no such compassion. In its severe Calvinism, the poem is marked as much by a harsh withholding of sympathy as by its enlargement. The levelling is often largely negative, in calling for divine judgement on sinners in all levels of society:

> Down every channel ran a mixèd flood,
> With streams of royal and of common blood.
> The princes were with vulgar prisoners chained,
> Lords with their slaves one servitude sustained. (15.197–200)

The poet is concerned with the reduction of princes to slaves rather than with the evils of slavery; and it is not hard to see how the idea of a cursed seed, here deployed against the nobility, might be used to justify the enslavement of subject peoples. On the verge of an age of colonization, Hutchinson's narrative of the expansion of the chosen people through the world and their suppression of their enemies has harsh resonances. She can unsettle worldly hierarchies in speaking of 'vulgar angels' (1.267), but can also dismiss the rebellious impulses of 'vulgar breasts' (12.83). We shall not, then, be surprised to find similar tensions in her treatment of the status of women.

Eve's Version? Genesis, Women and the Woman Writer

Genesis contains texts which have become standard declarations of female subordination, and have received extensive critique and analysis from feminist scholars (Bach; Brenner; Jeansonne; Nyquist). It also contains some of the Bible's most striking portrayals of independent-minded women – leading Harold Bloom provocatively if unpersuasively to suggest that the J-text, often regarded as the most misogynistic, must have been the work of a woman. In *Order and Disorder* we do have a telling of the story by a woman, and it is particularly interesting to see how she steers her narrative.

For women readers, the first two chapters of Genesis have stood as an obstacle fronting the whole Bible. At Genesis 1.26–7 God declares, 'Let us make man in our image, after our likeness . . . So God created man in his own image, in the image of God created he him; male and female created he them'. At 2.18–25 he announces that he will give Adam a helper; Adam names the other creatures but none of them is suitable; God sends him to sleep and creates Eve out of one of his ribs.

From these narratives, Paul formed the view that women must learn in silence with subjection but should not teach or usurp authority over men (1 Corinthians 11.7–9, 1 Timothy 2.11–14).

Medieval and Renaissance women writers had often tried to reinterpret the Genesis story to counter its misogynistic use (Gössman), and in England such reinterpretations can be found in figures like Aemilia Lanyer and Rachel Speght (Lewalski 1993 165–9, 231–2). In Lucy Hutchinson's time Quaker women were continuing the challenge, setting the spirit above the authority of Scripture. Hutchinson did not go this far, however; for her and her husband, Paul's letters were the key to the deepest meanings of Scripture, and she would have been wholly resistant to questioning their literal authority. And yet, if his injunctions are interpreted in their narrowest form, writing *Order and Disorder* at all – even in order to versify them – was itself a challenge to Pauline authority. In finding a space for her own voice and for the voices of other women, Hutchinson proceeds by a more indirect path than the Quakers. If on one level Paul insists on rigid hierarchy, on another level he presents the true faith as a challenge to all traditions; faith cuts across any received value, and he supports this belief with repeated examples from Genesis (e.g. Galatians 4.22–4, Isaac and Ishmael; Hebrews 11 – then thought to be by Paul). As has been seen, in political terms this commitment to faith enables Hutchinson to contest the traditions of kingship. It is less easy to establish how far the same commitment allows her to contest traditions of female subordination.

Hutchinson's treatment of Genesis necessarily encounters complexities that Paul's brief allusions avoided. Modern scholarship recognizes that chapters 1 and 2 represent very different, 'Priestly' and 'Yahwist', accounts of the creation. In the first version, man and woman are created at the same time; and most early modern commentators rejected Paul's implication that man alone was made in God's image. If that was true, it was so not at the level of the soul but only within the sphere of the household, where the man should hold authority. The Yahwist narrative gives Adam the priority, in his ability to name the creatures and in Eve's being formed from his body. From the Renaissance to the present day, commentators seeking to emphasize female subordination have tended to read the Yahwist into the Priestly account, while their opponents have tried to privilege the Priestly account (Nyquist). Tensions between the two emphases can be found within Genesis 1.27 in the shift from 'him' to 'them'.

In her treatise to her daughter, Hutchinson deploys aspects of each version. She inverts the order of the shift from singular to plural: 'God created man, male and female, in his own image and likenesse . . . happie in the favour of God . . . who had made him Lord of all the other creatures' (*R* 28). She thus implies that 'him' from now on applies to both sexes (as was indeed the case in Hebrew: '*Adam* was the common name of man & woman', Ainsworth at Genesis 5.1). She omits the story of the rib. In describing the Fall, she places less emphasis on Eve in particular than on the couple's common culpability: 'The chiefe of these [devils] seduced Eve, and she her husband . . . and this they committed willingly' (*R* 33–4). In the explication of the 'sinne of Adam', no further mention is made of Eve.

In her poem, Hutchinson is committed to following the details of the Genesis narrative, and the pressure of the Yahwist story leads her to revise her recounting of the earlier version, leaving woman for a later appearance:

> 'Let us', said God, 'with sovereign power endued,
> Make man after our own similitude,
> Let him our sacred impressed image bear,
> Ruling o'er all in earth and sea and air.' (3.9–12)

The poem proceeds with a long discussion of Adam as king of the created world. Hutchinson follows the Yahwist narrative as Adam names the creatures and God puts him to sleep and takes Eve from his rib to be his companion. Her commentary, however, draws an unusual conclusion. The creation from the rib, rather than illustrating inferiority (Adam has asked for an 'equal mate', 3.233), is used to show mankind's dependency: as she was formed in his sleep, so human actions are helpless without divine grace. In declaring that 'Our choicest mercies out of dead wombs flow' (3.466), Hutchinson gives a new twist to the Biblical imagery of male birth. The poem proceeds by splicing together Priestly and Yahwist narratives. Genesis 1.29–30, in which dominion is offered to both Adam and Eve, is paraphrased at 3.417–28; the passage then jumps to Genesis 2.16–17, a warning given to Adam before Eve's creation. We then move back to Eve in a further allegorization: Adam and Eve figure Christ and the Gospel Church, deploying the symbolism of the Song of Songs. In a poem where female beauty is often associated with illusion and temptation, this introduction of the naked Eve as a revelation of divine truth offers a counterweight. It is Adam who is described in terms of his physical beauty, in strikingly androgynous terms (3.111–22). The narrative now jumps back to the Priestly version of the end of the sixth day (1.21, 2.1), but this time Eve has dropped out of the picture: Adam alone is viceroy of God (3.503–24).

These inconsistencies suggest that Hutchinson was having some difficulty in finding a place for Eve, under the dual pressure of Pauline interpretation and her inhibitions about going beyond the Biblical text; but the experiment is interesting. Eve comes into focus only with the temptation scene, and here Paul is very much in evidence: her fault springs from her failure to listen to her husband. The marginal note refers us to 2 Timothy 3.6, which warns against reprobates who 'creep into houses, and lead captive silly women laden with sins, led away with divers lusts'. This passage was quoted by Hutchinson in her treatise to her daughter, as a warning that women were especially liable to be misled by 'fancies'; and she admitted that she had herself been guilty of lapses (*R* 6). The concerns of her Lucretius preface emerge here: Eve is motivated by 'unbelief quenching religious dread' (4.205). The godly household is a bastion against atheism. So concerned is Hutchinson with the present that she even observes that 'unexperience might excuse Eve's fault' (4.179); the women of today should be able to benefit from their pious reading.

This orthodoxy then makes it all the more striking to encounter the narrator's response to God's judgement in making Eve's husband her ruler. However just it is that women should be subordinated to their husbands, marriage may feel like fetters, even though golden ones; women may well 'despise the rule / Of an unmanly, fickle, froward fool' (5.145–6). Though the margin quotes Peter on the evils of women's golden ornaments, the text reminds us that the ornaments may be chains imposed by the husband; and other notes look forward to the stories of Rebecca and Rachel, who will be presented sympathetically later in the poem. In this speech, for the first time in the poem, the narrator identifies herself with a female 'we'. When she writes that 'we shall trample on the serpent's head' (5.252), the 'we' unites male and female (cf. 5.64–6, 104). It is Eve who is given the first human utterance in the poem that breaks away from the Biblical text to dramatize an individualized voice. The intensity of Hutchinson's own feelings of guilt emerges here; and Adam's long reply is a palimpsest of her husband's favourite Biblical texts, with Romans especially prominent. In cramming the margins with those texts, she was reduplicating the gesture in which she had copied out in the *Memoirs* manuscript the texts he had noted in his own Bible. Even though she presented herself as following her husband's lead in his Biblical researches, however, her own intense familiarity with Scripture had enabled her to internalize those texts to the point where the language spoke through them both. It is noteworthy that Adam does not cite any of Paul's censures of women, and near the end he re-emphasizes the union of man and woman in a recurring 'we shall trample on the monster's head' (5.574), and in the birth imagery of 5.580. In a remarkable moment Hutchinson emphasizes this reciprocity by breaking the poem's frame:

> Ah! can I this in Adam's person say,
> While fruitless tears melt my poor life away? (5.599–600)

If Adam's voice represents male rationality consoling female emotion, she is herself the creator of that voice.

In the later part of the poem, Hutchinson is concerned with the endless struggle between the Holy State and the Worldly State. As has been seen, her ideology is strongly anti-courtly; and in the early modern period, critics of monarchical corruption often identified tyranny with effeminacy. Equitable rule was identified with the dominance of reason over the passions, and women were held to find it harder to control their passions. The ideal state was one where public interests prevailed over private concerns; monarchy tended inexorably towards the private interests of the prince and his favourites, subsuming the whole nation under a single household. Hutchinson joined Milton and others who attacked Charles I because he allowed himself to be unduly swayed by his Catholic queen, Henrietta Maria, allowing his personal sentiments to overcome his sense of the public good. Charles's court had been a centre for female literary and, to some extent, political patronage. Hutchinson agreed with the republicans who wanted such malign female influence to be purged. She viewed even the rule of Queen Elizabeth favourably only because of her 'submission to her masculine and wise counsellors' (*M* 70). *Order and Disorder* reveals similar sentiments. Satan's first strategy after the Fall is to tempt the holy seed with women, re-enacting Eve's role (6.473). The 'female empire' parodies and reinforces the structures of monarchy, in a vainglorious struggle for personal honour. Wars, which should serve only the public good, are 'undertaken at a whore's command'. The artifice of seductive cosmetics is another form of shutting out the divine order, as court ladies

> Their curls in well-becoming order set;
> Nature's defects, and time's wastes to repair[.] (6.520–1)

The poem's dominant contrast between divine *kósmos* and the fallen world here works against the female. The virtuous women of Genesis are no pattern for the learned lady of Hutchinson's time; the closest they come to linguistic activity is in their involvement in naming their children – notably in the elaborate word-fight between Leah and Rachel (19.391–480).

   If Hutchinson had adhered quite rigidly to the notion that women should confine themselves to a public sphere, however, her poem would never have been written. Puritan republicans attacked monarchs who turned states into households; conversely, they tended to view households as effectively mini-states. The households of Genesis, units which are broadly autonomous of a larger state structure, and whose heads take charge of religious as well as civil functions, can be seen as an idealized version of the experience of Puritan households like that of John Hutchinson, who would lead prayers with his kin and with his servants. This religious function of the household gave wives an important ideological role. If John Hutchinson encouraged his wife in her reading and writing, it was partly because she could thus become an informed educator. It is clear that the Hutchinson household was a centre of vigorous debate about the meaning of Scripture, and in this period such debate inevitably raised 'public' issues about the state. Strong political activity centred on the household unit was characteristic of the seventeenth-century radicals (Hughes). Though the male was the prime mediator with the public world, wives would be expected to be capable of such mediation in exceptional circumstances – as Lucy Hutchinson had to do when her husband was in prison. Though the Genesis narrative primarily sees its women as instruments of succession, Hutchinson makes Abraham share her own concern for education:

> And since that both the parents' godliness
> To children's education is required,
> He for his son a virtuous wife desired,
> And lest his unexperienced youth should be
> Betrayed by fond love to idolatry,
> The father's harsh prerogative doth use,
> Nor leaves it in his young son's power to choose[.] (16.10–16)

Abraham's patriarchal authority is unchallenged, but it does imply a dependence on unusual women.

There are some signs that Hutchinson viewed the restriction of her role with ambivalence. Perhaps the most remarkable female figure in the poem is Divine Vengeance, the instrument of God's judgement against Sodom. As she and another female, Death, wield their divine powers against Sodom, the words 'blaze' and 'blazing' recur (13.185–250), recalling references elsewhere to 'blazing females' (6.479), the courtly ladies who are 'blazing stars' to corrupt the state (16.67). If this passage is of later date, it is possible that Hutchinson was glancing at Margaret Cavendish's absolutist *The Blazing World* (1666), where an empress – at a time when Charles was at war with the Dutch – uses her 'fire-stones' to destroy the enemy fleet (Cavendish 203–16). Hutchinson would have had a different view of Charles's wars, and of the role of women at court in general. Yet her Vengeance is in her own way a blazing female. Her triumph, however, immediately succeeds the punishment of Lot's wife for female curiosity (13.173–6).

A certain ambivalence was likely to emerge given Hutchinson's Calvinist contempt for all unregenerate institutions, male or female. Hutchinson presented herself as her husband's 'mirror' or 'shadow' (Keeble 1990), accepting the idea that within the household woman was less in the image of God than man. But there was an important qualification: she worried that in her love for her husband she might have delighted 'more than I ought to have done in the mirror that reflected the Creator's excellence'; it was God's grace alone that changed 'that wretched fallen nature . . . into such a blessed image of his own glory' (*M* 17). The poem has hard words for manliness as well as effeminacy. Atheists believe themselves to be showing 'manly courage' in shutting themselves off from God (7.134); debauched rakes jeer at 'unmanly shame' (9.27); the corrupt Sodomites engage in 'manly exercises' (13.8). True humanity in male and female shows itself closest to the image of God when furthest from the vainglorious impositions that block out the divine order.

The tension between Pauline restrictions on women and a strongly Pauline predestinarianism emerges in Hutchinson's portraits of the women of Genesis. As has been seen, the very lack of a clear link between moral virtue and divine providence intrigued commentators on Genesis; and in the case of the women, there were persistent problems for traditional moralists (see Whately). Women are, after all, 'the kink in the works of a patrilineal descent system' (Schwartz 84). The narrative sources, especially J, often adopt a comic tone, delighting in the ingenuity with which these female tricksters can get their way. Reworking the texts to make them part of her providential narrative, Hutchinson sometimes presents the women as a diversion of patriarchal purposes; but on occasion she can relish their trickery as part of the divine purpose. She is less consistently critical than Calvin of Sarah and of Rachel, both of whom repay closer study than is possible here. It is Rebecca, however, who engages Hutchinson most – and she had few parallels in contemporary divine poetry to work from. As first seen, Rebecca conforms to the mould of the submissive, industrious, austere woman as contrasted with the courtly sinner (16.61–8). Her parents 'freely . . . resign her' (16.154; Genesis 24.58), a point taken by some Biblical commentators as evidence that children should always submit to their parents' decisions. Rebecca, however, turns her obedience to the parental will into something more complex. She will go right away lest her 'virtuous courage' relent, she must choose the 'occasion' (16.188, 194), for

> Tedious consideration checks the bold;
> Whilst cautious men deliberating be,
> They oftener lose the opportunity
> Which daring minds embrace than with their wise
> Foresight escape the threatened precipice.
> Where choice is offered we may use the scales
> Of prudence, but where destiny prevails,
> Consideration then is out of date
> Where courage is required to meet our fate. (16.216–24)

The language here is that of Machiavelli, for whom the statesman of manly energy, of *virtù*, should seize the *occasione*, should master the female Fortune. This was the language conventionally used of action in the public world. The non-Machiavellian concept here is 'destiny'; Rebecca sees that this marriage involves obeying not just her parents but the will of God.

Her insight extends to her understanding of her children. Genesis 26.34–5 briefly discusses Esau's wives, but Hutchinson brings in material from later chapters to emphasize his love of idolatrous, courtly women. Rebecca and Isaac have significantly different responses. Rebecca, having tried in vain to educate her daughters-in-law in divine worship, favours Jacob over Esau, while Isaac still prefers the elder son. The end of canto 17 states categorically that Rachel is right, 'Confirmed with powerful reason' (17.541). Hutchinson thus introduces the story of the blessing with the readers already predisposed in Rebecca's favour. She leaves no doubt that Rebecca takes the lead in deceiving her husband: it is her 'plot' (18.17). Isaac is slowly brought to realize that he has 'doted' (18.155), that he has failed to allow grace to modify his 'natural inclination' (18.159). When Rebecca's 'spies' find out Esau's anger, she urges the 'prudent', 'politic' course (18.210–11). Lacking this context, the narratorial comment might seem straightforwardly misogynistic:

> What power like that of subtle women when
> They exercise their skill to manage men,
> Their weak force recompensed with wily arts!
> While men rule kingdoms, women rule their hearts. (18.219–22)

Many commentators condemned Rebecca for her artifice, some of them seeing it as distinctly and negatively female. Indeed, not so long ago a commentator could still take the Elohist's 'shifting the blame from Jacob to Rebekah' as evidence of a 'heightening of moral sensitivity' (Interpreter's I.679). For Hutchinson, however, there is no doubt that Rebecca is at this point more open to the divine image than Isaac.

It is then not quite unexpected, but still surprising, that as her favourite son continues on his journey, he should be described in a strikingly androgynous simile:

> Night's chariot hasted on, by swift Hours drawn,
> And the next day brought on his early dawn,
> When with like diligence as dames that feel
> The spur of urging need rise to the wheel,
> Rake by the cinders, and rush-candles light,
> Calling their drowsy maids up while 'tis night,
> Then ply their tasks and labour hard to gain
> An honest maintenance for their small train,
> The son of Isaac from his hard bed rose,
> The stone on which he did that night repose
> Erects and consecrates unto the Lord,
> And like a pillar sets it to record
> The memorable vision . . . (19.101–13)

A disparity between the world of a simile and the world it evokes was a feature of epic poetry, and has often been noticed in *Paradise Lost* – including, interestingly, another simile evoking Jacob's ladder (3.511–

15). In this case, however, the disparity between the vigorous young male and the ageing women is so great that it seems to need a further term. Women had traditionally been supposed to turn to the spinning wheel instead of the pen. In her Lucretius dedication, Hutchinson had tried to integrate the different spheres of activity by declaring that she had numbered the syllables of her translation by the threads of the canvas she was working on (*L* 23–4). Jacob is seeking to immortalize his dream with his stone; the spinning of the dames hints at Hutchinson's poetic labours. She was indeed experiencing 'the spur of urging need' in her later years, having sold off the family estates and being involved in endless lawsuits. Her decision to begin publishing *Order and Disorder* in 1679 may have been spurred by such need as well as by the political opening. This may be the closest we come to a self-portrait of the artist in later years: clinging to a little gentility; trying to care for a family she can barely support; finding in her work an improbable strength beyond merely natural expectations – and beyond conventional distinctions between male and female; writing on.

Note on the Text and Editing

The aim of this edition is to make *Order and Disorder* as accessible as possible to a wide readership. Glosses indicate words that might give difficulty. The annotations are necessarily selective. For the first five cantos, Hutchinson has been her own annotator, and reading selected passages along with the Biblical texts she notes will provide the best guide into the way her poem relates to Scripture. For the later portions, it is impossible to guess just how she would have glossed her text; selected Biblical texts and other points of note from commentators have been given.

The first five cantos of *Order and Disorder* were published by Henry Mortlock, a publisher who had two years earlier produced the first great work of Nottinghamshire history, Robert Thoroton's *The Antiquities of Nottinghamshire*, which is advertised along with some of his other books at the back of *Order and Disorder*. Mortlock's Nottinghamshire and Derbyshire connections may have drawn Hutchinson to publish with him. It is interesting, but in the publishing conditions of the time not necessarily significant, that the printer was a woman – Margaret White was continuing a business previously run by her husband. There is good reason to consider the 1679 edition as representing the author's final views, and it has been taken as the copy-text for the first five cantos.

For the remainder of the poem we are dependent on the manuscript now in Yale University Library, which belonged to the Countess of Rochester, and is indicated in the textual notes as *MS*. The inscription 'Anne Rochester her book' appears at the front of the notebook, immediately preceding the poem. 'Rochester 1664' appears upside down at the other end, many leaves after the end of the poem, so that it is not entirely clear whether the date refers to the manuscript book or to the poem. The poem has no title, beginning merely 'Genesis Chap. 1st. Canto 1st.'. The manuscript is in two different scribal hands, neither of which can be identified with the scribes of other Hutchinson manuscripts. The first scribe takes the story to line 392 of canto 8, breaking off at mid-sentence. The second, rather more elegant, hand carries the poem to the end of page 324 and breaks off in mid-line. A note at the start of canto 10 (*MS*, page 190), possibly but not definitely in the second scribe's hand, reads 'There [*sic*] were copied out of the old notes after they were dead'. If 'they' were the Hutchinsons, the note must be later than Lucy Hutchinson's death in October 1681. Though the note seems to imply that the sections of cantos 8 and 9 copied out by the second scribe were done when 'they' were alive and from a different, more reliable, manuscript source, there is no sign of a break in ink or handwriting at canto 10. The evidence is thus frustratingly enigmatic.

It seems that at least two other manuscripts of part or all of the poem were in circulation. During the 1730s Julius Hutchinson copied an extract from Eve's speech after the Fall 'out of my other Book'. Since the extract does not identify the speech as part of a longer work, and Julius Hutchinson takes it to have been written in Hutchinson's own voice, presumably the 'other Book' was not a manuscript of *Order and Disorder* but perhaps a collection of drafts. The 1679 edition must have been set from a manuscript other than the Countess of Rochester's, for it differs in many minor and some major elements. The Countess inserted in her manuscript, at the end of canto 5, 'thus far printed', and she made several corrections which brought the manuscript closer to the printed text (or to the manuscript on which that text was based), though this was not done consistently. Throughout the manuscript there are also corrections in at least two other hands. These seem to have been motivated in part by a desire for euphony rather than any special textual authority, for example by changing the occasional tetrameter lines to pentameters; since tetrameters are frequent in the Lucretius translation it is not clear that this reflects any special knowledge of authorial preferences. All changes not in the scribe's hand are identified as *MSC*; for this edition it has not been possible to indicate full details of all the minor changes, some of which can be found in Norbrook 2000a. A few lines not found in 1679 occur in the Rochester manuscript and in the 'Elegies' manuscript.

It is to be hoped that another manuscript of the poem, obscured under some general title like 'Poem on Genesis', may eventually surface from an archive and bring more certainty into the textual situation. For the present, any text must be provisional. For the first five cantos, the status of 1679 as reflecting the author's final thoughts is reasonably secure, and I have taken this as my copy-text, with some minor emendations where they seem necessary for the sense. At the cost of inconsistency in editorial policy, I have also included a few lines whose omission from 1679 seems to weaken a passage's sense. Unless otherwise noted, all variants listed for cantos 1–5 are from the manuscript. For cantos 6–20, the Yale manuscript is the only authority and has been taken as copy-text; where the editor has changed apparent errors, the manuscript reading appears in the textual notes. The later corrections are noted and have been followed where there seems good reason to doubt the manuscript reading. Original spelling has been retained in the apparatus.

Marginal references from the 1679 text have been included in roman type. I have modernized the forms of the references and occasionally silently corrected them. In the manuscript the references are much more sparing, after the first few pages; I have recorded, in italics, only those which do not repeat 1679. Marginal notes in square brackets are editorial insertions to indicate the passage in Genesis being treated.

The spelling and punctuation for this edition have been modernized. Something will inevitably be lost in this process. Modernizing spelling may obscure changes in meaning or pronunciation, while seventeenth-century conventions differed significantly from today's. An old-spelling edition is in preparation. For the present edition, however, accessibility is the prime consideration; a wholly unfamiliar poem from this period presents enough obstacles without interposing further ones. Hutchinson's syntax, with its fondness both for long, expansive sentences and for compressed absolute constructions, can be hard to untease without some help. In any case, we do not possess any text which clearly preserves the author's preferences in these matters. Conventions of punctuation differ considerably between the printed text and the manuscript, and between the two scribal transcriptions. When texts went to the printer, authors normally expected that their spelling and punctuation might be changed. The present edition offers punctuation that is lighter than the 1679 edition but heavier than the manuscript. In some cases it is difficult to decide whether an old spelling constitutes a different word; I have preserved some word-forms that are necessary to complete a rhyme, such as 'drownd' for 'drown', 'begun' where modern English would have 'began'; but have regularized 'murther' and 'burthen' to 'murder' and 'burden'. I have, however, preserved elided forms such as 'th'Almighty' since they can sometimes help to highlight the metre, and marked with accents syllables whose stress is required for the metre; though I have been reluctant to emend possible irregularities to the extent of some of the corrections in the Yale manuscript. I have normally regularized Biblical names to the spelling of modern Authorized Version editions, but have followed the manuscript where it regularly uses a different spelling, as with 'Rebecca'. The manuscript does not register Genesis's shift from 'Abram' to 'Abraham', 'Sarai' to 'Sarah'. Biblical quotations are from the Authorized Version unless otherwise stated.

Acknowledgements

The Yale manuscript is reproduced by permission of the James Marshall and Marie-Louise Osborn Collection, Beinecke Rare Book and Manuscript Library, Yale University, whose staff have been extremely helpful. Nottinghamshire Archives DD/HU1, DD/HU2 and DD/HU3 are the copyright of the Hutchinson family and I am grateful to Mrs Hugh Priestley and to the Principal Archivist of the Nottinghamshire Archives for permission to reproduce extracts, and to many other members of the Hutchinson family for their cooperation.

The earlier stages of my work on this project were enormously facilitated by the award of a Research Readership by the British Academy, which also granted research expenses. Magdalen College, Oxford and the Oxford University English Faculty also helped with leave and expenses. At the University of Maryland, I have been fortunate to receive research assistance from the Department of English and research expenses from the College of Arts and Humanities. Carole Breakstone and Anita Sherman provided a firm foundation for this edition in their help with transcription and with much other research assistance. Hugh Craig energetically took up the question of authorship and generously provided me with his findings and files. I am very grateful to Dr G. F. Nuttall for sharing with me his unrivalled knowledge of the world of Dissent. Katherine Narveson's discovery that Lucy Hutchinson's 'Of Theology' was a translation from John Owen shed a flood of light on the understanding of her later life from which I have greatly benefited. Another invaluable clue that opened up the subject was a reference to the Yale manuscript in a note in a Folger Shakespeare Library manuscript; cataloguing beyond the call of immediate duty is a great source of the accidents or providences of scholarship, and I thank Laetitia Yeandle. For other help and advice I am grateful to Peter Beal, Hugh de Quehen, Arthur Freeman, Nicholas Green, Germaine Greer, Theodore Hofmann, the late Jeremy Maule, Joad Raymond, Jason Rosenblatt, Nigel Smith, Nicholas von Maltzahn and Steven N. Zwicker. The late Asher Achinstein gave me one of his numerous Genesis commentaries, and I am very fortunate to have been able to use his excellent library for this edition. Sharon Achinstein helped to sustain the project in its many changes and migrations and to suggest many new lines of thought. Finally, warm thanks to Andrew McNeillie for believing in the book and working so hard to make it a reality.

— Order and Disorder —

Order and Disorder:

OR, THE

WORLD MADE

AND

UNDONE.

BEING

MEDITATIONS

UPON THE

CREATION and the FALL ;

As it is recorded in the beginning
of GENESIS.

apsley, allen

A 3594

LONDON,

Printed by *Margaret White* for *Henry Mortlock* at the
Phœnix in St. *Paul's* Church-yard, and at the *White
Hart* in *Westminster* Hall. 1679.

Plate 1 Title-page of *Order and Disorder*, 1679. Reproduced by permission of the James Marshall and Marie-Louise Osborn Collection, Beinecke Rare Book and Manuscript Library, Yale University.

The Preface

These meditations were not at first designed for public view, but fixed upon to reclaim a busy roving thought from wandering in the pernicious and perplexed maze of human inventions; whereinto the vain curiosity of youth had drawn me to consider and translate the account some old poets and philosophers give of the original of things:[1] which though I found it blasphemously against God, and brutishly below the reason of a man, set forth by some erroneously, imperfectly and uncertainly by the best; yet had it filled my brain with such foolish fancies, that I found it necessary to have recourse to the fountain of Truth, to wash out all ugly wild impressions, and fortify my mind with a strong antidote against all the poison of human wit and wisdom that I had been dabbling withal. And this effect I found; for comparing that revelation God gives of himself and his operations in his Word with what the wisest of mankind, who only walked in the dim light of corrupted nature and defective traditions, could with all their industry trace out or invent; I found it so transcendently excelling all that was human, so much above our narrow reason, and yet so agreeable to it being rectified, that I disdained the wisdom fools so much admire themselves for;[2] and as I found I could know nothing but what God taught me, so I resolved never to search after any knowledge of him and his productions, but what he himself hath given forth. Those that will be wise above what is written may hug their philosophical clouds,[3] but let them take heed they find not themselves without God in the

---

[1] Cf. *L* 24: 'this Lunatick, who not able to dive into the true Originall and Cause of Beings and Accidents, admires them who devizd this Casuall, Irrationall dance of Attomes'; LH also translated parts of Ovid.

[2] Cf. the first chapters of Romans and 1 Corinthians, which LH emphasizes in *R* 12.

[3] Alludes to the myth of Ixion, tricked into making love to a cloud.

world, adoring figments of their own brains, instead of the living and true God.

Lest that arrive[4] by misadventure, which never shall by my consent, that any of the puddled water my wanton youth drew from the profane Helicon of ancient poets should be sprinkled about the world,[5] I have for prevention[6] sent forth this essay; with a profession that I disclaim all doctrines of God and his works, but what I learnt out of his own word, and have experienced it to be a very unsafe and unprofitable thing for those that are young, before their faith be fixed, to exercise themselves in the study of vain, foolish, atheistical poesy. It is a miracle of grace and mercy, if such be not deprived of the light of Truth, who having shut their eyes against that sun, have, instead of looking up to it, hunted glow-worms in the ditch bottoms. It is a misery I cannot but bewail, that when we are young, whereas the lovely characters of Truth should be impressed upon the tender mind and memory, they are so filled up with ridiculous lies, that 'tis the greatest business of our lives, as soon as ever we come to be serious, to cleanse out all the rubbish our grave tutors laid in when they taught us to study and admire their inspired poets and divine philosophers.[7]

But when I have thus taken occasion to vindicate my self from those heathenish authors I have been conversant in, I cannot expect my work should find acceptance in the world, declaring the more full and various delight I have found in following Truth by its own conduct; nor am I much concerned how it be entertained, seeking no glory by it but what is rendered to him to whom it is only due. If any one of no higher a pitch than myself be as much affected and stirred up in the reading as I have been in the writing, to admire the glories and excellencies of our great Creator, to fall low before him, in the sense of our own vileness, and to adore his power, his wisdom, and his grace, in all his dealings with the children of men, it will be a success above my hopes; though

---

[4] happen
[5] Cf. *L* 26: 'those walkes of witt which poore vaineglorious schollars call the Muses groves, are enchanted thicketts, and while they tipple att their celebrated Helicon, they loose their lives, and fill themselves with poyson, drowning their spiritts in those pudled waters'.
[6] anticipatory refutation
[7] Cf. *L* 24: 'I am perswaded, that the Encomiums given to these Pagan Poets and Philosophers, wherewith Tutors put them into the hands of their pupills, yet unsetled in the Principles of Devine Truth, is one greate means of debauching the learned world, at least of confirming them in that debauchery of soule, which their first sin led them into, and of hindring their recovery, while they puddle all the streames of Truth, that flow downe to them from devine Grace, with this Pagan mud'.

my charity makes me wish everyone that hath need of it the same mercy I have found.

I know I am obnoxious[8] to the censures of two sorts of people: first, those that understand and love the elegancies of poems: they will find nothing of fancy in it; no elevations of style, no charms of language, which I confess are gifts I have not, nor desire not in this occasion; for I would rather breath forth grace cordially[9] than words artificially. I have not studied to utter anything that I have not really taken in. And I acknowledge all the language I have, is much too narrow to express the least of those wonders my soul hath been ravished with in the contemplation of God and his works. Had I had a fancy, I durst not have exercised it here; for I tremble to think of turning Scripture into a romance; and shall not be troubled at their dislike who dislike on that account, and profess they think no poem can be good that shuts out drunkenness, and lasciviousness, and libelling satire, the themes of all their celebrated songs. These (though I will not much defend my own weakness) dislike not the poem so much as the subject of it.

But there are a second sort of people, whose genius not lying that way, and seeing the common and vile abuse of poesy, think Scripture profaned by being descanted on in numbers; but such will pardon me when they remember a great part of the Scripture was originally written in verse; and we are commanded to exercise our spiritual mirth in psalms and hymns and spiritual songs; which if I have weakly composed, yet 'tis a consenting testimony with the whole Church, to the mighty and glorious truths of God which are not altogether impertinent,[10] in this atheistical age; and how imperfect soever the hand be that copies it out, Truth loses not its perfection, and the plainest as well as the elegant, the elegant as well as the plain,[11] make up a harmony in confession and celebration of that all-creating, all-sustaining God, to whom be all honour and glory for ever and ever.

---

[8] liable
[9] from the heart
[10] irrelevant
[11] Hutchinson's carefully structured language (the figure of antimetabole) shows that, as was conventional in literary prefaces, her profession of complete plainness is not to be taken too literally.

MEDITATIONS ON THE CREATION, as recorded in the First Chapter of Genesis[12]

Canto 1

My ravished soul a pious ardour fires
To sing those mystic wonders it admires,[i] [13]
Contemplating the rise of everything
That with Time's birth flowed from th'eternal
    spring:
And the no less stupendous Providence
By which discording natures ever since
Have kept up universal harmony,
While in one joint obedience all agree,
Performing that to which they were designed
With ready inclination; but Mankind   10
Isaiah 10.5–7   Alone rebels against his Maker's will,
Which, though opposing, he must yet fulfil.[ii]
And so that wise power who each crooked stream
Most rightly guides becomes the glorious theme
Of endless admiration, while[iii] we see,

[i] desires
[ii] Which yet he by opposeing doth fullfill
[iii] whilest

[12] This title heads the 1679 text; the manuscript is headed merely 'Genesis Chap. 1st. Canto 1st.'.
[13] wonders at

Eccl. 6.10	Whatever mortals' vain endeavours be,
Isaiah 27.4	They must be broken who with power contend,
Gen. 45. 4–5	And cannot frustrate their Creator's end,
Acts 2.23	Whose wisdom, goodness, might and glory shines
Gen. 50.20	In guiding men's unto his own designs. 20

In these outgoings would I sing his praise,
But my weak sense with the too glorious rays
Is struck with[iv] such confusion that I find
Only the world's first Chaos in my mind,
Where light and beauty lie wrapped up in seed
And cannot be from the dark prison freed
Except[14] that Power by whom the world was made
My soul in her imperfect[v] strugglings aid,
Her rude conceptions into forms[vi] dispose,
And words impart which may those forms disclose.[15]   30
    O thou eternal spring of glory, whence

James 1.17   All other streams derive their excellence,
From whose love issues every good desire,
Quicken my dull earth with celestial fire,
And let the sacred theme that is my choice
Give utterance and music to my voice,

Romans 1.15   Singing the works by which thou art revealed.
What dark Eternity hath kept concealed
From mortals'[vii] apprehensions, what hath been
Before the race of time[16] did first begin,   40

Deut. 29.29   It were presumptuous folly to inquire.
Let not my thoughts beyond their bounds[viii] aspire:[17]

The Creator   Time limits mortals, and Time had its birth,

Gen. 1.1   In whose *Beginning God made Heaven and Earth.*

[iv] in
[v] vnperfect
[vi] forme
[vii] Mortall
[viii] bounds] *MS* bound *1679*

[14] unless
[15] For Hutchinson's parallel between poetic and divine creation cf. *PL* 1.17–22.
[16] Cf. *PL* 12.554; the phrase also occurs in Joseph Beaumont, *Psyche* 9.24 (Beaumont I.164).
[17] LH follows Du Bartas's Muse, which 'keepes the middle Region', *DWW* I.1.136, whereas Milton aims to soar 'with no middle flight', *PL* 1.14.

Bara Elohim	God, the great *Elohim*,[18] to say no more,
	Whose sacred name we rather must adore
	Than venture to explain; for he alone
Job 11.7	Dwells in himself, and to himself is known,
1 Tim. 6.16, 1.17	His essence wrapped up in mysterious clouds
	While he himself in dazzling glory shrouds:[ix] 50
	And so even that by which we have our sight
Ps. 104.2	His covering is: *He clothes himself with light.*
	Easier we may the winds in prison shut,
	The whole vast ocean in a nutshell put,
Isaiah 40.12	The mountains in a little balance weigh,
	And with a bulrush plumb the deepest sea,
	Than stretch frail[x] human thought unto the height
	Of the great God, immense and infinite,
Job 38	Containing all things in himself alone,
	Being at once in all, contained in none. 60
	Yet as a hidden spring appears in streams,
	The sun is seen in its reflected beams,
	Whose high-embodied glory is too bright,
	Too strong an object for weak mortal[xi] sight;
Romans 1.20	So in God's visible productions we
Hebrews 11.27	What is invisible in some sort see;
	While we, considering each created thing,
	Are led up to an uncreated spring,
	And by gradations of successive time
Isaiah 44.6	At last unto Eternity do climb; 70
	As we in tracks of second causes tread,
	Unto the first uncausèd cause are led;
	And know, while we perpetual motion see,
	There must a first self-moving Power be,
Romans 11.36	To whom all the inferior motions tend,
Acts 17.24,26,28	In whom they are begun, and where they end.[19]

ix His . . . shrouds] *MS, not in 1679*
x vaine
xi mortalls

18 The Hebrew words in the margin mean literally 'created the Lord'. *Elohim* gives its name to the Elohist narrative as opposed to the 'Jehovah/Yahweh' of the J narrative.
19 A 'poore fleshly finite creature cannot ascend up to that inaccessible, incomprehensible light, wherein God dwells, to see or consider him as he is absolutely in himselfe; but by

This first eternal Cause, th'original
Of being, life, and motion, God we call;
In whom all wisdom, goodness, glory, might,
Whatever can himself or us delight,   80
Unite,[xii] centring in his perfection,

Ephesians 4.5,6 Whose nature can admit but only one:
Divided sovereignty makes neither great,
Wanting what's shared to make the sum complete.

The Trinity   And yet this sovereign sacred Unity
1 John 5.7 Is not alone, for in this One are Three,[20]
Matt. 28.19, Distinguished, not divided, so that what
3.16,17 One person is, the other is not that;
Yet all the three are but one God most high,
One uncompounded, pure Divinity,   90
Wherein[xiii] subsist so the mysterious three
That they in power and glory equal be;
John 14.10 Each doth himself and all the rest possess
Proverbs 8.22,30 In undisturbèd joy and blessedness.[xiv]
John 1.1 There's no inferior, nor no later[xv] there,
Philippians 2.6 All coeternal, all coequal, are.
John 5.18 And yet this parity order admits:
The Father first eternally begets,
John 1.14 Within himself, his Son, substantial Word
1 Cor. 1.14 And Wisdom as his second, and their third   100
The ever-blessèd Spirit is, which doth
John 16.13,14 Alike eternally proceed from both.
John 15.16 These three distinctly thus in one divine,
Pure, perfect, self-supplying essence shine;

[xii] Vnitie
[xiii] In which
[xiv] happynesse
[xv] latter

considering ourselves, as creatures produced in time, we are led to the knowledge of an eternall, uncreated Being before all time, who is the first cause, the last and noblest end of all beings, and this is God, whose nature is so farre transcending ours, that wee cannot know him as he is absolutley in himselfe, but by his operations manifested in ourselves, and all things elce which wee contemplate', *T* 10.

[20] The length and doctrinal explicitness of LH's account of the Trinity in 1679 contrasts not only with *PL* but also with Du Bartas's warning that 'fraile Reason' was not fit to probe the mysteries of this doctrine (*DWW* I.1.102).

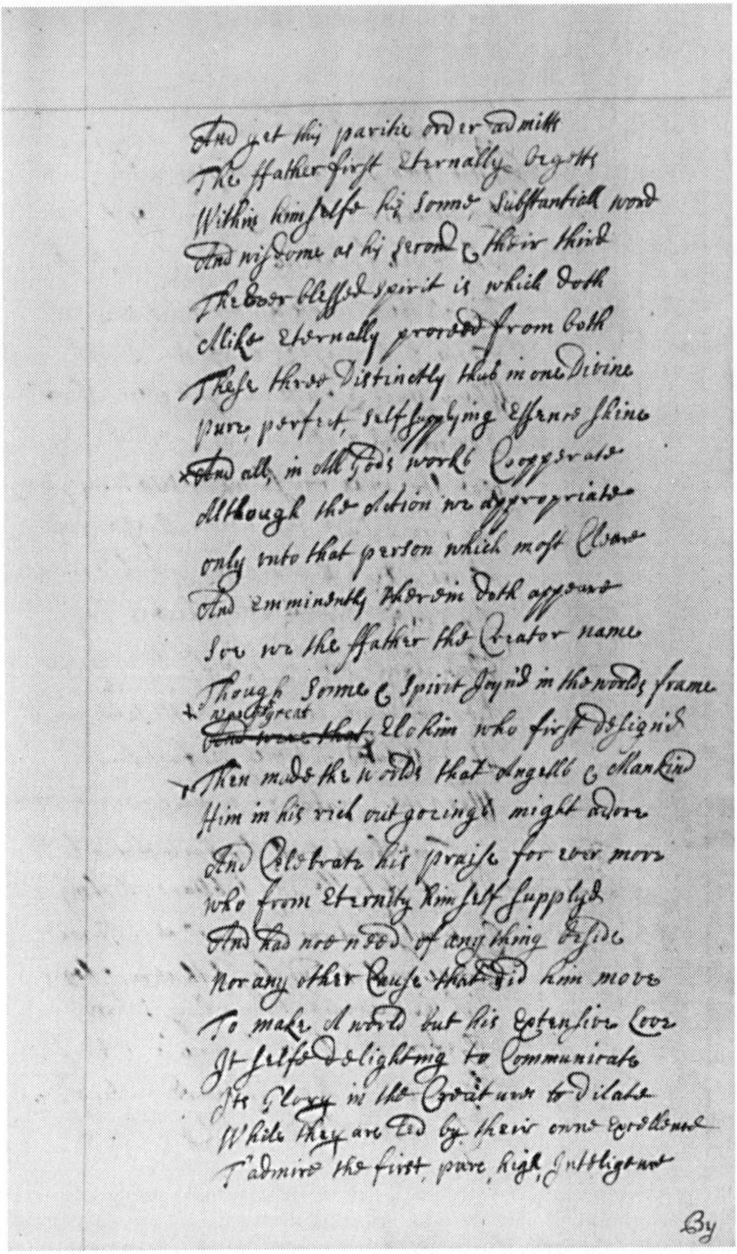

Plate 2   Canto 1, lines 97–135: New Haven, Yale University, Osborn Collection fb 100, p. 7. (Original size 303 × 188 mm.) Reproduced by permission of the James Marshall and Marie-Louise Osborn Collection, Beinecke Rare Book and Manuscript Library, Yale University.

John 5.17	And all cooperate in all works done	
	Exteriorly, yet so as every one	
	In a peculiar manner suited to	
	His person doth the common action do.[21]	
Hebrews 12.19	Herein the Father is the principal,	
Isaiah 42.4	Whose sacred counsels are th'original	110
John 5.26	Of every act; producèd by the Son,	
1 Cor. 8.6	By'the Spirit wrought up to perfection.[22]	
John 5.19	I'the Creation thus, by'the Father's wise decree	
Eph. 1.11	Such things should in such time, and order be,	
2 Tim. 1.9	The first foundation of the world was laid.	
John 1.3	The fabric by th'eternal Word was made	
Hebrews 1.2	Not as th'instrument, but joint actor, who	
John 5.19, etc.	Joyed to fulfil the counsels which he knew.	
Genesis 1.2	By the concurrent Spirit all parts were	
Job 26.13	Fitly disposed, distinguished, rendered fair,	120
	In such harmonious and wise order set	
	As universal Beauty did complete.	
	This most mysterious triple Unity,	
	In essence one, and in subsistence three,	
	Was that great *Elohim*[23] who first designed,[xvi]	
	Then made, the worlds, that angels and mankind	
Rev. 4.11	Him in his rich out-goings might adore,	

[xvi] And all . . . designed] *1679*

And all, in All God's works Coopperate
Although the Action we appropriate
Only vnto that person which most Cleare
And emminently therein doth appeare
Soe we the ffather the Creator name
Though Sonne & Spirit Joyn'd in the worlds frame
And were that Elohim who first design'd
MS

And all . . . Was yᵉ great Elohim who first design'd *MSC*

[21] In 'all the workes of God, both Father, Sonne, and Spirit co-operate each in his owne manner of working, and the worke in Scripture is attributed cheifely to that Person whose distinctt manner of working appeares cheifely in the worke': *R* 25.

[22] In 'every great work of God, the *concluding, completing, perfecting acts* are ascribed unto the Holy Ghost': Owen, *Works* III.94.

[23] On the textual variants cf. *R* 26: 'Some thinke the plurall word Elohim, by which God is namd in the creation, ioynd to the singular verb created, intimates the Trinity'.

Ps. 147,148	And celebrate his praise for evermore;
Acts 17.24	Who from eternity himself supplied,
	And had no need of anything beside, 130
	Nor any other cause that did him move
	To make a world but his extensive love,
	Itself delighting to communicate,
	Its glory in the creatures to dilate,[24]
	While they are led by their own excellence
Job 33.12	T'admire the first, pure, high Intelligence;
Ps. 95.31	By all the powers and virtues which they have,
Rev. 19.6	To that Omnipotence who those powers gave;
	By all their glories and their joys to his
Ps. 16.11	Who is the fountain of all joy and bliss; 140
Genesis 17.10	By all their wants and imbecilities[25]
	To the full magazine[xvii] [26] of rich supplies,
	Where Power, Love, Justice, and Mercy shine[xviii]
	In their still[27]-fixèd heights, and ne'er decline.
	No streams can shrink the self-supplying spring,
Job 35.7	No retributions can more fullness bring
Ps. 16.2	To the eternal fountain which doth run
Rev. 1.8	In sacred circles, ends where it begun,
Isaiah 41.4	And thence with inexhausted life and force
	Begins again a new, yet the same course 150
	It instituted in Time's infant birth,
Gen. 1.1	When the Creator first made *Heaven and Earth*.
Time	Time, though it all things into motion bring,
Be resheth	Is not itself any substantial thing,
In Capite,	But only Motion's measure, as a twin
Principio	Born with it; and they both at once begin
	With the existence of the rolling sphere,
	Before which neither Time nor Motion were;[28]

[xvii] Magazines
[xviii] Where power, Love, Wisdome, Justice, Mercy shine

[24] spread abroad
[25] weaknesses
[26] storehouse
[27] always, continually
[28] Aristotle believed that the world was eternal and that time and motion were inseparable; Genesis implies that time began before the world; on commentators' attempts to reconcile time and motion see Williams 41–2 and Fowler's note to *PL* 5.580–2.

Time being a still-continued number, made
By the vicissitude[xix] of light and shade,　　　　　160
By the moon's growth, and by her waxing old,
By the successive reign of heat and cold,
Thus leading back all ages to the womb
Of vast Eternity from whence they come,[29]
And bringing new successions forth until
Heaven its last revolutions[30] shall fulfil,
And all things unto their first state restore

Rev. 10.6　　When, Motion ceasing, Time shall be no more,
　　　　　　But with the visible heavens shall expire
2 Peter 3.12　　While they consume in the world's funeral fire.　　170
Hebrews 12.27,28 Th'invisible heavens, being still the same,
　　　　　　Shall not be touched by the devouring flame.
　　　　　　Treating of which, let's waive Platonic dreams
　　　　　　Of worlds made in Idea,[31] fitter themes
　　　　　　For poets' fancies than the reverent view
　　　　　　Of contemplation, fixed on what is true
　　　　　　And only certain, kept upon record
　　　　　　In the Creator's own revealèd Word,
　　　　　　Which, when it taught us how our world was made,
　　　　　　Wrapped up th'invisible in mystic shade.　　　　180
Heaven　　　　Yet through those clouds we see God did create
　　　　　　A place his presence doth irradiate,
Hebrews 11.10　Where he doth in his brightest lustre shine;
Isaiah 66.1　　Yet doth not his own Heaven him confine,
Matt. 5.34, 6.9 Although the paradise of the fair world above,[xx]

[xix] vicissitudes
[xx] Although the paradice of the faire world above *MS* Though the faire paradice of the world above *MSC* Though the paradice of the faire world above *MSC*

[29] Cf. *L* 5.272–3: 'Earth for her part made by her fruitfull womb / The generall mother, is the common tomb'; and *PL* 2.911.
[30] Rotations of the celestial spheres. Medieval cosmology assumed that the seven planets were fixed to concentric spinning spheres; outside these was a fixed sphere of stars; some commentators posited a ninth, crystalline sphere between these eight and God, the Unmoved Mover (cf. *PL* 3.482).
[31] The belief that God had patterned the world on a pre-existing Idea emerged in part to account for the lapse between the beginning of time and the creation, and borrowed from Plato's *Timaeus*, 37C–D. This 'fantastike fore-conceipted plot' was strongly rejected by Du Bartas, *DWW* I.1.202, though hinted at by Milton, *PL* 7.557: Williams 42.

1 Kings 8.27,28	Each-where perfumed with sweet-respiring love,
Luke 23.43	Refreshed with pleasure's never shrinking streams,
	Illustrated[32] with light's unclouded beams,
1 Cor. 13.13	The happy land of peace and endless rest
1 John 4.16	Which doth both soul and sense with full joys feast,[xxi] 190
Ps. 16.11	Feasts that extinguish not the appetite,
Rev. 20.5	Which is renewed to heighten the delight.
Hebrews 4.9	Here stands the Tree of Life, decked with fair fruit,
Rev. 14.13, 22.2	Whose leaves health to the nations contribute:
	The spreading,[xxii] true, celestial vine
John 15.1	Where fruitful grafts and noble clusters shine.
	Here majesty and grace together meet;
	The grace is glorious, and the glory sweet.
Rev. 21.25,26	Here is the throne of th'universal King,
	To which the suppliant world addresses bring. 200
	Here next him doth his Son in triumph sit,
Ps. 110.1	Waiting till all his foes lie at his feet.
Exodus 15.17,18	Here is the temple of his holiness,
	The sanctuary for all sad distress.
Rev. 7.17	Here is the saints' most sure inheritance,
1 Peter 1.4	To which they all their thoughts and hopes[xxiii] advance.
Col. 3.1,2,24	Here their rich recompense and safe rest[xxiv] lies,
Heb. 12.2	For this they all th'inferior world despise;
	Yet not for this alone, though this excel,
	But for that[xxv] Deity who here doth dwell; 210
Ps. 73.25	For Heaven itself to saints no Heaven were
	Did not their God afford his presence there.
Luke 12.33	But now, as he inhabits it, it is
1 Cor. 12.4	The treasure-house of everlasting bliss,
2 Tim. 4.8	The Father's house, the pilgrim's home, the port
John 14.21	Of happiness, th'illustrious regal[xxvi] court,

[xxi] Which . . . feast] *1679* Which doth both soule & body with full Joyes feast *MS* Which soule & body with full Joyes doth feast *MSC*

[xxii] The spreading] *1679, MS* Th'eternall spreading *MSC*

[xxiii] hopes & thoughts

[xxiv] saftie

[xxv] the

[xxvi] Royall

[32] illuminated

Hebrews 11.16 The city that on the world's summit stands,
Ps. 15.1, 122.3 United in itself, not made with hands;
Hebrews 12.22 Whose citizens, walls, pavements are so bright
2 Cor. 5.1 They need no sun in God's more radiant light.   220
Rev. 21.23 The pure air being not[xxvii] thickened with dark clouds,
No sable night the constant glory shrouds;
Nor needs there[xxviii] night, when no[xxix] dull lassitude
Doth[xxx] into the unwearied soul intrude;
New vigour flowing in with that dear joy
Whose contemplation doth their lives employ.
2 Cor. 12.2 This Heaven, the[xxxi] third to us within,[33]
The first, if from the outside we begin,
1 Pet. 1.4 Is incorruptible and still the same,
Confirmed by him who[xxxii] did its substance frame.   230
No time its strong foundations can decay,
Its renewed glory fadeth not away.
Joel 2.30 The other heavens which it doth enfold
Isaiah 34.4 In tract[34] of time as garments shall wax old,
Ps. 102.26 And all their outworn glory shall expire
1 Pet. 3.7,12 In the world's dreadful last devouring[xxxiii] fire;
But this shall still unchangeable remain,
While all the rolling spheres which it contains
Shall be again into their Chaos whirled
At the last dissolution of the world.   240
For God, who made this blessèd place to be
The habitation of his sanctity,
Rev. 21.27 Admitting nothing to it that is vile,[xxxiv]
Nothing that can corrupt or can defile,

[xxvii] not being
[xxviii] their
[xxix] where a
[xxx] Doth not
[xxxi] Heaven, the] *1679* Heaven the *MS* Heaven is the *MSC*
[xxxii] that
[xxxiii] Consumeing
[xxxiv] Admitting nothing into it that's vile

[33] 'The Scripture tells us that God was the creator of things invisible, as well as of those things which appeare; among these are the 3d heavens, called in the Scripture Paradice, and the dwelling of God', *R27*. The note refers us to Paul's account of being miraculously caught up to the third heaven (2 Cor. 12.2).
[34] passing

Never withdraws his gracious presence thence

Isaiah 4.5   But is on all the glory a defence.

Nor are his gates e'er shut by night or day;

His only dread[35] keeps all foes far away.

Angels   He[xxxv] not for need, but for majestic state,[36]

Innumerable hosts of angels did create   250

To be his out-guards, in respect of whom

Isaiah 48.2   He doth his name *El-tzeboim*[37] assume.

Matt. 26.53   These perfect, pure intelligences be,

2 Sam. 14.17 Excel in might and in celerity,

Whose sublime natures and whose agile powers

2 Thes. 1.7   Are vastly so superior unto ours

Dan. 9.21   Our narrow thoughts cannot to them extend

Isaiah 6.6   And things so far above us comprehend

Col. 2.18   As in themselves, although in part we know

Some scantlings[38] by appearances below   260

And sacred writ, wherein we find there be

Rom. 8.38   Distinguished orders in their hierarchy:

1 Thes. 4.16   Archangels, cherubims, and seraphims,

Who celebrate their God with holy hymns;[39]

Some raised to thrones and principalities,

Some power, some dominion exercise;[xxxvi]

Ps. 103.20,21 Ten thousand thousand vulgar[40] angels stand

Gen. 3.24   All in their ranks, waiting the Lord's command,

Dan. 7.10   Which with prompt inclination of their will

Matt. 6.10   And cheerful, swift obedience they fulfil;   270

Whether he them to save poor men employ

Ps. 91.11,12   Or send them armed, proud rebels to destroy;

2 Kings 19.35 Whether he them to mighty monarchs send

Gen. 32.1   Or bid them on poor pilgrim saints attend;

Luke 2.13,14   Whether they must in heavenly lustre go,

---

xxxv Who
xxxvi Some raised . . . exercise] *MS; not in 1679*

[35] the very fear of him
[36] Cf. *PL* 8.239.
[37] Hebrew: 'the Lord of hosts'.
[38] estimates
[39] Catholic commentators distinguished nine orders of angels arranged in a strict hierarchy; LH, like Milton and other Protestant writers, is less specific: West 132–4.
[40] Ordinary, common: the term emphasizes their lack of social pretension.

Or walk in mortal mean[xxxvii] disguise below;

Gen. 32.1,2 So kind, so humble are they, though so high,

Gen. 19.1 They do it with the same alacrity.

Ps. 104.4 Why blush we not at our vain pride, when we

Luke 16.20 Such condescension in Heaven's courtiers see,   280

That they who sit on heavenly thrones above

Scorn not to serve poor worms with fervent love,

And joyful praises to th'Almighty sing,

When they a mortal to their own home bring?

Matt. 13.29 How gracious is the Lord of all, that he

Should thus consider poor mortality,

Such powers for us into those powers diffuse,

Such glorious servants in our service use,

Who, whether they with Light or Heaven had

Creation, were within the six days made?[41]   290

But leave we looking through the veil, nor[xxxviii] pry

Too long on things wrapped up in mystery,

Heb. 12.22 Reserved to be our wonder at that time

When we shall up to their high mountain[xxxix] climb.

Besides th'empyrean Heaven, we are told

Of divers other heavens which we behold

Only by reason's eye; yet were not they,

If made, at least distinguished the first day.

Then from the height[xl] we cannot comprehend,

Let us to our inferior world descend.   300

Earth's Chaos   The Earth at first was a vast empty place,

A rude congestion[42] without form or grace,

Gen. 1.2 A confused mass of undistinguished seed.

Darkness the deep, the deep the solid hid,

Where things did in unperfect[xli] causes sleep,

Until God's Spirit moved the quiet deep,

[xxxvii] poore
[xxxviii] not *MS* nor *MSC*
[xxxix] Mountaines
[xl] Heights
[xli] imperfect

---

[41] Genesis does not specifically mention the creation of angels. Milton, *Christian Doctrine* I.7, *CPW* VI.313, concluded that they had already been created before the six days; LH follows the more orthodox view that they were created on the first or second days.

[42] heap, mass

Brooding the creatures under wings of love,
As tender birds hatched by a turtle-dove.[43]

Light   Light first of all its[xlii] radiant wings displayed,
Gen. 1.3,4,5 God called forth Light: that Word the creature
     made.   310
Whether it were the natures more divine,
Or the bright mansion where just souls must shine,
Or the first matter of those tapers which
The since-made firmament do still enrich,
It is not yet agreed among[xliii] the wise:[44]
But thus the day did out of Chaos rise,
And casts[xliv] its bright beams on the floating world,
O'er which soon envious Night her black mists
  hurled,
Damping[xlv] the new-born splendour for a space
Till the next morning did her shadows[xlvi] chase, 320
With restored beauty and triumphant force
Returning to begin another course:

John 3.19,20,21 An emblem of that everlasting feud
'Twixt sons of light and darkness still pursued;
Col. 1.12,13 And of that frail imperfect[xlvii] state wherein
The wasting lights of mortal men begin;
1 Pet. 1.24 Whose comforts, honours, lives, soon as they shine
Must all to sorrows, changes, death resign;
Even their wisdom's and their virtue's light
Are hid by envy's interposing night.   330
But though these splendours all in graves are
  thrown,
Wherever the true seed of light is sown

---

xlii his
xliii determin'd by
xliv Cast
xlv Dampning
xlvi shadow
xlvii imperfect] *1679, MS* vnperfect *MSC*

[43] Cf. Du Bartas, *DWW* I.1.323, 'as a Henne that faine would hatch a brood'; *PL* 1.21–2: 'Dovelike satst brooding on the vast abyss / And mad'ʃt it pregnant'.
[44] Since light was created before the heavenly bodies, commentators assigned different locations and identities to this pre-solar light: LH considers the alternatives of the angels, Heaven, or the stars.

Ps. 97.11   The powers of darkness may contend in vain,
It shall a conqueror rise and ever reign.
For when God the victorious morning viewed,
Approving his own work he said 'twas good,
And of inanimate creatures sure the best,
As that which shows and beautifies the rest;
Those melancholy thoughts which night creates
And feeds^{xlviii} in mortal bosoms, dissipates;   340
In its own nature subtle, swift, and pure,
Which no polluted mirror can endure.
By it th'Almighty Maker doth dispense
To earthly^{xlix} creatures heavenly influence;
By it with angels' swiftness are our eyes
Exalted to the glory of the skies,
In whose bright character the light divine,
Which flesh cannot behold, doth dimly shine.
Thus was the first day made; God so called Light,
Severed from darkness; darkness was the Night.   350

Canto 2

Gen. 1.6   Again spoke God; the trembling waters move.
Part fly up in thick mists, made^l clouds above,
The Firmament   Part closer shrink about the earth below,
But did not yet the mountains' dry heads show.
Th'all-forming Word stretched out the firmament
Ps. 104.2,3   Like azure curtains round his glorious tent,
And in its hidden chambers did dispose
The magazines^{li} of hail, and rain, and snows,
Job 38.22,23 Amongst those thicker clouds from whose dark
         womb
Th'imprisoned winds in flame and thunder^{lii} come;   10
Clouds   Those clouds which over all the wondrous arch

---

^{xlviii} seeds
^{xlix} earthly] *MS* earthy *1679*
^l make
^{li} Magazine
^{lii} Thunders

Like hosts of various-formèd creatures march,[liii]
And change the scenes[liv] in our admiring eyes;
Who sometimes see them like vast mountains rise,
Sometimes like pleasant seas with clear waves glide,
Sometimes like ships on foaming billows ride;
Sometimes like mounted warriors they advance,
And seem to fire[lv] the smoking ordinance;[45]
Sometimes like shady forests they appear,
Here monsters walking, castles rising there.   20
Scorn, princes, your embroidered canopies
And painted roofs: the poor whom you despise
With far more ravishing delight[lvi] are fed
While various clouds sail o'er th'unhousèd head,
And their heaved[lvii] [46] eyes with nobler scenes present
Than your poetic courtiers can invent.

2 Pet. 3.5   Thus the exalted waters were disposed
And liquid skies the solid world enclosed,

Job 37.18   To magnify the most almighty hand
That makes thin floods like rocks of crystal stand,   30
Not quenching, nor drunk up by that bright wall
Of fire which, neighbouring them, encircles all.[lviii] [47]
The new-built firmament God Heaven named,
And over all the arch his windows[lix] framed;

[liii] Like . . . march] *1679* Like Hosts of various Creatures march *MS* Like spreading Hosts of various Creatures march *MSC*
[liv] scene
[lv] shoot
[lvi] delights
[lvii] erected
[lviii] Not . . . all]*1679; not in MS*
[lix] Windores

[45] artillery
[46] raised
[47] Genesis 1.6–8: 'And God said, Let there be a firmament in the midst of the waters, and let it divide the waters from the waters. And God made the firmament, and divided the waters which were under the firmament from the waters which were above the firmament . . . and God called the firmament Heaven.' LH combines different interpretations of this passage: the older view that the firmament was the eighth sphere enclosing the planets' seven spheres and surrounded by a further layer of water, which became ice, and the increasingly common view that the 'firmament' was the air and the upper waters were cloud; Du Bartas, *DWW* I.2.1067–90, strongly defended the first view; Milton's position, *PL* 7.261–73, is ambiguous.

From whence his liberal hand at due time pours
Ps. 147.16–18 Upon the thirsty earth refreshing showers;
Job 26 to the end And clothes her bosom with descending snow
To cherish the young seeds when cold winds blow:
Ps. 18.8–14 Hence every night his fattening dews he sheds,
And scatters pearls[lx] amidst th'enamelled beds.   40
But when presumptuous sins the bright arch scale,
Job 38.27 etc. He beats them back with terrifying hail,
Which like small shot amidst his foes he sends,
Till flaming thunder,[lxi] his great ordnance, rends
The clouds which, big with horror, ready stand
Exodus 9.2 To pour their burdens forth at his command.
But th'unpolluted air as yet had not
From mortals' impious breath infection got;
Enlightened then by a superior ray,
A serene lustre decked the second day.   50
Gen. 1.10 etc.   Th'inferior globe was fashioned on the third,
When waters at the all-commanding Word
Ps. 104.6–10 Did hastily into their channels glide,
And the uncovered hills as soon were dried.
In the same body thus, distinct and joined,
Water and earth, as flesh and blood, we find.
The late-collected waters God called seas.
The sea & rivers Springs, lakes, streams, and broad rivers are from
        these
Branched, like life-feeding veins, in every land,
Yet wheresoe'er they seem to flow or stand,   60
Eccl. 1.7 As all in the vast ocean's bosom bred,
They daily reassemble in their head,
Which thorough secret conduits back conveys
To every spring the tribute that it pays.
Eccl. 1.4 So ages from th'eternal bosom creep,
So lose themselves again in that[lxii] vast deep.
So empires, so all other human things,
With winding streams run to their native springs.
Rom. 4.22 So all the goodness mortals exercise

[lx] pearle
[lxi] Thunders
[lxii] the

Eph. 2.6 Flows back to God out of his own supplies.   70
         Now, the great fabric in all parts complete,
         Beauty was called forth to adorn the seat;[48]
Ps. 102.25 Where Earth, fixed in[lxiii] the centre, was the ground,
Job 26.7 A mantle of light air compassed it round;
         Then first the watery, then the[lxiv] fiery wall,
         And glittering Heaven last involving all.
Plants Earth's fair green robe vied with the azure skies,
         Her proud woods near[lxv] the flaming towers did rise.
         The valleys' trees, though less in breadth and height,
Gen. 2.9 Yet, hung with various fruit, as much delight.   80
         Beneath these little shrubs and bushes sprung,
         With fair flowers clothed, and with rich berries hung,
         Whose more delightful fruits seemed to upbraid
         The tall trees yielding only barren shade.
Ps. 104.14   Then sprouted grass and herbs[lxvi] and plants,
         Prepared to feed the earth's inhabitants,
         To glad their nostrils and delight their eyes,
         Revive their spirits,[lxvii] cure their maladies.
         Nor by these are the senses only fed,
         But th'understanding too, while we may read   90
         In every leaf, lectures of Providence,
         Eternal wisdom, love, omnipotence;
         Which th'eye that sees not with hell's mists[lxviii] is
             blind,
         That which regards not is of brutish kind.
         The various colours, figures, powers of these
         Are their Creator's growing witnesses;
Ps. 90.5–6 Their glories emblems are wherein we see

[lxiii] on
[lxiv] the . . . the] A . . . A
[lxv] to
[lxvi] grass and herbs] Grasse and hearbs and Flowers *MSC*
[lxvii] spirits and
[lxviii] mist

---

[48] Many commentators divided the creation into the stages of creation, distinction and orna-
mentation, Williams 51, 57. Cf. Owen, *Works* III.96: 'Hence the Vulgar Latin in this place
renders that word by "ornatus eorum", all their beauty and adorning; for the creation and
beautiful disposal of these hosts gave them beauty and ornament: and thence do the Greeks
call the world *kósmos* – that is, an adorned thing'.

	How frail our human lives and[lxix] beauties be:
Job 14.2	Even like those flowers which at the sunrise[lxx] spread
Isaiah 40.6–8	Their gaudy leaves, and are at evening dead,

How frail our human lives and[lxix] beauties be:
Job 14.2 Even like those flowers which at the sunrise[lxx] spread
Isaiah 40.6–8 Their gaudy leaves, and are at evening dead,   100
Yet while they in their native lustre shine,
Matt. 6.28–30 The eastern monarchs are not half so fine.
In richer robes God clothes the dirty soil
James 1.10–11 Than men can purchase by their sin and toil.
Then rather fields[lxxi] than painted courts admire,
Yet seeing both, think both must feed the fire:
Job 14.7–8 Only God's works have roots and seeds, from
    whence
They spring again in grace and excellence,
But men's have none: like hasty lightning they
1 Cor. 3.15 Flash out, and so forever pass away.   110
This fair creation finished the third day,
In whose end God did the whole work survey,
The seas, the skies, the trees, and less plants viewed,
And by his approbation made them good;
Gen. 1.12 In all the plants did living seeds enclose,
Whence their successive generations rose;
Gave them those powers which in them still remain,
Whereby they man and beast with food sustain.
The fourth day   Thrice had the day to gloomy night resigned,
And thrice victorious o'er the darkness shined,   120
Before the mediate cause of it, the sun
Or any star had their creation,
For with th'Omnipotent it is all one
To cause the day without, or by the sun.
God in the world by second causes reigns,
But is not tied to those means he ordains.[49]
Hab. 3.17–18 Let no heart faint, then, that on him depends,
When the means fail that[lxxii] lead to their wished ends;
For God the thing, if good, will bring about

[lxix] lives
[lxx] suns rise
[lxxi] Rather the fields
[lxxii] which

---

[49] An emphasis on 'second causes' was characteristic of thinkers with a secular tendency who minimized God's direct intervention in history; cf. 2.189, 18.88.

With instruments we see not, or without.   130
The fourth light having now expelled the shade,

Gen. 1.14 etc.   God on that day the luminaries[50] made,
And placed them all in their peculiar spheres
To measure out our days, and months, and years,
Which by their various motions are renewed,
And heat and cold have their vicissitude.
So springs and autumns still successive be,
Till ages lose them in eternity.

Sun   The sun, whom th'Hebrews God's great servant
           call,[51]
Placed in the middle orb, as lord of all,   140
Is in a radiant flaming[lxxiii] chariot whirled,

Ps. 19.4–6   And daily carried round about the world
By the First Mover's force, who in that race
Scatters his light and heat[lxxiv] in every place,
Yet not at once. Now in the east he shines,
And then again to'the western deep declines,
Seeming to quench his blazing taper there
While it enlightens the other hemisphere.
Thus he their share of day and night divides
Unto each world in their alternate tides.   150
But then its[lxxv] orb, by its own motion rolled,
Varies the seasons, brings in heat and cold,
As it projects its rays in a straight line
Or more obliquely on the earth doth shine.
And thus doth he to the low world dispense
Life-feeding and engendering influence.

Moon   This lord of day with his reflected light
Gilds the pale moon, the empress of the night,
Whose dim orb monthly wastes[lxxvi] and grows,
Doth at the first sharp-pointed horns disclose,   160
Then half, then her full-shining globe reveals,

---

lxxiii flameing Radiant
lxxiv Heat & Light
lxxv this
lxxvi waites

50 light-giving bodies
51 The Hebrew words for sun and servant were closely similar.

Which, waning, she by like degrees conceals.
Stars   The other glittering planets now appear
Each as a king enthroned in his own sphere;
Then the eighth heaven in fuller lustre shines
Thick-set with stars.[52] All these were made for signs,
That mortals by observing them might know
Due times to cultivate the earth below,
To gather fruits, plant trees, and sow their seed,
To cure their herds and let their fair flocks breed,   170
Acts 27.10   Into safe harbours to retire their ships,
Again to launch out into the calm deeps,
Their wandering vessels in broad seas to guide[lxxvii]
When the lost shores no longer are descried;
Physicians to direct in their great art,
And other useful knowledge to impart.
Nor were they only made for signs to show
Fit opportunities for things we do,
But in their various aspects too we read
Various events which shall in time succeed: 180
Droughts, inundations, famines, plagues and wars,
By several conjunctions of the stars
At least shown, if not[lxxviii] caused, through the strong
     powers
And workings astral bodies have on ours,
Which, as above they variously are joined,
So are their subjects here below inclined
To sadness, mirth, dread, quiet, love or hate,
All that may calm or trouble any state.
Yet are they but a second cause, which God
Shakes over sinners as a flaming rod,   190
And further[lxxix] manages in his own hands
To scourge the pride of all rebellious lands.
Falsely and vainly do blind mortals then
To them impute the fates and ills of men,

[lxxvii] in . . . guide] *1679* on . . . quiet *MS* on . . . ride *MSC*
[lxxviii] Not only shewne but
[lxxix] farther

---

[52] In the old cosmology the seven then-known planets were believed to be fixed to concentric
spheres surrounded by an eighth sphere.

When their sinister[53] operations be
Only th'effects of men's iniquity,
Which makes the Lord his glittering hosts thus send
Judges 5   To execute the just threats they portend.[54]
Nor are they characters of wrath alone,
They sometimes have God's grace to mankind
    shown.   200
Matt. 2   Such was that new star which did heaven adorn
When the great king of the whole world[lxxx] was
    born.
Such were those stars that fought for Israel
When Jabin's vanquished host by God's host fell.
Even those stars which threaten misery and woe
To wicked men, to saints deliverance show:
Luke 2.28   For when God cuts the bloody tyrant[lxxxi] down,
He will their lives with peace and blessings crown.
Thus the fourth evening did the fourth day close,
And where the sun went down, the stars arose.   210
   New triumph now the fifth day celebrates.
The perfumed morning opes her purple gates,
Ps. 19   Through which the sun's pavilion doth appear
And he, arrayed in all his lustre there,
Like a fresh bridegroom, with majestic grace
And joy diffusing vigour in his face,
Comes gladly forth to greet[lxxxii] his virgin bride
Tricked up[55] in all her ornaments and pride;
Her lovely maids at his approach unfold
Their gaudy vests,[56] on which he scatters gold,   220
Both cheering and enriching every place

---

lxxx the whole world] *ed.* all the world *MS* the whole word *1679*
lxxxi Tyrants
lxxxii Comes . . . greet] *1679* Come . . . meet *MS*

---

[53] Inauspicious, indicating disaster. Belief in astrological prediction was still widespread; the variant at 2.183 indicates LH's unease about reconciling this belief with Scripture.
[54] The marginal note refers to the great victory song of Deborah and Barak, which celebrates female audacity in Jael's murder of Sisera, military commander of the idolatrous king Jabin. Restoration authorities were worried about Dissenters' reading of divine judgements in the stars: on the licenser's response to a comparable passage in *PL* 1.594–9, see von Maltzahn.
[55] adorned
[56] gowns

Through which he passes^{lxxxiii} in his glorious race.
But though he found a noble theatre,^{lxxxiv}
As yet in it no living creatures were;
Though flowery carpets spread the whole earth's
    face
And rich embroideries the upper arch did grace,
And standards on the mountains stood between,
Bearing festoons like pillars wreathed with green,
The velvet couches and the mossy seats,
The open walks and the more close retreats   230
Were all prepared; yet^{lxxxv} no foot trod the woods,
Nor no mouth yet had touched the pleasant floods;
No weary creature had reposed its head
Among the sweet perfumes of the low bed;
The air was not respired in living breath,
Throughout a general stillness reigned, like death;
The king of day came forth but, unadmired,
Like unpraised gallants blushingly retired;
As an uncourted beauty, night's pale queen
Grew sick to shine where she could not be seen;   240

Fishes   When the Creator first for mute herds calls,
And bade^{lxxxvi} the waters bring forth animals.
Gen. 1.20 etc. Then was each^{lxxxvii} shell-fish and each scaly race
At once produced in their assigned place;
The crooked dolphins,[57] great Leviathan,
And all the monsters of the ocean
Job 41   Like wanton kids among^{lxxxviii} the billows played;
Nor was there after on the dry land made
Any one beast of less or greater^{lxxxix} kind
Whose like we do not in the waters find;   250
Where every greater fish devours the less,

---

^{lxxxiii} passeth
^{lxxxiv} Threatre] *1679* Theatre *MS*
^{lxxxv} but
^{lxxxvi} bid
^{lxxxvii} each] *MS* all *1679*
^{lxxxviii} amongst
^{lxxxix} less or greater] *1679* greater or lesser *MS* great or lesser *MSC*

[57] Following the Latin poetic epithet *curvus delphinus*; Milton's version, *PL* 7.410, is 'bended dolphins'.

As mighty lords poor commoners oppress.[58]
Next the Almighty by his forming word

Fowls

Made the whole plumy race, and every bird
Its proper place assigned, while with light wings
All mounted[xc] heaven. Some o'er the lakes and
   springs,
Some over the vast fens and seas did fly,
Some near the ground, some in the cloudy sky,
Some in high trees their proud nests built, some
   chose
The humble shrubs for their more safe repose,   260
Some did the marshes, some the rivers love,
Some the cornfields, and some the shady grove.
That Silence which reigned everywhere before
Its universal empire held no more.
Even Night and Darkness, its own[xci] dear retreat,
Could not preserve it in their reign complete.
The nightingales with their complaining notes,
Ravens and owls with their ill-boding throats,
And all the birds of night, shrill-crowing cocks
Whose due-kept times made them the world's first
   clocks,   270
All interrupted it, even in the night;
But at the first appearance of the light
A thousand voices, the greenwood's whole choir,
With their loud music do the day admire.
The lark doth with her single carol rise
To welcome the fair morning in the skies;
The amorous and still-complaining dove
Courts not the day, but woos her own fair love;
The jays and crows against each other rail,
And chattering pies[59] begin their gossips' tale.   280
Thus life was carried on, which first begun
In growth of plants, in fishes' motion,

[xc] mount to'wards
[xci] most

[58] The belief in correspondences between earthly and marine creatures was commonplace (cf.
DWW I.5.33–48); the link with social criticism was not.
[59] magpies

And next declared itself in living sound,
Whilst various noise the yielding air did wound.
   Various instincts the birds by nature have,
Which God to them in their creation gave,
That unto their observers do declare
The storms and calms approaching in the air;
That teach them how to build their nests at spring
And hatch their young under their nursing wing,   290
To lead abroad and guard their tender brood,
To know their hurtful and their healing food,
To feed them till their strength be perfect grown,
And after teach them how to feed alone.
   Could we the lessons they hold forth improve,
We might from some learn^{xcii} chaste and constant
   love,
Conjugal kindness of the pairèd swans,
Paternal bounty of the pelicans,^{xciii}
While they are prodigal of their own blood
To feed their chickens with that precious food.[60]   300
Wisdom of those who, when storms threat the sky,
In thick assemblies to their shelter fly,
And those who, seeing devourers in the air,
To the safe covert of the wing repair.^{xciv}

Matt. 10.16   The gall-less doves would^{xcv} teach us innocence,
Matt. 8.26 and   And the whole race to hang on Providence;
10.19   Since not the least bird that divides the air
Exempted is from the Almighty's care,
Whose bounty in due seasons feeds them all,
Prepares them berries when the thick snows fall,   310
Clothes them in many-coloured plumes, which vain
Men borrow; yet the peacock's gaudy train
More beautifully is by nature dressed

---

^{xcii} Turtles would teach vs
^{xciii} Storks piety, Conjugall kindnesse Swans / Would teach, paternall Bounty pellycans
^{xciv} Wisdom . . . repair] *1679; not in MS*
^{xcv} will

[60] Mother pelicans were believed to wound their own breasts to feed their offspring, and became emblems of charity.

Than art can make it on the gallant's crest.
This privilege these creatures had, to raise
Their voices first in their great Maker's praise,
Which when the morning opes her rosy gate,
They with consenting[61] music celebrate;
Again, with hunger pinched, to God they cry,
And from his liberal hand receive supply;   320
Who them and all his watery creatures viewed,
And saw that they in all their kinds were good,
Then blessed them that for due successions they
Might multiply. So closed he the fifth day.
    And now the sun the third time raised his head

Gen. 1.24   And rose the sixth day[xcvi] from his watery bed,
When God commands the teeming earth to bring

Beasts   Forth great and lesser beasts, each reptile[62] thing
That on her bosom creeps; the Word obeyed;
Immediately were all the[xcvii] creatures made.   330
Like hermits some made hollow rocks their cell,
And did in their preparèd mansions dwell.[xcviii]
The vermin, weasels, fulmots[63] and blind moles
Lay hid in clefts of[xcix] trees, in crannies and in holes.
The serpents lodged in marishes and[c] fens,
The savage beasts[ci] sought thickets,[cii] caves and dens.
Tame herds and flocks in open pastures[ciii] stayed,
And wanton kids upon the mountains played.
Here life almost to its perfection grew
While God these various creatures did endue   340
With various properties and various sense,

[xcvi] the sixth day rose
[xcvii] these
[xcviii] Like Hermits . . . dwell] *1679* And did in their prepared Mansions dwell / Like Hermits Made hollow Rocks their Cell *MS* And did . . . Like Hermits some made . . . *MSC*
[xcix] clefts of] *1679; not in MS*
[c] and in
[ci] Beast
[cii] thickest
[ciii] pasture

---

[61] agreeing, harmonizing
[62] Latin *reptilis* = 'creeping'.
[63] foulmarts, polecats

But little short of human excellence,
Save[64] what we in the Brutes dispersèd find
Is all collected in Man's nobler mind,
Who to the high perfection of his sense
Hath added a more high intelligence.
Yet several brutes have noble faculties:
Some apprehensive are, some subtle, wise,
Some have invention and[civ] docility,
Some wonderful in imitation be,[cv]   350
Some with high generous courage are endued,
With kindness some, and some with gratitude,
With memory[cvi] some, and some with providence,
With natural love, and with meek innocence:
Some watchful are, and some laborious be,
Some have obedience, some true loyalty.
Among them too, we all the passions find,
Some more to love, some more to hate inclined.
The musing hare and the light-footed deer
Are under the predominance of fear;   360
Goats and hot monkeys are with lust possessed,[65]
Rage governs in the savage tiger's breast;
Jealousy doth the hearts of fierce bulls move,
Impatient of all rivals in their love.
Some sportive and some melancholy be,
Some proner to revenge and cruelty.
The kingly lion in his bosom hath
The fiery seed of self-provoking wrath.[cvii]
Joy is no stranger to the savage breast,
As oft with love, hate and desire possessed,   370
Through the aversion and the appetite
Which all these passions in their hearts excite.
God clothed them all in several wools and hair,

[civ] some
[cv] *Followed in MS by* Some past things, long in Memory doe keepe / Some have a ffancey
working in their sleepe
[cvi] prudence
[cvii] The . . . wrath] *1679; not in MS*

[64] save that
[65] Cf. Shakespeare, *Othello* 3.3.406, 4.1.263.

Whereof some meaner, some more precious are,
Which men now into garments weave and spin,
Nor only wear their fleeces, but their skin;
Besides employ their teeth, bones, claws, and horn;
Some medicines be, and some the house adorn.
A thousand other various ways we find,
Wherein alive and dead they serve mankind,   380
Who from th'obedience they to him afford
Isaiah 1.3   Might learn his duty to his Sovereign Lord.[66]

Canto 3

Now was the glorious universe complete
And everything in beauteous order set,
When God, about to make the king of all,
Did in himself a sacred[cviii] council call;
Not that he needed to deliberate,
But pleased t'allow solemnity and state
To wait upon that noble creature's birth
Ps. 8.6   For whom he had designed both heaven and earth:
Gen. 1.26 etc. 'Let us', said God, 'with sovereign power endued,
Make man after our own similitude,   10
Eph. 4.24   Let him our sacred impressed image bear,
Ps. 8   Ruling o'er all in earth and sea and air.'
Man   Then made the Lord a curious mould of clay
Which lifeless on the earth's cold bosom lay
When God did it with living breath inspire,
A soul in all, and every part entire,
Where life ris'[cix] [67] above motion, sound and sense
To higher reason and intelligence;
And this is truly termèd life alone
Which makes life's fountain to the living known.   20
This life into itself doth gather all

---

cviii second
cix Live rise

[66] The passage from Isaiah gives a political resonance: at the book's opening the prophet denounces the Israelites as entirely corrupt except for a small remnant.
[67] rose

The rest maintained by its original,
Which gives it being, motion, sense, warmth, breath,
And those chief powers that are not lost in death.
  Thus was the noblest creature the last made,
As he in whom the rest perfection had,
In whom both parts of the great world were joined,
Earth in his members, Heaven in his mind;
Whose vast reach the whole universe comprised,

Eccl. 3.11   And saw it in himself epitomized.[68]   30
Yet not the centre nor circumference can
Fill the more comprehensive soul of man,
Whose life is but a progress of desire,
Which still, enjoyed, doth something else require,
Unsatisfied with all it hath pursued

Matt. 11.25   Until it rest in God, the sovereign good.
  The earthly mansion of this heavenly guest
Peculiar privileges too possessed.
Whereas all other creatures clothèd were
In shells, scales, gaudy plumes, or wools,[cx] or hair,   40
Only a fair smooth skin o'er man was drawn,
Like damask roses blushing through pure lawn.[69]
The azure veins, where blood and spirits flow,
Like violets in a field of lilies show.
As others have a down-bent countenance,
He only doth his head to heaven advance,

Ps. 144.12   Resembling thus a tree whose noble root
In heaven grows, whence all his graces shoot.[70]
He only on two upright columns stands,
He only hath, and knows, the use of hands,   50
Which God's rich bounties for the rest receive,
And aid to all the other members give.[cxi]

[cx] wool
[cxi] ... God's ... give, / ... aid ... receive] *1679; lines inverted in MS*

[68] The idea of the body as a miniature world was a Renaissance commonplace: cf. Du Bartas, *DWW* I.6.424. Moore compares this allegorized description of the human body with Phineas Fletcher's *The Purple Island* (1633), though the parallels are not especially close. LH follows the generic conventions of the formal, part-by-part praise of the body, the blazon: cf. Milton's famous blazon of Adam and Eve together (*PL* 4.288–318).
[69] fine linen
[70] See Chambers, and Marvell, 'Upon Appleton House', lines 567–8.

He only hath a voice articulate,
Varied by joy, grief, anger, love and^{cxii} hate,
And every other motion of the mind
Which hereby doth an apt expression find.
Hereby glad mirth in laughter is alone
By man expressed; in a peculiar groan
His grief comes forth, accompanied with tears,
Peculiar shrieks utter his sudden fears.   60
Herein is music too, which sweetly charms

Prov. 15.1   The sense, and the most savage heart disarms.
       The gate of this God in the head did place,
The head which is the body's chiefest grace,
The noble palace of the royal guest
Within by Fancy and Invention^{cxiii} dressed,
With many pleasant useful ornaments
Which new Imagination still presents,
Adorned without by^{cxiv} Majesty and Grace:
O who can tell the wonders of a face!   70
In none of all his fabrics more than here
Doth the Creator's glorious power appear,
That of so many thousands^{cxv} which we see
All human creatures like, all different be.
If the front⁷¹ be the glory of man's frame,
Those lamps which in its upper windows^{cxvi} flame
Illustrate⁷² it, and as day's radiant star
In the clear heaven of a bright face are.

1 John 2.26   Here Love takes stand, and here ardent Desire
Matt. 5.28   Enters the soul, as fire drawn in by fire.   80
1 Pet. 2.14   At^{cxvii} two ports on each side, the hearing sense
Still waits to take in fresh intelligence,
But the false spies both at the ears and eyes

---

^{cxii} or
^{cxiii} phansey, wit, Invention
^{cxiv} with
^{cxv} thousand
^{cxvi} windores
^{cxvii} As

⁷¹ forehead
⁷² illuminate, glorify

Conspire^{cxviii} with strangers for the soul's surprise

James 5.11   And let all life-perturbing passions in,

Which with tears, sighs^{cxix} and groans issue again.

Nor do those labyrinths which like breast-works are

About those secret ports serve for a bar

To the false sorcerers conducted by

Prov. 1.10–12   Man's own imprudent curiosity.   90

There is an arch i'the middle of the face

Of equal-necessary use and grace,

For there men suck up the life-feeding air,

And panting bosoms are dischargèd there.

Beneath it is the chief and beauteous gate

About which various pleasant graces wait,

When smiles the ruby doors^{cxx} a little way

Unfold, or laughter doth them quite display,

And, opening the vermilion curtains,^{cxxi} shows

The ivory piles set in two even rows   100

Before the portal, as a double guard

Prov. 25.11   By which the busy tongue is helped and barred;

Eccl. 12.11   Whose sweet sounds charm, when love doth it
    inspire,

James 3.6   And when hate moves it, set^{cxxii} the world on fire.

Within this portal's inner vault is placed

The palate, where sense meets its joys in taste.

On rising cheeks, beauty in white and red

Strives with itself, white on the forehead spread

Its undisputed glory there maintains,

And is illustrated with azure veins.   110

The brows Love's bow and Beauty's shadow are.

A thick-set^{cxxiii} grove of soft and shining hair

Adorns the head, and shows^{cxxiv} like crowning rays,

While th'air's soft breath among the loose curls
    plays.

^{cxviii} Conspires
^{cxix} sighs, Teares
^{cxx} doore
^{cxxi} Curtaine
^{cxxii} sets
^{cxxiii} thickest
^{cxxiv} looks

Besides the colours and the features, we
Admire their just and perfect symmetry,[73]
Whose ravishing resultance[74] is that air
That graces all, and is not anywhere;
Whereof we cannot well say what it is,
Yet beauty's chiefest excellence lies in this;   120
Which mocks the painters in their best designs,
And is not held by[cxxv] their exactest lines.
    But while we gaze upon our own fair frame,
Let us remember too from whence it came,
And that, by sin corrupted now, it must

Job 4.19   Return to its originary dust.
How undecently doth pride then lift that head
On which the meanest feet must shortly tread?

Eccl. 7.29   Yet at the first it was with glory crowned,
Till Satan's fraud gave it the mortal wound.   130
This excellent creature God did Adam call
To mind him of his low original,[75]
Whom he had formed out of the common ground
Which then with various pleasures did abound.

Paradise   The whole Earth was one large delightful field
That, till man sinned, no hurtful briars did yield,

Gen. 2.8   But God, enclosing one part from the rest,
A paradise in the rich spicy East
Had stored with Nature's wealthy magazine,
Where every plant did in its lustre shine,   140
But did not grow promiscuously[76] there:
They all disposed in such rich order were
As did augment their single native grace
And perfected the pleasure of the place
To such a height that th'apelike art of man,
Licentious pens or pencils,[77] never can,
With all th'essays[78] of all-presuming wit,

cxxv in

73 beauty, proportion
74 reflection
75 origin
76 mingled confusedly
77 artist's brushes
78 attempts

Or form or feign[cxxvi] aught that approaches it.
Whether it were a fruitful hill or vale,
Whether high rocks or trees did it impale,[79]　　　150
Or rivers with their clear and kind embrace
Into a pleasant island formed the place,
Whether its noble situation were
On earth, in the bright moon, or in the air,
In what forms stood the various trees and flowers,
The disposition of the walks and bowers,
Whereof no certain word nor sign remains,
We dare not take from men's inventive brains.[80]
　　We know there was pleasant and noble shade
Which the tall-growing pines and cedars[cxxvii] made,　　160
And thicker coverts,[81] which the light and heat
Even at noonday could scarcely[cxxviii] penetrate.
A crystal river, on whose verdant banks
The crownèd fruit-trees stood in lovely ranks,
His gentle wave thorough the garden led,
And all the spreading roots with moisture fed;
But past th'enclosure, thence the single stream,
Parted in four, four noble floods became:
Pison, whose large arms Havilah enfold,
A wealthy land enriched with finest gold,　　170
Where also many precious stones are found;
The second river, Gihon, doth surround
All that fair land where Chus inhabited,
Where tyranny first raised up her proud head
And led her bloodhounds all along the shore,
Polluting the pure stream with crimson gore.[82]
Eden's third river Hiddekel they call,
Whose waters eastward in Assyria fall.

Gen. 3.8
Gen. 2.10

Gen. 2.11

Gen. 2.13

[cxxvi] frame
[cxxvii] tall pines and growing Cedars
[cxxviii] not

[79] enclose, fence in
[80] On different theories of the location of Paradise see Williams 95ff.
[81] thickets
[82] Chus was the father of Nimrod: see canto 10. It was unusual to bring such direct political commentary into the topography of Eden.

Gen. 2.14   The fourth, Euphrates, whose swift stream did run
About the stately walls of Babylon   180
And in the revolution[83] of some years
Swelled high, fed with the captived Hebrews'[cxxix]
    tears.
God in the midst of Paradise did place
Gen. 2.9   Two trees that stood up dressed in all the[cxxx] grace,
The verdure, beauty, sweetness, excellence,
With which all else could tempt or feast the sense.
On one, apples of knowledge did abound,
And life-confirming fruit the other crowned.
    And now did God the new-created king
Into the pleasures of his earthly palace bring.   190
The air spice, balm, and amber did respire,
His ears were feasted by[cxxxi] the sylvan choir;
Like country girls, gross[cxxxii] flowers did dispute
Their humble beauties with the high-born fruit;
Both high and low their gaudy colours vied,
As courtiers do in their contentious pride,
Striving which of them should yield most delight
And stand the finest in their sovereign's sight.
The shrubs, with berries crowned like precious gems,
Offered their supreme lord their diadems,   200
Which did no single sense alone invite,
Courting alike the eyes and appetite.
Among all these the eye-refreshing green,
Sometimes alone, sometimes in mixture seen,
O'er all the banks and all the flat ground[cxxxiii] spread,
Seemed an embroidered or plain velvet bed.
And, that each sense might its refreshment have,
The gentle air soft pleasant touches gave
Unto his panting limbs, whenever they
Upon the sweet and mossy couches lay.   210

[cxxix] Hebrew Captives
[cxxx] their
[cxxxi] with
[cxxxii] gross] *MS* grass *1679*
[cxxxiii] Ore all the ground, and all the fat banks spread

[83] going round, passing

A shady eminence there was whereon

Gen. 2.19 etc.   The noble creature sat, as on[cxxxiv] his throne,

When God brought every fowl and every brute

That he might names unto their natures suit,

Whose comprehensive understanding knew

How to distinguish them at their first view;

And they,[cxxxv] retaining those names ever since,

Are monuments of his first excellence

And the Creator's providential grace,

Who in those names left us some prints[cxxxvi] to trace;   220

Nature, mysterious grown since we grew blind,

Whose labyrinths we should less easily find

If those first appellations as a clue

Did not in some sort serve to lead us through

And rectify that frequent gross mistake

Which our weak judgements and sick senses make

Since, man ambitious to know more, that sin

Brought dullness, ignorance and error in.[84]

Society   Though God himself to man did condescend,

Though his[cxxxvii] knowledge to all natures did extend,   230

Though heaven and earth thus centred in his mind,[85]

Yet, being the only one of his whole[cxxxviii] kind,

He found himself without an equal mate

To whom he might his joys communicate

And by communication multiply.

Too far out of his reach was God on high,

Too much below him brutish creatures were.

God could at first have made a[cxxxix] human pair,

But that it was his will to let man see

The need and sweetness of society;   240

[cxxxiv] in
[cxxxv] the
[cxxxvi] points
[cxxxvii] Though's
[cxxxviii] owne
[cxxxix] an

[84] On the belief that language in Paradise mirrored reality in a particularly close way see Leonard.
[85] Cf. *R* 135: God 'exalted him to the angelicall nature, making him the center where heaven and earth meete'.

Who, though he were his Maker's favourite,
Feasted in paradise with all delight,
Though all the creatures paid him homage, yet
Was not his unimparted joy complete,
While there was not a second of his kind
Endued with such a form and such a mind
As might alike his soul and senses feast:
He saw that every bird and every beast
Its own resemblance in its female viewed,
And only union with its like pursued.   250
Hence birds with birds, and fish with fish abide,
Nor those^{cxl} with beasts, nor beasts with these
    reside:
According to their several species too,
As several households in one city do,
So they with their own kinds associate:
The kingly eagle hath no buzzard mate;
The ravens more their own black feather^{cxli} love
Than painted pheasants, or the fair-necked dove.
So bears to rough bears rather do incline
Than to majestic lions, or fair kine.⁸⁶   260
    If it be thus with brutes, much less then can
The brutish conversation suit with man.
'Tis only like desires like things unite:
In union likeness only feeds delight.
Where unlike natures in conjunction are,
There is no product but perpetual war,
Such as there was in Nature's troubled womb
Until the severed births from thence did come.
For the whole world nor order had, nor grace,
Till severed elements each their own place   270
Assignèd were, and while in them they keep
Heaven still smiles above, th'untroubled deep
With kind salutes embraces^{cxlii} the dry land,
Firm doth the Earth on its foundation stand,

^{cxl} these
^{cxli} feathers
^{cxlii} embraceth

⁸⁶ cows

A cheerful light streams from th'ethereal fire
And all in universal joy conspire.[87]
But if with their unlike they attempt[cxliii] to mix,
Their rude congressions[88] everything unfix;
Darkness again invades[cxliv] the troubled skies,
Earth trembling under angry heaven lies;   280
The sea, swollen high with rage, comes to the shore
And swallows that which it but kissed before;
Th'unbounded fire breaks forth with dreadful
    light
And horrid cracks which dying nature fright,
Till that high Power which all powers regulates
The disagreeing natures separates,
The like to like rejoining as before,
So the world's peace, joy, safety[cxlv] doth restore.
Yet if man could not find in bird or brute
That conversation[89] which might aptly suit   290
His higher nature, was it not sublime
Enough, above the lower world to climb
And in angelic converse to delight,
Although it could not reach the supreme height?
No; for though man partake intelligence,
Yet that, being joined to an inferior sense,
Dulled by corporeal vapours, cannot be
Refined enough for angels' company:
As strings screwed up too high, as bows still bent
Or[cxlvi] [90] break themselves, or crack the instrument;   300
So drops neglected flesh into the grave,
If it no share in the soul's pleasures have.
Man like himself needs an associate,

cxliii 'tempt
cxliv Invests
cxlv So 'th'worlds peace, Joy, & Saftey
cxlvi Doe

[87] unite
[88] Collisions. Cf. 5.333, in a similar context of cosmic civil war; this relatively unusual word occurs three times within ten lines of LH's Lucretius translation (*L* 5.434–43).
[89] Beyond the modern sense, more generally society, intimacy; cf. *PL* 8.418 and *CPW* II.235, on the importance of marriage as conversation.
[90] either

Who doth both soul and sense participate:
Not the swift horse, the eager hawk or hound,
Dogs, parrots, monkeys, 'mongst whom Adam
    found
No meet companion, thinking them too base
For the society of human race,
Though his degenerate offspring choose that now
Which his sound reason could not then allow,   310
But found himself amongst them all alone.
    Whether he begged a mate it is not known.[91]
Likely his want might send him to the spring;
For God, who freely gives us everything,
Mercy endears by instilling the desire,

Ezekiel 36.37   And granting that which humbly we require.
Howe'er it was, God saw his solitude
And gave his sentence that it was not good.

Gen. 2.18   Yet not a natural, nor a moral ill,
Because his solitude was not his will,   320
Opposing his creator's[cxlvii] end, as they
Who into caves and deserts run away,
Seeking perfection in that state wherein
A good was wanting when man had no sin.
For without help to propagate mankind
God's glory had been to one breast[cxlviii] confined,
Which multiplièd saints do now conspire[92]

Hebrews 12.23   Throughout their generations to admire.
Man's nature had not been the sacred shrine,
Partner and bride of that which is divine;   330
The Church, fruit of this union, had not come
To light, but perished, stifled in the womb.
Again, 'tis not particularly good
For man to waste his life in solitude,
Whose nature, for society designed,
Can no full joy without a second find

Eccl. 4.8 etc.   To whom he may communicate his heart,

---

cxlvii Creation's
cxlviii to one Brest had bin

[91] Contrast *PL* 8.357ff.; LH is more reluctant to venture beyond Scripture.
[92] combine

And pay back all the pleasures they impart;
For all the joys that we enjoy alone,
And all our unseen lustre, is as none.   340
If thus want of a partner did abate
Man's happiness in man's most perfect state,
Much more hath human nature, now decayed,
Need of a suitable and a kind aid.
It is not good virtue should lie^{cxlix} obscure,
That barren rocks rich treasures should immure,

1 Cor. 12.5–12   Which our kind Lord to some, for all men gave,
That all might share of all his bounties have;

Matt. 5.15–16   Not good, dark lanterns should shut up the light
Of fair example, made for the black^{cl} night;   350
Not good, experience should her candle hide,
When weak ones perish, wanting her bright guide;
Not good to let unactive graces chill,
No lively warmth receive, no good^{cli} instil
By quickening converse. Thus nor are the great,
The wise, and firm, permitted to^{clii} retreat,
Betraying so deserted innocence,
To which God made them conduct and defence;
Nor may the simple and the weak expose
Themselves alone to strong and subtle foes;   360
Men for each other's mutual help were made,
The meanest may afford the highest aid,
The highest to necessity must yield:

Eccl. 5.9   Even princes are beholding[93] to the field.
He that from mortal converse steals away
Injures himself, and others doth betray
Whom Providence committed to his trust,
And in that act nor^{cliii} prudent is nor just.
For^{cliv} sweet friends, both in pleasure and distress,

^{cxlix} be
^{cl} black] *MS* dark *1679*
^{cli} heat
^{clii} A
^{cliii} that act nor] *1679* that nor *MS* that act nor *MSC*
^{cliv} As

[93] beholden; the passage in Ecclesiastes attacks oppression and insists that the profit of the earth is for all

Augment the joy and make the torment less.   370
Equal delight it is to learn and teach,
To be held up to that we cannot reach,
And others from the abject earth to raise
To merit, and to give deservèd praise.
Wisdom imparted, like th'increasing bread
Matt. 15.36   Wherewith the Lord so many thousands fed,
By distribution adds to its own store,
And still the more it gives it hath the more.
Extended power reaches itself a crown,
Gathering up those whom misery casts[clv] down.   380
Love raiseth us, itself to heaven doth rise
By virtue's varied mutual exercise,
Rom. 13.9–10   Sweet love, the life of life, which cannot shine
But lies like gold concealèd in the mine,
1 Cor. 13   Till it through much exchange a brightness take
And conversation doth it current make.[clvi]
     God, having showed his creature thus the need
Woman   Of human helps,[clvii] a help for man decreed.
'I will,' said he, 'the man's meet aid provide.'
But that he from his waking view might hide   390
Such a mysterious work, the Lord did keep
Gen. 2.21–2   All Adam's senses fast locked up in sleep;
Then from his opened side took without pain
A clothèd rib, and closed the flesh again,
And of the bone did a fair virgin frame
Who, by her maker brought, to Adam came
And was in matrimonial union joined,
By love and nature happily combined.
Adam's clear understanding at first view
His wife's original and nature knew;   400
His will, as pure, did thankfully embrace
His father's bounty, and admired his grace;
And as her sweet charms did his heart surprise,
He spoke his joy in these glad ecstasies:
     'Thou art my better self, my flesh, my bone,

[clv] cast
[clvi] ... it ... take / ... conversation ... make] *1679; these lines inverted in MS, which also reads* doe *for* doth
[clvii] help

Gen. 2.23–4 We, late of one made two, again in one
Shall reunite, and with the frequent birth
Of our joint issue, people the vast earth.
To show that thou wert taken out of me,
Isha shall be thy name;[94] as unto thee,   410
Ravished with love and joy, my soul doth[clviii] cleave,
So men hereafter shall their fathers leave,
Eph. 5.31 And all relations else which are most dear,
Matt. 19.5 That they may only to their wives adhere;
When marriage male and female doth combine,
Children in one flesh shall two parents join.'
Lastly, God, who the sacred knot had tied,
With blessing his own ordinance sanctified:
'Increase,' said he, 'and multiply your race,
Gen. 1.28 etc. Fill th'Earth allotted for your dwelling-place.   420
I give you right to all her[clix] fruits and plants,
Dominion over her inhabitants;
The fish that in the flood's deep bosom lie,
All fowls that in the airy region fly,
Whatever lives and feeds on the dry land,
Are all made subject under your command.
The grass and green herbs let your cattle eat,
And let the richer fruits be your own meat,
Except the tree of knowing good and ill:
That, by the precept of my sovereign will,   430
You must not eat, for in the day you do,
Inevitable death shall seize on you.'
Marriage   Thus God did the first marriage celebrate
Gen. 2.22 While man was in his unpolluted state,
Hebrews 13.4 And th'undefilèd bed with honour decked,
Though perverse men the ordinance reject,
And, pulling all its sacred ensigns down,
Prov. 18.22 To the white virgin only give the crown.[95]
Nor yet is marriage grown less sacred since

[clviii] shall
[clix] the

[94] The Hebrew plays on the similarity between *ishshah* (woman) and *ish* (man).
[95] A typically Protestant elevation of the married life above the contemplative celibate life: cf.
PL 4.744–7.

Man fell from his created excellence: 440
Necessity now raises^{clx} its esteem,
Which doth mankind from death's vast jaws redeem,
Who even in their graves are yet alive
While they in their posterity survive.
In it they find a comfort and an aid
In all the ills which human life invade.

Ps. 127.3–5   This curbs and cures wild passions that arise,
Repairs time's daily wastes^{clxi} with new supplies;
When the declining mother's youthful^{clxii} grace
Lies dead and buried in her wrinkled face,   450
In her fair daughters it revives and grows
And her dead cinder in their new flames glows.
And though this state may sometimes prove accursed,
For of best things, still the corruption's worst,^{clxiii}
Sin so destroys an institution good,
Provided against death and solitude.

     Eve, out of sleeping Adam formèd^{clxiv} thus,
A sweet instructive emblem is to us

Ps. 121.3–5   How waking Providence is active still
To do us good, and to avert our ill   460

Job 32.15–17 etc.   When we locked up in stupefaction lie,
Not dreaming that our blessings are so nigh,

Deut. 32.36   Blessings wrought out by Providence alone
Without the least assistance of our own.

Rom. 4.19   Man's help produced in death-like sleep doth show

John 19.34
1 John 5.6   Our choicest mercies out of dead wombs flow.

     So from the second Adam's bleeding side

[1] Tim. 5.5
Phil. 4.13   God formed the Gospel Church, his mystic bride,
2 Cor. 12.9   Whose strength was only of his firmness made:
John 5.2   His blood quick spirits into ours conveyed,   470
Eph. 2.1,5–6 etc.   His wasted flesh our wasted flesh supplied,
2 Tim. 1.10
Isaiah 53.5   And we were then revivèd when he died;
Acts 20.28   Who, waked from that short sleep, with joy did view
Eph. 5.25–7   The virgin fair that out of his wounds grew,

---

^{clx} raiseth
^{clxi} wast
^{clxii} vsefull
^{clxiii} Corruptions still ye worst
^{clxiv} sleeping Adam formed] *1679* sleeping formed Adam *MS* sleeping Adam formed *MSC*

Rev. 5.19
John 17.9–10

Presented by th'eternal Father's grace
Unto his everlasting kind embrace.[96]
　　'My spouse, my sister,' said he, 'thou art mine;

Ps. 2.8
Cant. 2.16 and 4.10
1 Cor. 3.22–3
John 6.38–9
Rev. 5.9–10
Phil. 2.9
John 19.27
Col. 2.13–15
1 Cor. 15.54–5, 21–2
John 17.23–4, 14.3

I and my death, I and my life are thine;
For thee I did my heavenly Father quit
That thou with me on my high throne mayst sit,　　480
My mother's human flesh in death did leave
For thee, that I to thee might only cleave,
Redeem thee from the confines of dark hell,
And evermore in thy dear bosom dwell:
From heaven I did descend to fetch up thee,
Rose from the grave that thou mightst[clxv] reign
　　with me.

Eph. 4.9–10 etc.
Rom. 8.17–18
2 Tim. 2.12
Col. 1
Eph. 1
John 1.16
Acts 9.24
Matt. 25.34ff.

Henceforth no longer two but one we are.
Thou dost my merit, life,[clxvi] grace, glory share:
As my victorious triumphs are all thine,
So are thy injuries and sufferings mine,　　490
Which I for thee will vanquish as my own,
And give thee rest in the celestial throne.'

Heb. 4.13, 10.19–20 etc.
1 Pet. 1.2
Heb. 13.12
1 Pet. 1.10–12
Eph. 3.9–10
Heb. 8.5

　　The bride, with these caresses entertained,
In naked beauty doth before him stand,
And knows no shame, purged from all foul desire
Whose secret guilt kindles the blushing fire.
Her glorious Lord is naked too, no more
Concealed in types[97] and shadows[clxvii] as before.
So our first parents innocently did
Behold that nakedness which since is hid,　　500

2 Pet. 2.14
Matt. 5.28

That lust may not catch fire from beauty's flame,
Engendering thoughts which dye the cheeks with
　　shame.

[clxv] mayst
[clxvi] Life, Merit
[clxvii] figures

---

[96] Adam's love for Eve prefigures Christ's love for the church, following a tradition of allegorical readings of the marital language in the Song of Songs (Canticles). Such readings were especially common amongst Dissenters. On the 'Gospel Church' cf. Owen, *The True Nature of a Gospel Church*, *Works* XVI.1–208.

[97] Christian interpreters took persons and events of the Old Testament to be anticipatory symbols of Christ's mission, accommodated to pre-Christian understandings: cf. *PL* 12.303: 'From shadowy types to truth'.

Gen. 2.1   Thus Heaven and Earth their full perfection had,
Thus all their hosts and ornaments were made.
Armies of angels had the highest place,
Bright starry hosts the lower heaven did grace,
The mutes encampèd in the waters were,
The wingèd troops were quartered in the air,
The walking animals, as th'infantry
Of th'universal host, at large did lie   510
Spread over all the Earth's most ample face,
Each regiment in its assignèd place.
Paradise the[clxviii] headquarter was, and there

Gen. 2.16 The Emperor to his Viceroy did appear,
Him in his regal office did instal,
A general muster of his hosts did call,

Gen. 2.19 Resigning up into his sole command
The numerous tribes that fill both[clxix] sea and land.
As each kind severally had before
Blessing and approbation, so once more,   520
When all together God his works reviewed,

Gen. 1.31 The blessing was confirmèd and renewed,
And with the sixth day the creation ceased.

Sabbath   The[clxx] seventh day the Lord himself did rest,
Gen. 2.2–3 And made it a perpetual ordinance then
Ex. 20.8 To be observed by every age of men,
That after six days' honest labour they
His precept and example should obey,
As he did his, their works surcease, and spend
That day in sacred rest till that day end,   530
And in its number back again return,
Still consecrated, till it have outworn
All other time, and that alone remain
When neither toil nor burden shall again
The weary lives of mortal men infest,
Nor intermit[clxxi] their holy, happy rest.[98]

clxviii their
clxix both] *MS* doth *1679*
clxx And the
clxxi Interrupt

[98] Belief that Sabbath observance was commanded at the first creation, by the moral rather than the ceremonial law, was a distinctively Puritan emphasis.

                    Nor is this rest sacred to idleness:
                    God, a perpetual act, sloth cannot bless.
                    He ceased not from his own celestial joy,
                    Which doth himself perpetually employ   540
Prov. 8.22,30–1   In contemplation of himself and those
Matt. 3.17   Most excellent works wherein himself he shows;
John 5.17,20–1   He only ceased from making lower things,
                    By which, as steps, the mounting soul he brings
                    To th'upmost height, and, having finished these,
Jer. 9.24   Himself did in his own productions please,
Ps. 104, 147, 145 Full satisfied in their perfection,
                    Rested from what he had completely done;
                    And made his pattern our instruction,
                    That we, as far as finite creatures may   550
                    Trace him that's infinite, should in our way
                    Rest as our Father did, work as he wrought,
Eccl. 9.10   Nor cease till we have to perfection brought
Heb. 6.1   Whatever to his glory we intend,
Phil. 3.19   Still making ours the same which[clxxii] was his end.
1 Cor. 10.30   As his works in commands begin, and have
                    Conclusion in the blessings which he gave,
1 John 5.3   So must his word give being to all ours;
Ps. 119.9   And since th'events[99] are not in our own powers,
                    We must his blessing beg, his great name bless,   560
                    And make our thanks the crown of our success.
                    As God first heaven did for man prepare,
                    Men last[clxxiii] for heaven created were:
Matt. 6.33   So should we all our actions regulate,
Col. 3.1   Which Heaven, both first and last, should terminate,
                    And in whatever circle else they run,
                    There should they end, there should they be begun,
                    There seek their pattern, and derive from thence
                    Their whole direction and their influence.
                    As, when th'Almighty this low world did frame,   570
                    Life by degrees to its perfection came,
                    In vegetation first sprung up, to sense

[clxxii] that
[clxxiii] last of all

[99] outcomes

Heb. 5.12–14 Ascended^{clxxiv} next, and climbed to reason thence,
So we, pursuing our attainments, should
Press forward from what's positively good,
Still climbing higher, until^{clxxv} we reach the best,
And, that acquired, forever fix our rest,
Our souls so ravished with the joys divine
That they no more to creatures can decline.
As God's^{clxxvi} rest was but a more high retreat   580
From the delights of this inferior seat,
So must our souls upon our Sabbaths^{clxxvii} climb
Isaiah 58.13 Above the world, sequestered for that time
From those legitimate delights which may
Rejoice us here upon a common day.
As God, his works^{clxxviii} completed, did retire
To be adored by the angelic choir,
So, when on us the seventh day's light doth shine,
Should we ourselves to God's assemblies join,
Job 1.6 Thither all^{clxxix} hearts as one pure offering bring,   590
Hebrews 10.25 And all with one accord adore our King.
This seventh day the Lord to mankind gave,
Matt. 2.27 Nor is it the least privilege we have:
Ezekiel 20.12 And ours peculiarly. The orbs above
As well the seventh as the sixth day move,
The rain descends^{clxxx} and the fierce tempest blows,
On^{clxxxi} it the restless ocean ebbs and flows;
Bees that day fill the hive,^{clxxxii} and on that day
Ants their provisions^{clxxxiii} in their store-house lay;
All creatures ply their works, no beast   600
But those which mankind use share in that rest,
Which God indulged only to human race,

^{clxxiv} Extended
^{clxxv} till
^{clxxvi} his
^{clxxvii} sabboth
^{clxxviii} worke
^{clxxix} our
^{clxxx} Raines descend
^{clxxxi} In
^{clxxxii} their hives
^{clxxxiii} provision

That they in it might come before his face
To celebrate his worship and his praise,
And gain a blessing upon all their days.
    O wretched souls of perverse men, who slight
So great a grace, refuse such^{clxxxiv} rich delight,
Which the inferior creatures cannot share,
To which alone their natures fitted are,
Heb. 4.9 and And whereby favoured men admitted be   610
12.22 Into the angels' blessed society.
Yet is this rest but a far distant view
Of that celestial life which we pursue,
By Satan oft so interrupted here
That little of its glory doth appear,
Nor can our souls' sick, languid appetite
Feast upon such substantial, strong delight.
As music pains the grievèd^{clxxxv} aching head,
Amos 8.5 With which the healthful sense is sweetly fed;
So duties wherein sound hearts full joys find   620
Fetters and sad loads are to a sick mind
Till it thereto by force itself inure,
And from a loathing fall to love its cure.
    God for his worship kept one day of seven;
The other six, to^{clxxxvi} man for man's use given,
Adam, although so highly dignified,
Was not to spend in idle ease and pride,
Nor supine sleep, drunk with his sensual pleasures,
Profusely wasting th'Empire's sacred treasures,
As now his fall'n sons do, that arrogate   630
His forfeited dominion and high state;
But God his daily business did ordain
That kings, hence taught, might in their realms
    maintain
Fair order, serving those whom they command
Romans 13.3–4 As guardians, not as owners of the land,
Not being set there to pluck up and destroy

---

^{clxxxiv} soe
^{clxxxv} grieved] *1679* Greivous *MS* Greived *MSC*
^{clxxxvi} to] *1679* for *MS* to *MSC*

Those plants whose culture[clxxxvii] [100] should their
    cares employ.

1 Thes. 4.11   Nor doth this precept only kings comprise,

1 Tim. 5.8   The meanest must his little paradise

With no less vigilance and care attend   640

Than princes on their vast enclosures[clxxxviii] spend.

All hence must learn their duty, to suppress

Prov. 19.5,   Th'intrusions[clxxxix] of a sordid idleness.

10.26   Who[101] formed, could have preserved the garden
    fair

Without th'employment of man's busy care,

But that he willed that our delight[cxc] should be

The wages of our constant industry,

That we his ever-bounteous hand might bless

Crowning our honest labours with success,

And taste the joy men reap in their own fruit,   650

Loving that more to which they contribute

Either the labour of their hands or brains

Than better things produced by others' pains.

Led by desire, fed with fair hope,[cxci] the fruit

Oft-times delights not more than the pursuit.

For man a nature hath to action prone,

That languishes and sickens finding none.

As standing pools corrupt, water that flows

More pure by its continual[cxcii] current grows,

So human kind by active exercise   660

Do to the heights of their perfection rise,

While their stocked glory comes to no ripe growth

Whose lives corrupt in idleness and sloth,

Which is not natural, but a disease

That doth upon the flesh-cloyed spirit seize.

[clxxxvii] Cultures
[clxxxviii] Inclosure
[clxxxix] Instruction
[cxc] deligts
[cxci] Led . . . Hope] *1679* ffed with faire, led with desire *MS* ffed with faire hope, led with desire *MSC*
[cxcii] Constant

[100] cultivation
[101] he who

Where health untainted is, then[cxciii] the sound mind
In its employment doth its pleasure find.
But when Death or its representer Sleep
Upon the mortals' tired members creep,
This during its dull reign doth life suspend,   670
That, ceasing action, puts it to an end.
Lastly, since God himself did man employ
To dress up Paradise, that moderate joy
Which from this fair creation we derive
Is not our sin, but our prerogative,
1 Tim. 4.4–5   If bounded so as we fix not our rest
1 John 2.17   In creatures, which but transient are at best;
1 Cor. 7.31,20   Yet 'tis sin to neglect, not use or prize,
As well as 'tis to waste and idolize.

Canto 4

Gen. 1.31   Good were all natures as God made them all,
Rom. 9.21–3   Good was his will, permitting some to fall:
Rom. 11   That th'rest, renouncing their frail strength, might
    stand
Rom. 3.6   Humble and firm in his supporting hand;
Gen. 18.25   His wisdom and omnipotence might own
Rom. 11.33   When his foes' power and craft is overthrown;
1 Cor. 10.12   Seeing his hate of sin, might thence confess
His pure innate and perfect holiness,
Rom. 16.20   And that the glory of his justice might
Ps. 2   In the bold[cxciv] rebels' torturing flames[cxcv] seem bright;   10
Jos. 24.19   That th'ever-blessed Redeemer might take place
To illustrate[102] his rich mercy and free grace
Ps. 5.4–6, 7.11
etc., 11.5–6   Whereby he fallen sinners[cxcvi] doth restore
To fuller bliss than they enjoyed before;
1 Pet. 1–10   That virtue might in its clear brightness[cxcvii] shine,

[cxciii] there
[cxciv] bold] *MS; not in 1679*
[cxcv] flame
[cxcvi] sinners] *1679* natures *MS* sinners *MSC*
[cxcvii] Beauty

[102] render illustrious

Eph. 1.4,11
John 3.16
Eph. 2.5
Rom. 8.35–9
Rom. 5.5 etc.
1 Pet. 4.12–14

Eccl. 7.29

Jude 6

John 8.44

Jer. 2.13
Devils

Eph. 2.2
Acts. 26.18
Matt. 25.41
Rev. 20.10

Which, like rich ore concealèd in the mine,
Had not been known but that opposing vice
Illustrates it by frequent exercise.
    If all were good, whence then arose the ill?
'Twas not in God's, but in the creatures' will,   20
Averting[103] from that good which is supreme,
Corrupted so, as a declining stream
That breaks off its communion with its head,
By whom its life and sweetness late were fed,
Turns to a noisome, dead, and poisonous lake,
Infecting all who the foul waters take:[cxcviii]
Or as a branch cut from the living tree
Passes into contempt immediately,
And dies divided from its glorious stock;
So strength disjoinèd from the living rock   30
Turns to contemnèd imbecility,[104]
And doth to all its grace and glory die.
    Some new-made angels thus, not more sublime
In nature than transcending in their crime,
Quitting th'eternal fountain of their light,
Became the first-born sons of woe and night,
Princes of darkness and the sad abyss,
Which now their cursèd place and portion is,
Where they no more must see God's glorious face
Nor ever taste of his refreshing grace,   40
But in the fire of his fierce anger dwell,
Which though it burns, enlightens not their hell.
But circumstances that we cannot know
Of their rebellion and their overthrow
We will not dare t'invent,[105] nor will we take
Guesses from the reports themselves did make
To their old priests, to whom they did devise
To inspire some truths,[cxcix] wrapped up in many lies;

---

cxcviii Turns . . . take] *1679; not in MS*
cxcix truth

---

103 turning away
104 despised weakness
105 'What that sinne was particularly, with other circumstances of their fall, the Scripture doth not properly informe us', *R* 33: LH's refusal to go beyond Scripture here strongly contrasts with *PL.*

Such as their gross poetic fables are,
Saturn's extrusion, the bold Giants' war,   50
Division of the universal realm
To gods that in high heaven steer^{cc} the helm,
Others who all things in the ocean guide,
And those who in th'infernal^{cci} court preside,
Who there a vast and gloomy empire sway,
Whom all the furies and the ghosts obey.[106]
 But not to name these foolish impious tales,
Which stifle truth in her pretended veils,
Let us in its own blazing conduct go
And look no further than that light doth show;   60
Wherein we see the present powers of hell,
Before they under God's displeasure fell,
Were once endued with grace and excellence
Luke 10.18 Beyond the comprehension of our sense.
Pure holy lights in the bright heaven were
Jude 6 Blazing about the throne, but not fixed there;
Where, by the apostasy of their own will
Precipitating them into all ill,
2 Pet. 2.4 And God's just wrath, whose eyes are far too pure
Hab. 1.13 Stained and polluted objects to endure,   70
Luke 10.18 They fell like lightning, hurled in his fierce ire,
James 3.6 And, falling, set the lower world on fire:
John 8.44 Which their loose prison is where they remain,
Jude 6 And walk as criminals under God's chain
Until the last and great assizes come,
1 Cor. 6.3 When execution shall seal up their doom.
Matt. 8.29
Gen. 3.15   Thus are they now to their created light,
1 Pet. 5.8 Unto all truth and goodness opposite,
Job 1.7 etc. Hating the peace and joy that reigns above,
Rev. 12.10 Vainly contending to extinguish love,   80
Ruin God's sacred empire, and destroy
That blessedness they never can enjoy.
Mark 3.22–26 A Chief they have, whose sovereign power and place
Rev. 20.10 But adds to's sin, his torture, and disgrace.

^{cc} doth steere
^{cci} Inferall

[106] On the denunciation of pagan fictions cf. 'Preface' above, and *T*; cf. *PL* 1.507–21.

An order too there is in their dire state,
Though they all orders else disturb and hate.

Luke 8.30   Ten thousand thousand wicked spirits stand
Attending their black prince at his command,
To all imaginable evils pressed
That may promote their common interest.[107]   90
Nor are they linkèd thus by faith and love,
But hate of God and goodness, which doth move
The same endeavours and desires in all,

Matt. 12.25–6   Lest civil wars should make their empire fall.
     An empire which the Almighty doth permit,

Rev. 20.2,7–8   Yet so as he controls and limits it,
Job 2.6
Suffering their rage sometimes to take effect

Col. 2.14–15   Only to be the more severely checked
Heb. 2.9,14   When he produces a contrary end
From what they did maliciously intend,   100

Luke 22.3   Befools their wisdom, crosses their designs,
2 Tim. 2.25–6   And blows them up in their own crafty mines,
Allows them play in the entangling net

Eph. 6.11–12 etc. So to be faster in damnation set,
1 Pet. 5.8   Submits them to each other's tyrannies
Who did God's softer sacred bonds[ccii] despise,

Rev. 12.12   Lets them still fight who never[cciii] can prevail,
More cursed if they succeed than if they fail,
Since every soul the rebels gain from God
Adds but another scorpion to that rod,   110
Bound up, that they may mutual torturers be,

Luke 16.24   Tormented and tormenting equally.
Rev. 14.10–11
Matt. 25.41   As a wise general that doth design
To keep his army still in discipline
Suffers the embodying[108] of some slighter foes
Which he at his own pleasure can enclose
And vanquish, that he justly may chastise
Their folly, and his own troops exercise,
Their vigilance, their faith and valour prove;

[ccii] bands
[cciii] ever

[107] An ironic use of republican terminology, cf. 4.163, also *PL* 2.496–8.
[108] forming into a military body

Endearing them thereby to his own love,   120
Luke 22.31–2   As he alike endears himself to theirs
By his continual succours and kind cares:
John 17.20   So the Almighty gives the devils scope,
Matt. 4   Who, though they are excluded from all hope
Heb. 2.18, 4.15, Of e'er escaping, no reluctance[109] have,
7.25   But, like the desperate villains[cciv] they make brave,
Rom. 16.20   To death pursue their bold attempts, that all
O'er whom they cannot reign with them may fall.
And though God's watchful guards besiege them
          round
That none can pass their strict prescribèd bound,   130
Rev. 12.7–8   Yet make they daily sallies in their pride,
Matt. 4.11   Which, still repulsed, the holy host deride,
Jude 9   Their malice in itself and its event[110]
Being equally a crime and punishment.
Thus[ccv] though sin in itself be ill, 'tis good
That sin should be, for thereby rectitude
Thorough[111] opposed iniquity, as light
By shades, is more conspicuous and more bright.[ccvi]
     The wonderful creation of mankind,
For lasting glory and rich grace designed,   140
The blessèd angels looked on with delight,
Luke 15.10, 16.22 Gladded to see us climb so near their height,
Heb. 12.22   Above all other works, next in degree,
And capable of their society.
But 'twas far otherwise with those that fell:
Man's destined heaven increased their hell,
While they burned with a proud malicious spite
John 8.44   To see a new-made, earth-born[ccvii] favourite
For their high seats and empty thrones designed;
Therefore both against God and man combined[ccviii]   150

---

 cciv villains] *MS* villain *1679*
ccv That
ccvi and more bright] *1679* and bright *MS* and more bright *MSC*
ccvii new-made, earth-born] *1679* new borne Earth made *MS* new maid earth borne *MSC*
ccviii combined] *1679* design'd *MS* combind *MSC*

109 regret
110 outcome
111 through

To hinder God's decree from taking place,
And to divest man of his Maker's grace;

1 Pet. 3.13   Which while he in a pure obedience stood
They knew, not all their force nor[ccix] cunning could,
But if they could with any false pretence
Inveigle him to quit his innocence,
They hoped death would prevent[112] the dreaded
    womb
From whence their happier successors must come.
    Wherefore th'accursèd sovereign of Hell,
Thinking no other devil could so well   160

Gen. 3.1 etc.   Act this ill part, whose consequence was high
Enough to engage his hateful majesty,
Himself exposes for the common cause,
And with his hellish kingdom's full applause
Goes forth, putting himself into disguise,
And so within a bright-scaled serpent lies,
Folded about the fair forbidden tree,
Watching a wished-for opportunity;
Which Eve soon gave him, coming there alone
So to be first and easier overthrown;   170
On whose weak side th'assault had not been made
Had she not from her firm protection strayed;

2 Tim. 3.6   But so the Devil then, so lewd men now
Prevail, when women privacies allow,
And to those flattering whispers lend an ear
Which even impudence itself would fear
To utter in the presence of a friend,
Whose virtuous awe our frailty might defend.[113]
Though unexperience might excuse Eve's fault,
Yet those who now give way to an assault,   180

[ccix] that all their force nor Cunning

[112] precede
[113] 2 Timothy 3.6 denounces those who 'creep into houses, and take captive silly women laden with sins, led away with divers lusts'; LH warns her own daughter against heresy with the passage from Timothy here cited: 'The Apostle reproaches the weaknesse of our sex more than the other, when, speaking of the prevalency of seducers, he says they lead about silly weomen, who are ever learning, and never able to come to the knowledge of the truth . . . wee ought to take heed of presumption in ourselves' (*R* 5–6).

By suffering it alone, none can exempt
From the just blame that they their tempters tempt,
And by vain confidence themselves betray,
Fondly[114] secure in a known desperate way.
    As Eve stood near the tree, the subtle beast,
By Satan moved, his speech to her addressed:
'Hath God,' said he, 'forbid that you should taste
These pleasant fruits which in your eyes are placed?
Why are the tempting boughs exposed if you
May not delight your palates with your view?'   190
'God,' said the woman, 'gives us liberty
To eat without restraint of every tree
Which in the garden grows, but only one;
Restrained by such a prohibition,
We dare not touch it, for whene'er we do
A certain death will our offence ensue.'[115]
Then did the wicked subtle beast reply,
'Ah, simple wretch, you shall not surely die,
God enviously to you this fruit denies.
He knows that eating it will make you wise,   200
Of good and ill give you discerning[116] sense,
And raise you to a God-like excellence.'
    Eve, quickly caught in the foul hunter's net,
Believed that death was only a vain threat.
Her unbelief, quenching[ccx] religious dread,
Infectious counsel in her bosom bred,
Dissatisfaction with her present state
And fond ambition of a God-like height;
Who now applies[ccxi] herself to its pursuit,
With longing eyes looks on the lovely fruit,   210
First nicely plucks, then eats with full delight,
And gratifies her murderous appetite.
Poisoned with the sweet relish of her sin
Before her inward torturing pangs begin,

[ccx] vnbeleeveing quencht
[ccxi] applying

[114] foolishly
[115] follow
[116] distinguishing

The pleasure[ccxii] to her husband she commends,
And he by her persuasion too offends
As by the serpent's she before had done.

Prov. 1.10 etc.   Hence learn pernicious counsellors to shun.[ccxiii]
Within the snake the crafty tempter smiled
To see mankind so easily beguiled;   220
But laugh not, Satan: God shall thee deride.
The son of God and man shall scourge thy pride,

1 John 3.8   And in the time of vengeance shall exact
John 16.11   A punishment on thee[ccxiv] for this accursed fact.
Now wrought the poison on the guilty pair,
Who with confusion on each other stare
While death possession takes, and enters in

Rom. 5.12   At the wide breach laid open by their sin.
Sound health and joy before th'intruder fled,
Sickness and sorrow coming in their stead.   230
Their late sweet calm did now forever cease,
Storms in all quarters drove away their peace;

Isaiah 48.22   Dread, guilt, remorse in the benighted soul
Like raging billows on each other roll;
Death's harbingers[117] waste in each province make,
While thundering terrors man's whole island
      shake.[118]
Within, without, disordered in the storm,
The colour fades and tremblings change the form,
Heat melts their substance, cold their joints
      benumbs,
Dull languishment their vigour overcomes.   240
Grief-conquered beauty lays down all her arms,

Ps. 39.11   And mightier[ccxv] woe dissolves her late-strong charms.
Shame doth their looks deject, no cheerful grace,
No pleasant smiles, appear in their sad face,
They see themselves fooled, cheated, and betrayed,

[ccxii] pleasures
[ccxiii] *this line not in MS, space left blank*
[ccxiv] Thy punishment
[ccxv] mighty

[117] Cf. *PL* 9.13.
[118] Phineas Fletcher's *The Purple Island* (1633) allegorized the human body as an island.

And naked in the view of heaven made.
No glory compasses[ccxvi] the drooping head,
The sight of their own ugliness they dread,
And curtains of broad, thin fig-leaves[ccxvii] devise
To hide themselves from their own weeping eyes;   250
But ah! these coverings were too slight and thin
To ward their shame off, or to keep out sin,
Or the keen air's quick-piercing shafts, which
     through
Both leaves and pores into the bowels[ccxviii] [119] flew.
While they remained in their pure innocence
It was their robe of glory and defence;
But when sin tore that mantle off, they found
Their members were all naked, all uncrowned,
Their purity in every place defiled,
Their vest of righteousness all torn and spoiled.   260
Wherefore through guilt the late-loved light they
     shun,
And into the obscurest[ccxix] shadow run;
But in no darkness can their quiet find,
Carrying within them a disturbèd mind
Which doth their cureless folly represent
And makes[ccxx] them curse their late experiment,
Wishing they had been pure and ignorant still,
Nor coveted the knowledge of their ill.
Ah, thus it is that yet we learn our good,
Till it be lost but seldom understood;   270
Rich blessings, while we have them, little prize
Until their want their value magnifies,
And equally doth our remorse increase
For having cast away such happiness.
     O wretched man! who at so dear a rate
Purchased the knowledge of his own frail state,

Ps. 139.11 (margin, beside line 262)

[ccxvi] compasseth
[ccxvii] broad fig leaves they
[ccxviii] Body
[ccxix] obscurer
[ccxx] make

[119] interior of the body

Eccl. 1.18   Knowledge of small advantage to the wise,
Which only their affliction multiplies,
While they in painful[120] study vex their brain,
Pursuing what they never can attain   280
And what would not avail them if acquired,
Till at the length, with fruitless labour tired,
All that the learnèd and[ccxxi] the wise can find
Is but a vain disturbance of the mind,
A sense of man's inevitable woes,
Which he but little feels who little knows.
While mortals, holding on their error, still
Prov. 1.7   Pursue the knowledge both of good and ill,
Ps. 111.10   They neither of them perfectly attain
1 Cor. 1.20–21,2.14 But in a dark tumultuous state remain;   290
James 3.15–17   Till sense of ill, increasing like night's shade,
Or hath a blot of good impressions made,
Or good, victorious as the morning light,
Triumphs[ccxxii] over the vanquished opposite:
For both at once abide not in one place,
Good knowledge flies from them who ill embrace.
    So were our parents filled with guilt and fear
When in the groves they God's approaches hear,
And from the terror of his presence fled;
Whether their own convictions caused their[ccxxiii]
    dread,   300
For inward guilt of conscience might suffice
To chase vile sinners from his purer eyes;
Or Nature felt an angry God's descent,
Which shook the earth, and tore the firmament;
We are not told, nor will too far inquire.
Lightnings and tempests might speak forth his ire;
For at the day of universal doom
The great Judge shall in flaming vengeance come,
An all-consuming fire shall go before,

ccxxi or
ccxxii Triumphs] *MS* Triumph *1679*
ccxxiii that

120 laborious

Ps. 97.3–4	Whirlwinds and thunder^{ccxxiv} shall about him roar, 310
Isaiah 9.5 and *66.15–16*	Horror shall darken the whole troubled skies
[2] Thes. 1.8	And bloody veils shall hide the world's bright eyes,
2 Pet. 3.12	While stars from the dissolving heaven drop down
	And funeral blazes every turret crown.
Rev. 1.7	The clouds shall be confounded with the waves,
Joel 3.15–16	The yawning earth shall open all her graves,
	Loud fragors¹²¹ shall firm rocks in sunder rend,
Matt. 24.29	Cleft mountains shall Hell's fiery jaws distend,
	Vomiting cinders, sulphur, pitch, and flame,
	Which shall consume the world's unjointed frame 320
	And turn the paradises we admire
Rev. 19.20	Into an ever-boiling lake of fire.

    But God then^{ccxxv} in his rich grace did delay
These dismal terrors till the last great day.
Yet even his first approach created dread
And the poor mortals from his anger fled
Until a calmer voice their sense did greet.

Heb. 12.11	Love even when it chides is kind and sweet.
	The sense of wrath far from the feared power drives,
Ps. 89.31–3	The sense of love brings home the fugitives. 330
	Souls flying God into despair next fall,
Gen. 4.14	Thence into hate, till black Hell close up all.
	But if sweet Mercy meet them on the way,
Acts 9	That milder voice first doth their mad flight stay
	And their ill-quitted hope again restore,
Ps. 130.7,4	Then Love that was forsaking them before
	Returns with a more flaming strong desire
	Of those sweet joys from which it did retire,
Lam. 3.1 etc.	And in their^{ccxxvi} absence woe and terror found,
	And all those plagues that can a poor soul wound. 340
	While^{ccxxvii} thus this love with holy ardour burns,
	The bleeding sinner to his God returns
Matt. 27.46	And prostrate at his throne of grace doth lie,

^{ccxxiv} Thunders
^{ccxxv} them
^{ccxxvi} its
^{ccxxvii} Whiles

¹²¹ crashes

If death he cannot shun, yet there to die

Job 13.15
Hos. 6.1–3

Where Mercy still doth fainting souls revive

And in its kind embraces keep alive

A gentler fire than what it lately felt

Under the sense of wrath. The soul doth melt

Like precious ore, which when men would refine

Doth in its liquefaction brightly shine;   350

In cleansing penitential meltings so

Foul sinners once again illustrious grow,

Mal. 3.2–3

When Christ's all-heating, softening spirit hath

Rev. 1.5

Their furnace been, and his pure blood their

       bath.[ccxxviii]

Now though God's wrath bring not the sinner

       home,

Who only by sweet love attracted come,

Rom. 12.1

Yet is it necessary that the sense

John 16.9,10

Of it should make us know the excellence

Matt. 11.28

And taste the pleasantness of pardoning grace,

That we may it with fuller joy embrace;   360

Which, when it brings a frighted[ccxxix] wretch from

       Hell,

Luke 7.47
1 John 4.10

Makes it love more than those who[ccxxx] never fell:

But mankind's love to God grows by degrees

As he more clearly God's sweet mercy sees,

And God at first reveals not all his grace,

That men more ardently may[ccxxxi] seek his face,

Averted by their folly and their pride,

Which makes them their confounded faces hide.

As still the Sun's the same behind the clouds,

Lam 3.22–3

Such is God's love, which his kind anger shrouds,   370

Which doth not all at once itself reveal

But first in the thick shadows that conceal

Its glory doth attenuation cause;

Then the black, dismal curtain softly draws

Lam. 3.26,29
etc.

And lets some glimmering light of hope[ccxxxii] appear,

[ccxxviii] When Christ's . . . bath] *1679; not in MS;* furnace] *ed.* furnance *1679*
[ccxxix] frightned
[ccxxx] that
[ccxxxi] might
[ccxxxii] hope of Light

Hos. 2.15 Which rather is a lessening of our fear
Than an assurance of our joy and peace,
A truce with misery, rather than release.
  Thus had not God come in, mankind had died
Without repair; yet came he first to chide,   380
To urge their sin, with its sad consequence,
And make them feel the weight of their offence,
To'examine and arraign them at his bar
And show them what vile criminals they were.
But ah! our utterance here is choked with woe,
With tardy steps from Paradise we go.
Then let us pause on our lost joys a while
Before we enter on our sad exile.

Canto 5

Sad Nature's sighs gave the alarms,
And all her frighted hosts stood to their^{ccxxxiii} arms,
Waiting whom the great Sovereign would employ
His all-deserted rebels to destroy,
Gen. 3.8 When God descended out of heaven above
His disobedient viceroy to remove.
Yet, though himself had seen the forfeiture,
Which distance could not from his eyes obscure;
To teach his future substitutes how they
Should judgements execute in a right way,   10
2 Sam. 23.3 He would not unexamined facts[122] condemn,
Nor punish sinners without hearing them;
Therefore cites to his^{ccxxxiv} bar the criminals,^{ccxxxv}
And Adam first out of his covert calls.
Gen. 3.9–12   'Where art thou, Adam?' the Almighty said.
'Here, Lord,' the trembling sinner answer made,
'Amongst^{ccxxxvi} the trees I in the garden heard

---

^{ccxxxiii} stood to their] *1679* stood their *MS* stood to their *MSC*
^{ccxxxiv} the
^{ccxxxv} selfe Judg'd Criminalls
^{ccxxxvi} Among

[122] seeds, crimes

Thy voice, and being naked, was afeared,
Nor durst I so thy purer sight abide,
Therefore myself did in this shelter hide.'   20
'Hast thou,' said God, 'eat[123] the forbidden tree,
Or who declared thy nakedness to thee?'
'She,' answered Adam, 'whom thou didst create
To be my helper and associate[ccxxxvii]
Gave me the fatal fruit, and I did eat.'
Then Eve was also called from her retreat.

Gen. 3.13   'Woman, what hast thou done?' th'Almighty said;
'Lord,' answered she, 'the serpent me betrayed
And I did eat.' Thus did they both confess
Their guilt, and vainly sought to make it less   30
By such extenuations as, well weighed,
The sin, so circumstanced, more sinful[ccxxxviii] made:
A course which still half-softened sinners use:
Transferring blame their own faults to excuse,
They care not how, nor where, and oftentimes
On God himself obliquely charge their crimes,

Rom. 9.19   Expostulating in their discontent
Ezek. 18.2   As if he caused what he did not prevent;
James 1.13–15   Which Adam wickedly implies, when he
Cries, ''Twas the woman that[ccxxxix] thou gavest me';   40
Oft-times make that the Devil's guilt alone,
Which was as well and equally their own.
His lies could never have prevailed on Eve
But that she wished them truth, and did believe
A forgery that suited her desire,
Whose haughty heart was prone enough to'aspire.
The tempting and the urging was his ill,
But the compliance was in her own will.
And herein truly lies the difference
Of natural and gracious penitence: 50
The first transferreth and extenuates

ccxxxvii To be . . . associate] *1679; not in MS*
ccxxxviii sinfulls
ccxxxix which

123 eaten

Ps. 51.3–5, 32.5   The guilt, which the other owns and aggravates.
          While sin is but regarded slight and small
          It makes the value of rich mercy fall,
          But as our crimes seem greater in our eyes,
1 John 1.8–10   So doth our grateful sense of pardon rise.
            Poor mankind at God's righteous bar was cast
          And set for judgement by, when at the last
          Satan within the serpent had his doom,
          Whose execrable malice left no room   60
          For plea or pardon, but was sentenced first:
          'Thou,' said the Lord, 'above all beasts accursed,[ccxl]
          Shalt on thy belly creep, on dust shalt feed;
          Between thee and the woman, and her seed
1 Pet. 5.8   And thine, I will put lasting enmity;[ccxli]
          Thou in this war his heel shalt[ccxlii] bruise, but he
          Thy head shall break.' More various mystery
Matt. 13.25   Ne'er did within so short a sentence lie.[124]
Jude 6   Here is irrevocable vengeance, here
Mal. 3.6   Love as immutable. Here doth appear   70
Zac. 6.13   Infinite wisdom plotting with free grace,
1 Cor. 2.9   Even by man's fall, th'advance of human race.
Rom. 11.22   Severity here utterly confounds,
          Here Mercy cures by kind and gentle wounds,
          The Father here the gospel first reveals,
Isaiah 7.14   Here fleshly veils th'eternal Son conceals.[125]
Rom. 8.2–4   The law of life and spirit here takes[ccxliii] place,
Acts 13.10   Given with the promise of assisting grace.
Matt. 3.7   Here is an oracle foretelling all
Ps. 22.30   Which shall the two opposèd seeds befall.   80

[ccxl] art Curst
[ccxli] Emnitie
[ccxlii] shall
[ccxliii] take

[124] 'which text hath more grace and mistery in it, then is generally taken notice of', *R* 52.
[125] The 'first Gospell was preached to Adam in Paradice, before the sentence of death was pronounced; and from that time the covenant of grace, which was allwayes the same for substance, was held out to men under divers administrations in the time of the Law and the Gospell' (*R* 38).

Jer. 31.22 *Eph. 6.12* *John 8.44* *Jude 9*	The great war hath its first beginning here, Carried along more than five thousand year, With various success[126] on either side,
Gen. 6.2,4–5 *Heb. 2.10* *Acts 5.31*	And each age with new combatants supplied. Two sovereign champions[ccxliv] here we find,
Eph. 2.2	Satan and Christ contending for mankind.
John 15.18–19	Two empires here, two opposite cities rise, Dividing all in two societies:
Luke 12.32	The little Church and the World's larger State,
Ps. 105.12–15	Pursuing it with ceaseless spite and hate.[127]

The great war hath its first beginning here,
Carried along more than five thousand year,
With various success[126] on either side,
And each age with new combatants supplied.
Two sovereign champions[ccxliv] here we find,
Satan and Christ contending for mankind.
Two empires here, two opposite cities rise,
Dividing all in two societies:
The little Church and the World's larger State,
Pursuing it with ceaseless spite and hate.[127]   90
Each party here erecting their own walls,
As one advances, so the other falls.

Isaiah 9.6–7   Hope in the promise the weak Church confirms,
Hell and the World fight upon desperate terms:

Rev. 12.12   By this most certain oracle they know
Their war must end in final overthrow.

John 16.30, 20   Some little present mischief they may do,
And this with eager malice they pursue.

Matt. 10.34   The angels whom[ccxlv] God's justice did divide

Ps. 2.1   Engage their mighty powers on either side: 100

Rev. 12.7–9   Hell's gloomy princes the World's rulers made,

Dan. 10.13, 21   Heaven's unseen host the Church's guard and aid;

Ps. 104.4   Till the frail woman's conquering son shall tread

Romans 16.20   Beneath his feet the serpent's broken head.
    Though God the speech to man's false foe
      address,
The words rich grace to fallen man express,
Which God will not to him himself declare

Ps. 50.15   Till he implore it by submissive prayer;

Isaiah 41.9   Sufficient 'tis to know a latitude

Ps. 130.4   For hope, which doth no penitent exclude.   110

Luke 1.74   Had death's sad sentence passed on man before

Gal. 3.8, 16   The promise of that seed which should restore

1 Cor. 15.54, 57 His fallen state, destroying death and sin,
Cureless as Satan's had his misery been.

---

ccxliv Champion
ccxlv which

126 outcome
127 Introducing a theme to be developed later, cf. 6.351ff.

But though free grace did future help provide,
1 Cor. 3.15   Yet must he present loss and woe[ccxlvi] abide
And feel the bitter curse, that he may so
Gal. 3.13   The sweet release of saving mercy know.
Gen. 3.16 etc.   Prepared with late-indulgèd hope, on Eve
Th'Almighty next did gentler sentence give.   120
'I will,' said he, 'greatly augment thy woes,
And thy conceptions, which with painful throes
Thou shalt bring forth, yet shall they be to thee
But a successive crop of misery.
Thy husband shall thy ruler be, whose sway
Thou shalt with passionate desires obey'.
   Alas! How sadly to this day we find
Th'effect of this dire curse on womankind;
Eve sinned in fruit forbid,[128] and God requires
Her penance in the fruit of her desires.   130
When first to men their inclinations move,
Gen. 39.7   How are they tortured with distracting love![129]
What disappointments find they in the end;
Constant uneasinesses which attend
1 Cor. 7.34,39–40 The best condition of the wedded state,[130]
1 Pet. 3.5   Giving all wives sense of the curse's weight,
Which makes them ease and liberty refuse,
And with strong passion their own shackles choose.
Now though they easier under wise rule prove,
Gen. 29.20   And every burden is made light by love,   140
Yet[ccxlvii] golden fetters, soft-lined yokes, still be
Though gentler curbs, but curbs of liberty,
As well as the harsh tyrant's iron yoke;
More sorely galling them[ccxlviii] whom they provoke
To loathe their bondage, and despise the[ccxlix] rule

[ccxlvi] Woe and losse
[ccxlvii] Though
[ccxlviii] those
[ccxlix] their

[128] forbidden
[129] The note refers us to the adulterous passion for Joseph felt by the wife of his overseer.
[130] The Corinthians passage says that married women may be more concerned with pleasing their husbands than with religion.

1 Sam. 25.25	Of an unmanly, fickle, froward[131] fool.
Gen. 30.1, 35.18	Whate'er the husbands be, they covet fruit,
	And their own wishes to their sorrows[ccl] contribute.
Matt. 24.19	How painfully the[ccli] fruit within them grows,
	What tortures do their ripened births disclose, 150
	How great, how various, how uneasy are
	The breeding-sicknesses, pangs that prepare
John 16.21	The violent openings of life's narrow door,
	Whose fatal issues we as oft deplore![132]
	What weaknesses, what languishments ensue,
	Scattering dead lilies where fresh roses grew.
	What broken rest afflicts the careful nurse,
	Extending to the breasts the mother's curse;
	Which ceases not when there her milk she dries,
	The froward child draws new streams from her eyes. 160
	How much more bitter anguish do we find
	Labouring to raise up virtue in the mind
	Than when the members in our bowels grew:
Prov. 10.1	What sad abortions, what cross births ensue:
	What monsters, what unnatural vipers come
Prov. 15.20	Eating their passage through their parent's womb;
	How are the tortures of their births renewed,
	Unrecompensed with love and gratitude.
	Even the good, who[cclii] would our cares requite,
	Would be our crowns, joys, pillars, and delight, 170
	Affect us yet with other griefs and fears,
	Opening the sluices of our near-dried[ccliii] tears.
Luke 2.48,35	Death, danger, sickness, losses, all the ill
Matt. 2.18	That on the children falls,[ccliv] the mothers feel,[133]
	Repeating with worse pangs the pangs that bore
	Them into life; and though some may have more

ccl And by their Wishes, sorrowes
ccli their
cclii which
ccliii near-dried] *ed.* neare dry'd *MS* ne'er dried *1679*
ccliv fall

131 perverse, refractory
132 LH had eight children, one of whom died young after a difficult pregnancy.
133 The notes juxtapose Mary's delight in the birth of Christ with Rachel's mourning for her children.

Of sweet and gentle mixture, some of worse,
Yet every mother's cup tastes of the curse,
And when the heavy load her faint heart tires,

Gen. 27.46 Makes her too oft repent her fond desires. 180
    Now last of all, as Adam last had been
Drawn into the prevaricating sin,

Gen. 3.17 His sentence came: 'Because that thou didst yield,'
Said God, 'to thy enticing wife, the field,
Producing briars and fruitless thorns to thee,
Accursèd for thy sake and sins[cclv] shall be.
Thy careful brows in constant toils shall sweat,
Thus thou thy bread shalt all thy whole life eat
Till thou return into the earth's vast womb,
Whence, taken first, thou didst a man become; 190
For dust thou art, and dust again shalt be[cclvi]

Prov. 103.14, When life's declining spark goes out in thee.'
104.29   In all these sentences we strangely find
God's admirable love to lost mankind;
Who, though he never will his word recall
Or let his threats like shafts at random fall,
Yet can his wisdom order curses[cclvii] so
That blessings may out of their bowels flow.

2 Cor. 4.6 Thus death the door of lasting life[cclviii] became,
Dissolving nature to rebuild her frame 200
2 Tim. 1.10 On such a sure foundation as shall break
All the attempts Hell's cursèd empire make.
Thus God revenged man's quarrel on his foe,
To whom th'Almighty would no mercy show,

Luke 18.7–8 Making his reign, his respite, and success,
All augmentations of his cursedness.

Zac. 9.10-12 Thus gave he us a powerful Chief and Head,
By whom we shall be out of bondage led,
And made the penalties of our offence
Precepts and rules of new obedience, 210
Matt. 11.29–30 Fitted in all things to our fallen state
Under sweet promises that ease their weight.

[cclv] sin
[cclvi] shalbe
[cclvii] Cures
[cclviii] the door . . . life] *1679* the lasteing dore of Life *MS* the dore of lasting Life *MSC*

Our first injunction is to hate and fly

Prov. 1.10 etc.   The flatteries of our first grand enemy;

To have no friendship with his cursèd race,

Eph. 5.11   The interest of the opposite seed t'embrace,[134]

1 Tim. 6.12   Where though we toil in fights,[cclix] though bruised
                         we be,

Jude 3   Yet shall our combat end in victory,

Rev. 2.10   Eternal glory healing our slight wound

Micah 7.6–17   When all our labours are with triumph crowned.   220
                     The next command is, mothers should maintain

Posterity, not frighted with the pain,

Which, though it make us mourn under the sense

Of the first mother's disobedience,

1 Tim. 2.16   Yet hath a promise that thereby she shall

Recover all the hurt[cclx] of her first fall[135]

Isaiah 9.6   When, in mysterious manner, from her womb

Heb. 2.12–13   Her father, brother, husband, son shall come.

Subjection to the husband's rule enjoined

Eph. 5.25 etc.   In the next place: that yoke with love is lined,   230

Luke 1.35   Love too a precept made, where God requires

1 Peter 3.1–2   We should perform our duties with desires;

And promises t'incline our averse[136] will,

Whose satisfaction takes away the ill

Of every toil and every suffering

That can from unenforced submission spring.

The last command God with man's curse did give

Was that men should in honest callings live,

Eating their own bread, fruit of their own sweat,

1 Thes. 4.11–12   Nor feed like drones on that which others get: 240

And this command a promise doth imply[cclxi]

2 Thes. 3.12   That bread should recompense our industry.

---

cclix fight
cclx hurts
cclxi employ

---

[134] 'Oftentimes [JH] would say, if ever he were at liberty in the world he would flee the
conversation of all the Cavaliers . . . it was a resolution he would oftener repeat than any other
he had, telling us that he was convinced there was a serpentine seed in them' (*M* 322).
[135] Paul writes that woman may be saved by childbearing, having just declared that she should
remain silent rather than teaching.
[136] reluctant

One mercy more his sentence did include,
Rev. 14.13   That mortal toils, faintings and lassitude
Should not beyond death's fixèd bound extend,
Matt. 10.28   But there in everlasting quiet end.
When men out of the troubled air depart,
Job 3.17–19   And to their first material dust revert,
Eccl. 3.20   The utmost power that death or woe can have
Is but to shut us prisoners in the grave,   250
Bruising the flesh, that heel whereon we tread;
1 Thes. 4.14   But we shall trample[cclxii] on the serpent's head.
Our scattered atoms shall again condense,
Isaiah 26.19   And be again inspired with living sense;
Captivity shall then a captive be,[137]
Job 19.26–7   Death shall be swallowed up in victory,
1 Cor. 15.20–2,26, And God shall man to Paradise restore,
54–57   Where the foul tempter shall seduce no more.
Acts 2.24   How far our parents, whose sad eyes were fixed
Ps. 68.18   On woe and terror, saw the mercy mixed   260
We can but make a wild uncertain guess,
As we are now affected in distress,
Isaiah 43.2 etc.   Who less regard the mitigation still
1 Pet. 4.12–13   Than the slight smart of our afflicting ill;
And while we groan under the hated yoke,
Jer. 30.11 etc.   Our gratitude for its soft lining choke.
Mic. 7.18–19   But God, having th'amazèd sinners doomed,
Put off the judge's frown and reassumed
Isaiah 49.15   A tender father's kind and melting face,
Jer. 31.20   Opening his gracious arms for new embrace,   270
Ps. 50.5   Taught them to expiate their heinous guilt
1 Pet. 1.19   By spotless sacrifice and pure blood spilt,
Heb. 11.4   Which, done in faith, did their faint hearts sustain
Dan. 9.26–7   Till the intended Lamb of God was slain,
John 1.29   Whose death, whose merit, and whose innocence
Ps. 40.6–7   The forfeit paid and blotted out th'offence.
1 John 2.2   The skins of the slain beasts God vestures made
Rev. 1.5 etc., 9–10 Wherein the naked sinners were arrayed,

cclxii Triumph

[137] Cf. Ephesians 4.8, cited in *R* 48, and at *PL* 10.188.

Rom. 5.10,19	Not without mystery, which typified
Col. 2.14	That righteousness that[cclxiii] doth our foul shame
	hide. 280
Ps. 32.1–2	As when a rotting patient must endure
Rev. 19.8	Painful excisions to effect his cure,
Rom. 3.22, 13–14	His spirits we with cordials fortify,
Gal. 3.27	Lest, unsupported, he should faint and die,
Zac. 3.4–5	So with our parents the Almighty dealt:
	Before their necessary woes they felt,
Deut. 33.27	Their feeble souls rich promises upheld
	And their deliverance was in types revealed.
	Even their bodies God himself did arm
Matt. 6.30	With clothes that kept them from the weather's
	harm; 290
Ps. 89.32–4	But after all, they must be driven away,
	Nor in their forfeit Paradise must stay.
Gen. 3.22	Then said the Lord with holy irony,
	Whence man the folly of his pride might see,
	'The earthly[cclxiv] man like one of us is grown,
	To whom, as God, both good and ill is known.
	Now lest he also[cclxv] eat of th'other tree,
	Whose fruit gives life, and an immortal be,[cclxvi]
	Let us by just and timely banishment
	His further[cclxvii] sinful arrogance prevent.' 300
	Then did he them out of the garden chase
	And set a cherubim[138] to guard the place,
	Who waved a flaming sword before the door
	Through which the wretches must return no more.
	May we not liken to this sword of flame
Heb. 12.7,	The threatening law which from Mount Sinai came,
12.18–21	With such thick flashes of prodigious fire
	As made the mountains[cclxviii] shake and men retire,
	Forbidding them all forward hope that they

[cclxiii] which
[cclxiv] earthly] *MS [cf. 1 Cor. 15.47–9]* earthy *1679*
[cclxv] alsoe least he
[cclxvi] and Imortallitie
[cclxvii] farther
[cclxviii] Mountaine

[138] archaic as a singular form (*OED* 2a( ).

Could enter into life that dreadful way?   310
Whate'er it was, whate'er it signifies,
It kept our parents out of Paradise,
Who now, returning to^{cclxix} their place of birth,
Found themselves strangers in their native earth.

1 Pet. 2.11   Their fatal breach of God's most strict command
Heb. 11.13   Had there dissolved all concord, the sweet band
Ps. 39.12   Of universal loveliness and peace,
And now the calm in every part^{cclxx} did cease;
Love, though immutable, its smiles did shroud
Rev. 3.19   Under the dark veil of an angry cloud,   320
And while he seemed withdrawn whose^{cclxxi} grace upheld
Ps. 75.3   The order of all things, confusion filled
The universe. The air became impure
And frequent dreadful conflicts did endure
With every other angry element;
The whirling fires its tender body rent.
From earth and seas gross vapours did arise,
Turned to prodigious meteors in the skies;
The blustering winds let loose their furious rage
Ps. 107.25–7 And in their battles did the floods engage.   330
The sun confounded was with Nature's shame
Jude 5.20   And the pale moon shrunk in her sickly flame;
The rude congressions of the angry stars
In heaven begun the universal wars,
While their malicious influence from above
On Earth did various perturbations move.
Droughts, inundations, blastings, killed the plants;
Worse influence wrought on th'inhabitants,
Ps. 78.45–8   Inspiring lust, rage, ravenous appetite,
Which made the creatures in all regions fight.   340
The little insects in great clouds did rise
And, in battalias^{cclxxii} spread, obscured the skies;
Armies of birds encountered in the air,
With hideous cries deciding battles there;

^{cclxix} revisiting
^{cclxx} place
^{cclxxi} his
^{cclxxii} Battallions

The birds of prey, to gorge their appetite,
Seized harmless fowl in their unwary flight.[cclxxiii]
When the dim evening had shut in the day,
Troops of wild beasts, all marching out for prey,

Ps. 104.20–22   To the resistless[cclxxiv] flocks would go, and there
Oft-times by other troops assailèd were,   350
Who snatched out of their jaws the[cclxxv] new-slain food
And made them purchase it again with blood.
    Thus sin the whole Creation did divide
Into th'oppressing and the suffering side.
Those, still employing craft and violence
T'ensnare[cclxxvi] and murder simple innocence,
True emblems were of Satan's craft and power

1 Pet. 5.8   In daily ambuscado[139] to devour;
Rev. 12.8,12   Nor only emblems were, but organs too,
In and by whom he did his mischiefs[cclxxvii] do,   360
While persecuting cruelty and rage
Them in his cursèd party did engage.
Love, meekness, patience, gentleness, combined
The tamer brood with those of their own kind;
Wherefore God chose them for his sacrifice
When he the proud and mighty did despise,

Rom. 8.20–1   And his most certain oracles declare
They man's restorèd peace at last shall[cclxxviii] share.

Isaiah 11.7, 65.25   But to our parents then, sad[cclxxix] was the change
Which them from peace and safety did estrange,   370
Brought universal woe and discord in,

Isaiah 57.20–1 The never-failing consequents[140] of sin;

[cclxxiii] *Followed in MS by* But Cocks more generous, murther'd not for food / But for their Hono.ʳ spilt each others blood / Through Lust and Jealousy the Gulls Contend / Till flight or Death the Cruell Combate End
[cclxxiv] resistless] MS restless *1679*
[cclxxv] their
[cclxxvi] To engage
[cclxxvii] Mischiefe
[cclxxviii] should
[cclxxix] But then to our parents sad

[139] ambush
[140] consequences

Eph. 2.12–14 Nor only made all things without them jar
But in their breasts raised up a civil war.
Reason and sense maintained continual fight,
Urging th'aversion and the appetite,
Which led two different troops of passions out,
Confounding all in their tumultuous rout.
The less world with the great proportion held:
As winds[cclxxx] the caverns, sighs the bosoms[clxxxi] filled;   380
So flowing tears did beauty's fair fields drown,
As inundations kept within no bound.
Fear earthquakes made, lust in the fancy whirled,
Turned into flame and, bursting, fired the world:
Spite, hate, revenge, ambition, avarice
Made innocence a prey to monstrous vice.
The cold and hot diseases represent
The perturbations of the element.
Thus woe and danger had beset them round,
Distressed without, within no comfort found.   390
Even as a monarch's favourite in disgrace
Suffers contempt both from the high and base,
And the most abject most insult o'er[cclxxxii] them
Whom the offended sovereigns[cclxxxiii] condemn;
So after man th'Almighty disobeyed,
Each little fly durst his late king invade
As well as the wood's[cclxxxiv] monsters, wolves and
    bears,
And all things else that exercise[cclxxxv] his fears.
Methinks I hear sad Eve in some dark vale
Her woeful state with[cclxxxvi] such sad plaints bewail: 400
   'Ah! why doth Death its[cclxxxvii] latest stroke
       delay?'[141]

[cclxxx] wind
[cclxxxi] bosome
[cclxxxii] on
[cclxxxiii] Soveraigne
[cclxxxiv] Wood
[cclxxxv] Excerciz'd
[cclxxxvi] in
[cclxxxvii] his

[141] Cf. *PL* 10.771–3.

If we must leave the light, why do we stay
By slow degrees more painfully to die,
And languish in a long calamity?
Have we not lost by one false cheating sin
All peace without, all sweet repose within?
Is there a pleasure yet that life can show,
Doth not each moment multiply our woe:
And while we live thus in perpetual dread,
Our hope and comfort[cclxxxviii] long before us dead,   410

Job 3
Why should we not our angry Maker pray
Jonah 4.3
At once to take[cclxxxix] our wretched lives away?
Hath not our sin all Nature's pure leagues rent
And armed against us every element?
Have not our subjects their allegiance broke,
Doth not each worm[ccxc] scorn our unworthy yoke?
Are we not half with griping hunger[ccxci] pined
Before we bread amongst[ccxcii] the brambles find?
All pale diseases in our members reign,
Anguish and grief no less our sick souls pain.   420
Wherever I my eyes or thoughts convert,
Each object adds new tortures to my heart.
If I look up, I dread Heaven's threatening frown,
Thorns prick my eyes when shame hath cast them
      down,
Dangers I see, looking on either hand,
Before me all in fighting posture stand.
If I cast back my sorrow-drownèd eyes,
I see our ne'er to be recovered Paradise,
The flaming sword which doth us thence exclude,
By sad remorse and ugly guilt pursued.   430
If on my sin-defilèd self I gaze,
My nakedness and spots do me amaze.[ccxciii] [142]

---

cclxxxviii hopes & comforts *'Elegies'*
cclxxxix To take at once *'Elegies'*
ccxc flie *'Elegies'*
ccxci with griping hunger] *1679, MS* wth hungar *'Elegies'*
ccxcii amongst] *1679, MS* among *'Elegies'*
ccxciii If on . . . amaze] *'Elegies'; not in 1679 or MS*

[142] terrify, stupefy

If I on thee a private glance reflect,[143]
Confusion doth^{ccxciv} my shameful eyes deject,
Seeing the man I love^{ccxcv} by me betrayed,
By me, who for his mutual help was made,
Who to preserve thy life ought to have died,
And I have killed thee by my foolish pride,
Defiled thy glory and pulled down thy throne.
O that I had but sinned and died alone!   440
Then had my torture and my woe been less,
I yet had flourished in thy happiness.'^{ccxcvi}
   If these words Adam's melting soul did move,
He might reply with kind rebuking love:
'Cease, cease, O foolish woman, to dispute,

Ps. 115.3   God's sovereign will and power are absolute.
If he will have us soon or slow to die,

Rom. 9.20–3   Frail worms must yield, but must not question why.
When his great hand appears, we must conclude

Ps. 119.68   All that he doth is wise and just^{ccxcvii} and good;   450

Rom. 3.4   Though our poor, sin-benighted souls are blind,

Ps. 51.4   Nor can the mysteries of his wisdom find,

Gen. 18.25   Yet in our present case^{ccxcviii} we must confess
His justice and our own unrighteousness.
He warned us of this fatal consequence,

Rom. 6.23   That death must wait on disobedience;
Yet we despised his threat and broke his law,
So did destruction on our own heads draw;
Now under his afflicting hand we lie,
Reaping the fruit of our iniquity;   460

Gen. 6.3   Which, had not he prevented when we fell,

1 Pet. 3.20 At once had plunged^{ccxcix} us in the lowest Hell;
But by his mercy yet we have reprieve,

---

^{ccxciv} doth] *1679, MS* does *'Elegies'*
^{ccxcv} love] *1679, 'Elegies'* lov'd *MS*
^{ccxcvi} *'these verses were writ by Mrs Hutchinson on ye occasion of ye Coll: her Husbands being then a prisoner in ye Tower: 1664': note by Julius Hutchinson, 1730s, 'Elegies' 491*
^{ccxcvii} Just and wise
^{ccxcviii} Cause
^{ccxcix} plagu'd

[143] turn back

And yet are showed how we in death may live,
If we improve our short-indulgèd space
John 11.25   To understand, prize, and accept his grace.
        'Did all of us at once like brutes expire
And cease to be, we might quick death desire:
But since our chief and immaterial part,
Not framed of dust, doth not to dust revert,   470
Its death not an annihilation is,
Matt. 25.41,46   But to be cut off from its supreme bliss:
Whatever here to mortals can befall
Luke 16.21–2   Compared to future miseries is small.
The saddest, sharpest, and the longest have
Matt. 10.28   Their final consummations^{ccc} in the grave;
These have their intermissions and allays,
Though black and gloomy ones, these nights have
        days.
Ps. 130.1   The worst calamities we here endure
Admit a possibility of cure.   480
Ps. 107   Our miseries here are varied in their kind,
And in that change the wretched some ease find.
Isaiah 29.8   Sleep here our painèd senses stupefies
And cheating streams in our sick fancies rise,
But in our future sufferings 'tis not so,
There is no end, no^{ccci} intermitted woe,
Luke 16.26   No more return from the accursèd place,
No hope, no possibility of grace,
No sleepy intervals, no pleasant dreams,
No mitigations of those^{cccii} sad extremes,   490
Rom. 2.8–9   No gentle mixtures, no soft changes there,
Jude 13   Perpetual tortures heightened with despair,
Matt. 13.50   Eternal horror and eternal night,
Luke 16.24   Eternal burnings with no glance of light,
Matt. 8.12, 22.13 Eternal pain. O, 'tis a thought too great,
        Too terrible, for any to repeat
Rev. 19.20   Who have not 'scaped the dread. Let's not to shun
Hos. 13.9
Rom. 3.16   Heaven's scorching rays, into Hell's furnace run:

---

^{ccc} The finall Consummation
^{ccci} nor
^{cccii} their

Ps. 103–4	But having slain ourselves, let's fly to him
	Who only can our souls from death redeem. 500
	'To undo what's done is not within our power,
	No more than to call back the last fled hour.
	To think we can our fallen state restore,
	Or without hope our ruin to deplore,
	Are equal aggravating crimes; the first
Eph. 2.4,6–10	Repeats that sin for which we were accursed,
	While we with foolish arrogating pride
Rom. 3.27	More in ourselves than in our God confide;[144]
	The last is both ungrateful and unjust,
	That doth his goodness or his power distrust, 510
	Which wheresoe'er we look, without, within,
	Above, beneath, in every place is seen.
Ps. 36.5–6	Doth Heaven frown? Above the sullen shrouds
	God sits, and sees through all the blackest clouds[ccciii]
	Sin casts about us, like the misty night,
Isaiah 44.22	Which hides[ccciv] his pleasing glances from our sight;
Lam. 3.44,31–2, 25	Nor only sees, but darts on us his beams,
	Ministering comfort in our worst extremes.
Job 37.11–13	When lightnings[cccv] fly, dire storm[cccvi] and thunder roars,
	He guides the shafts, the serene calm restores. 520
Isaiah 40.1–2, 57.18–19	When shadows occupy day's vacant room,
	He makes new glory spring from night's dark womb.
	When the black prince of air lets loose the winds,
John 14.18	The furious warriors he in prison binds.
Isaiah 25.4	If burning stars do conflagrations threat,
	He gives cool breezes to allay the heat.
Ps. 78.16–17	When cold doth in its rigid season reign,
Ps. 30.5	He melts the snows and thaws the air again;

ccciii Doth . . . clouds] *1679* If Heaven doth frowne above the angry Clowds / God sitts and sees through all ye blackest shrouds *MS*
ccciv hides] *MS* hide *1679*
cccv Lightning
cccvi stormes

144 trust

Luke 8.24–5	Restoring the vicissitude of things,	
Isaiah 27.8, 4.6		
Cant. 2.11–12	He still new good from every evil brings.	530
Gen. 8.22		
Ps. 147.17–18	He holds together the world's shaken frame,	
Isaiah 45.6–8	Ordaining every change,^{cccvii} is still the same.	
Ps. 75.3		
James 1.17	If he permit the elements to fight,	
Ps. 102.26–7	The rage of storms, the blackness of the night;	
Mal. 3.6	'Tis that his power, love and wisdom may	
Isaiah 54.11	More glory have, restoring calm and day;	
Jer. 31.35–6	That we may more the pleasant blessings prize,	
	Laid in the balance with their contraries.	
2 Cor. 4.17	'Though dangers, then, like gaping monsters^{cccviii} stand	
Isaiah 54.6–10	Ready to swallow us on either^{cccix} hand,	540
	Let us despise them, firm in this faith still,	
Ps. 46.1–2	If God will save, they can nor^{cccx} hurt nor kill;	
	If by his just permission we are slain,	
Isaiah 8.9–14	His power can heal and quicken us again.	
	If briars and thorns which from our sins arise,	
Isaiah 51.11 etc.	Looking on earth, pierce through our guilty eyes,	
	Let's yet give thanks they have not choked the seed	
Gen. 50.20	Which should with better fruit our sad lives feed.	
2 Sam. 17.14	If discord set the inward world on fire,	
Esther 5.14, 6.13,	With^{cccxi} haste let's to the living spring retire,	550
7.10	There quench and quiet the disturbèd soul,	
	There on Love's sweet refreshing green banks roll,	
Ezek. 37.1 etc.	Where, ecstasied with joy, we shall not feel	
	The serpent's little nibblings^{cccxii} at our heel.[145]	
Isaiah 19.22	If we look back on Paradise, late lost,	
Jer. 30.17	Joys vanished like swift dreams, thawed like a frost,	
Acts 14.17	Converting pleasant walks to dirt and mire,	
John 7.37–8	Would we such frail delights again desire,	
Ps. 23.1–2, 6–7	Which^{cccxiii} at their best, however excellent,	

^{cccvii} Chance
^{cccviii} Though gapeing Monsters, Horrid dangers
^{cccix} every
^{cccx} canot
^{cccxi} In
^{cccxii} nibbling
^{cccxiii} Who

[145] Cf. Willet 51: 'Sathan shall be nibling and biting at the heele, as a serpent doth'.

Col. 3.1–2	Had this defect, they were not permanent? 560
Ps. 107.33–6 *1 Cor. 7.31*	If sin, remorse, and guilt give us the chase,
Eccl. 1.2	Let us lie close in Mercy's sweet embrace,
2 Cor. 4.18 *Ps. 49.4,15*	Which when it us ashamed and naked found,
Rev. 3.18,20	In the soft arms of melting pity bound,
Ps. 32.1–2	Eternal glorious triumphs did prepare,
	Armed us with clothes against the wounding air,
1 John 2.25	By expiating sacrifices taught
	How new life shall by death to light be brought.
	If we before us look, although we see
	All things in present fighting posture be: 570
	Yet in the promise we a prospect have
1 Cor. 15.54–5,26	Of Victory swallowing up the empty grave;
	Our foes all vanquished, Death itself lies dead,
Hos. 13.14	And we shall trample on the monster's head,
Rom. 16,20	Entering into a new and perfect joy
Matt. 25.21	Which neither sin nor sorrow can destroy:
Rev. 20.4	A lasting and refined felicity,
Mal. 3.2–3	For which even we ourselves refined must be.
Col. 1.12	Then shall we laugh at our now childish woes,
John 16.21–2	And hug the birth that issues from these throes. 580

      'Let not my share of grief afflict thy mind,
But let me comfort in thy courage find;
'Twas not thy malice, but thy ignorance
That lately my destruction did advance;
Nor can I my own self excuse; 'twas I
Undid myself by my facility.[146]
Let's not in vain each other[cccxiv] now upbraid,
But rather strive to'afford each other aid,
And our most gracious Lord with due thanks bless,
Who hath not left us single in distress.   590
When fear chills thee, my hope shall make thee
     warm,
When I grow faint, thou shalt my courage arm;
When both our spirits at a low ebb are,
We both will join in mutual fervent prayer

[cccxiv] each other now in vaine

[146] pliancy

To him whose gracious succour never fails
When sin and death poor feeble man assails,
He that our final triumph hath decreed
And promised thee salvation in thy seed.'
    Ah! can I this in Adam's person say,
While fruitless tears melt my poor life away?   600
Of all the ills to mortals incident,
None more pernicious is than discontent,
That brat of unbelief and stubborn pride
And sensual lust, with no joy[cccxv] satisfied,
That doth ingratitude and murmur nurse,
And is a sin which carries its own curse;
This is the only smart of every ill.
But can we without it sad tortures feel?
Yes; if our souls above our sense remain,
And take not in th'afflicted body's pain;   610
When they descend and mix with the disease,
Then doth the anguish live, reign, and increase,
Which when the soul is not in it, grows faint
And wastes its strength, not nourished with
    complaint.
Submissive, humble, happy, sweet content
A thousand deaths by one death doth prevent,
When our rebellious wills, subdued thereby
Gal. 2.20   Into th'eternal will and wisdom, die;
Nor is that will harsh or irrational,
Matt. 11   But sweet in that which we most bitter call,   620
Who err in judging what is ill or good,
Only by studying that will understood.
    What we admire in a low paradise,
If they our souls from heavenly thoughts entice,
Here terminating our most strong desire
Which should to perfect permanence aspire,
From being good to us they are so far
That they our fetters, yokes and poisons are,
The obstacles of our felicity,
The ruin of our souls' most firm healths[cccxvi] be,   630

[cccxv] Joyes
[cccxvi] health

Quenching that life-maintaining appetite
Which makes substantial fruit^{cccxvii} our sound delight.
The evils, so miscalled, that we endure
Are wholesome medicines tending to our cure;
Only disease to these aversion breeds,
The healthy^{cccxviii} soul on them with due thanks feeds.
If for a prince, a mistress, or a friend,
Many do joy^{cccxix} their blood^{cccxx} and lives to spend,

Luke 9.23–4 Wealth, honour, ease, dangers and wounds despise,
Should we not more to God's will sacrifice   640
And by^{cccxxi} free gift prevent that^{cccxxii} else-sure loss?
Whate'er our will is, we must bear the cross,
Which freely taken up, the weight is less
And hurts not, carried on with cheerfulness.
Besides, what we can lose are gliding streams,

Ps. 90.5–6,9, Light airy shadows, unsubstantial dreams,
Ps. 49.10–13 Wherein we no propriety[147] could have

Luke 12.20 But that which our own cheating fancy gave.
The right of them was due to God alone,
And when with thanks we render him his own   650
Either he gives us back our offerings
Or our submission pays with better things.

Job 1.21, 42.10–12 Were ills as real as our fancies make,
They soon must us, or we must them forsake;
We cannot miss ease and vicissitude
Till our last rest our labours shall conclude.
Natural tears^{cccxxiii} [148] there are which in due bound
Do not the soul with sinful sorrow drown;

2 Cor. 7.10 Repentant tears, too, are no fretting brine,
But Love's soft meltings, which the soul refine;   660
Like gentle showers that usher in the spring,

---

^{cccxvii} food
^{cccxviii} healthy] *1679* Heavenly *MS* Healthy *MSC*
^{cccxix} Men do rejoyce
^{cccxx} blood] *MS* bloods *1679*
^{cccxxi} with
^{cccxxii} their
^{cccxxiii} feares

[147] property, right
[148] Cf. *PL* 12.645.

These make the soul more fair and flourishing.
No murmuring winds of passions^cccxxiv here prevail,
But the life-breathing spirit's sweet fresh gale,
Which by those fruitful drops all graces feeds
And draws rich extracts from the soakèd seeds;
But worldly sorrow, like rough winter's storms,
All graces kills, all loveliness deforms,
Augments the evils of our present state
And doth eternal woes anticipate.   670
Vain is that grief which can no ill redress
But adds affliction to uneasiness,
Unnerving the soul's powers then when^cccxxv they
    should
Most exercise their constant fortitude.
    With these most certain truths let's wind up all:[149]
Whatever doth to mortal men befall
Not casual[150] is,^cccxxvi like shafts at random shot,
But Providence distributes every lot,
In which th'obedient and the meek rejoice,
Above their own preferring^cccxxvii God's wise choice.   680
Nor is his Providence less good than wise,
Though our gross sense pierce not its mysteries.
As there's but one most true substantial good,
And God himself is that beatitude:
So can we suffer but one real ill,
Divorce from him by our repugnant will,
Which when to just submission it returns
The reunited soul no longer mourns,
His serene rays dry up its former tears,
Dispel the tempest^cccxxviii of its carnal fears,   690
Which dread what either^cccxxix never may arrive,

cccxxiv passion
cccxxv Unnerving . . . when] *1679* Enervateing the Soules powers when *MS*
cccxxvi are
cccxxvii preferring] *MS* preserving *1679*
cccxxviii Tempests
cccxxix either dread what

[149] Suggesting that cantos 1–5 were originally conceived as a complete work. The 1679 text
ends with the end of canto 5.
[150] fortuitous

Or not as seen in their false perspective;
For in the crystal mirror of God's grace
All things appear with a new lovely face.
When that doth Heaven's more glorious palace
    show,
We cease t'admire a Paradise below,
Rejoice in that which lately was our loss,
And see a crown made up^{cccxxx} of every cross.

Ps. 116.7 Return, return, my soul, to thy true rest,
As young benighted birds unto their nest;   700
There hide thyself under the wings of Love
Till the bright morning all thy clouds remove.^{cccxxxi 151}

Canto 6

When midnight is the blackest, day then breaks;
But then the infant dawning's pleasant streaks,
Charging through night's host, seem again put out
In the tumultuous flying shadows' rout,
Often pierced through with the encroaching light
While shades and it maintain a doubtful fight.
Such was Man's fallen state when, at the worst,
Like day appeared the blessèd promise first.[152]
The temporary curse this overlaid;
Comfort again new cheering sallies made   10
When types the promises did represent
And clothes were given for new encouragement.
Then their expulsion and their sad exile
Again contracted[153] the late gracious smile.
When God their woeful state with pity viewed,
Again their consolation was renewed,

^{cccxxx} now
^{cccxxxi} *Note in non-scribal hand: 'thus far printed'*

[151] Cf. 8.189–94. LH links this narratorial invocation not only with Psalm 116 but with Song of Songs (6.13), a favourite text of Puritan poets.
[152] Cf. *M* 7: 'the dawn of the gospel's restored ray, when light and shades were blended and almost undistinguished'.
[153] shrank

[*Genesis 4.1*]   And made the woman man's first fruit conceive,
In hope of which her husband called her Eve;
And by this name[154] not only did imply
Her curse, in his superiority,   20
But the sweet mitigation of that doom,
Promising life to enter through her womb:
Faith in which promise the glad Father thus
Professed and made exemplary to us.
    Then brought she forth; and Cain she called his
        son,
'For God', said she, 'gives us possession'.[155]
Her teeming womb with new fruit swelled again,
And finding now his forward first hopes vain,
Abel she called the next, whose riper age
Accomplished what his sad name did presage,[156]   30
And by converting their delights to woe
Did the vain joy of earthly comforts show.
When Cain was born, exultingly she thought
She had into the world her champion brought;
But from the error of that fond conceit[157]
She learned that such as live on faith must wait
To have the promises whereon they stay
Performed alone in God's own time and way.
The'entail[158] of life and victory was not
To earthly man, of earthly man begot;   40
And such alone could Eve to Adam breed
Whose sin and curse was fixed in all his seed;
And to recover its corrupted fruit
It must be set into a nobler root,
Its ignominious parentage disclaim
And be adopted into a new name:
Which then obscured in th'oracle did lie
Till the full time revealed the mystery;
When God did into human nature come,

---

[154] Genesis 3.20: 'And Adam called his wife's name Eve; because she was the mother of all living', playing on similarities between the words for 'Eve' and 'life'.
[155] Cain: from Hebrew word for 'got, obtained'.
[156] Abel: linked by commentators with Hebrew words for mourning and vanity.
[157] conception, idea
[158] inheritance

Vesting himself in a pure virgin's womb,   50
Whence he a second stock of mankind grew
That dead grafts set in him might life renew.
    But Death was first to exercise its reign
Long ere new life to light came forth again.
Adam in his own likeness got a son
Infected with his own pollution,
Which wholly spread itself through all his race,
Conceived in sin and born in sad disgrace.
For that black crime which did his honour stain
Doth yet a taint on all his blood remain.   60
Acknowledging this truth, alas, from whence
Doth vain nobility raise its pretence,[159]
When the first monarch's sons, in slavery born,
Were taught those trades which upstart nobles
    scorn:
The eldest prince to agriculture bred,
The next white[cccxxxii] flocks in the cool shadow fed?
Nor were they only taught to exercise
Honest employments; but with sacrifice
To worship God in his appointed day
And seek his favour and their due thanks pay.   70
The ceremony with a diverse mind
They both performed, and such success did find.
    Cain some of his new corn and fruits did bring,
But God accepted not his offering:
For 'tis the heart more than the sacrifice
That must find grace in the Almighty's eyes.
He that with meal and pure devotion comes
Shall better please than pompous hecatombs
Which unbelievers in a formal[160] way
With ostentation on his altars slay,   80
Smothering their faith with overgrowing pride
While they in their[cccxxxiii] performances confide.[161]

---

cccxxxii white *MS* his *MSC*
cccxxxiii there

[159] ostentation, presumption
[160] Following external forms only: a Puritan usage.
[161] trust

Abel the fattest of his whole flock sought,
And humbly to the Lord his offering brought;
Whose steadfast faith and self-denying mind
Gracious acceptance with his God did find.
This made Cain's wicked heart with rancour swell,
At which his late-erected countenance fell,
While wrath like fire beneath the cauldron lies
And made his thoughts like filthy scum arise,   90
Till they confusedly run o'er and drowned
Every faint spark in his dark bosom found.
Envy, that most pernicious hag of Hell,[162]
Observing this, starts from the gloomy cell
Where she, maligning all things good and great,
With pining rage doth her own carcass eat,
And secretly into his sad breast creeps,
There all his thoughts in her black poison steeps.
Th'infection first his sick heart ulcerates,
And thence itself to every part dilates.   100
No more could his dim eyes Heaven's splendour
    brook,
But on the Earth fixed their dejected look;
Where while he walked with slow and sullen pace,
A thousand fancies heightened his disgrace.
Envy and spite thus reigning nourished hate,
And all together vengeance meditate.
    His ill surmisings with his guilt increase,
Destroying the last remnant of his peace,
When God from Heaven graciously did call
To the grieved wretch: 'Why doth thy countenance
    fall?   110
Why doth thy anger burn? Why art thou sad?
If thou dost well, shall not regard be had
To thy good deeds, to give them recompense?
If thou dost ill, the guilt of thy offence
As a tormentor at thy door shall wait
And ever shall perplex thy future state.
What hath thy brother done to cause thy ire?
To thee he bends, to thee is his desire.

---

[162] For this allegorization of envy cf. Spenser, *Faerie Queene* 5.12.29–32.

The favour he hath found doth not elate[163]
His thoughts against thee to an insolent height.   120
Thee as his elder he doth reverence,
And bears thy wrath with humble innocence'.
   These reasons could not Cain's dire wrath
      appease,
For such contagion had his wild disease
That, as a forge more violently burns
By casting water on, his sick mind turns
All cures to poison, and what should abate
Rather gives growth unto his cruel hate.
He with his brother talks, whose answers mild
Inflame his passion more, and make him wild   130
To see those virtues he can never reach.
Furious despair then entering at the breach
Did all the obstacles of sin remove,
Trod down his piety and fraternal love,
Advancing only his triumphant pride,
Which had no rest till guiltless Abel died:
Whom whilst his innocence no fear instilled
His cruel brother on the sudden killed,
And, better to conceal his wicked deed,
The lifeless carcass in a covert[164] hid.   140
   This vengeance pleased his impious mind a while;
But ah! how wicked men themselves beguile.
They think God sees not mischiefs he permits
And long unexecuted threats forgets,
And that because he is not in their view
He sees and marks as little what they do;
When no dark shroud, nor the thick veil of night,
Can hide the sin of sinners from his sight,
Which penetrates into all shades, all deeps,
All that the heart in its dark corners keeps.   150
The secret'st sins contrivèd there are known
To him even in their first conception.
He sees their growth, is present at their birth,
Though in the darkest entrails of the earth.

[163] raise
[164] thicket

Remote from him nor caves nor rocks, nor far-
Extended shores, nor distant islands are.
His view that stretches to the largest space
Is not excluded in the narrowest place.
Can anything from him obscurèd be
Who made all that is seen, and all that see?   160
He who by winking would put out the sun
Is not so worthy of derision
As he who, while God is not in his eyes,
Believes himself unseen by him he flies.
 This foolish[cccxxxiv] unbelief is the chief sin
That shuts out awe and lets all villainy in.[165]
Why else doth lust and treason seek a shade
Except[166] men hoped they thereby could evade
As well as man's, God's eyes, which are too pure
Foul deeds without abhorrence to endure.   170
Would not th'adulterer start from lewd embrace,
Dreading t'abuse God's house before his face;
Would not the swinish drunkard be afraid
To come before the judge in masquerade,
Reason, his sovereign's livery, to divest,[167]
Wearing the badge of devil and of beast;
Would not the stoutest murderer shrink with fear
God's sacred Image in his sight to tear,
Were not Hell's mists so in their senses rolled?
They think him far whom they cannot behold,   180
While th'old enchanter with[cccxxxv] his sorceries
Seals up their understanding's blinded eyes,
Till the fact's[168] done, then doth his charms unbind,
And they God's presence to their terror find.
So the first murderer was a little time
Falsely secure in his close[169]-acted crime

---

cccxxxiv falce, this *MS* foolish *MSC*
cccxxxv of *MS* with *MSC*

[165] Cf. *T* 331: 'the roote of Cains sin was unbeliefe'.
[166] unless
[167] put off
[168] crime
[169] secret

Till God himself did then appear in view;
When Satan all his treacherous blinds[170] withdrew,
And naked left the wretch, without defence
But what he sought in lies and impudence;   190
Though he a witness in his own breast bore
As much convincing as a thousand more,
And in his blushes, guilt it self betrayed
When inquisition[171] of the fact was made.
For God, who suffers many sins to lie
Buried in darkness or hypocrisy
Till that day which all secrets shall reveal,
Seldom permits foul murderers to conceal
Their guilt till death, but makes them oftentimes
In dreams and ravings to disclose their crimes,   200
Oft to betray themselves by their own dread,
Oft-times by the fresh bleedings of the dead,
By complices,[172] by ghosts wandering in night,
And various other ways to come to light.
Oft have the murderers themselves been slain
And at their deaths confessed their bloody stain,
Finding themselves by their own crimes pursued
And crying out that blood must expiate blood.
    Cain's vengeance to its utmost stretch had run
And where that ended, God's revenge begun,   210
Which unexpected did the wretch surprise,
Asking where Abel was. In surly wise,
'Am I his keeper?' said the parricide.
'I know not where he is.' The Lord replied:
'What hast thou done? his blood spilt on the
    ground
To Heaven cries, and there hath audience[173] found.
The Earth, your common parent, shall no more
Indulge thee her rich blessings as before;
No more her fertile strength impart when thou
Openest her rich womb by thy labouring plough.   220

170 deceptive obstructions to sight
171 inquiry
172 accomplices
173 hearing

Thou with thy brother's blood her mouth
    hast[cccxxxvi] filled,
And that seed shall no crop but curses yield.
No portion shalt thou henceforth have in her,
But be a fugitive and wanderer.'
    Sad Cain, thus sentenced for his cruel fact,
Cried out to God, 'O Lord, thou dost exact
My punishment greater than I can bear.
Behold, I am an exile everywhere.
This day I have in all the Earth no place
And am forever banished from thy face.   230
Thou dost me from all habitation drive,
And whosoe'er shall meet this fugitive,
This bloody vagabond, with justice will
So vile a wretch as the first murderer kill'.
    Thus was vile Cain convicted[174] with deep sense
Not of his[cccxxxvii] sin but of its consequence,
When God assured him sevenfold vengeance should
Seize on whatever man should shed his blood,
And to confirm it set a mark on Cain
To show 'twas not God's will he should be slain.   240
Was't God's will, then, that parricide should be
At first encouraged by impunity?
Not so, but the first execution
Was more severely by the Lord's hand done
Than could by any minister have been,
And magistrates did not their power begin
Till mankind grew into societies
On whom that power hath its exercise.[175]
Before the Lord his substitutes ordained,
Himself immediately in judgement reigned,   250
His rebels by his own mouth did condemn
And by his own hand executed them.
The sword is God's, and who without his leave

[cccxxxvi] hath
[cccxxxvii] it's

[174] overcome
[175] For discussion of death penalty before the Flood cf. *Westminster Annotations*, Genesis 9.6; cf. 9.303–6.

Usurps it shall a double stroke receive.
   Yet did not this first impious criminal
'Scape punishment, nor was it light and small:
No more allowed unto the Lord to bring
With bloody hands his loathèd offering;
No more with pure Saints to associate,
Their sacred mysteries to communicate;[176]   260
No more to come before th'Almighty's face,
That is, into his favour and his grace,
Though he can nowhere from his justice run,
Nor nowhere can his dreadful terror shun;
By which he up and down the world was thrown,
As a light bark[177] by raging tempest blown.
Horror like thunder on his bare sides knocks;
Remorse, rage, spite, split him like pointed rocks;
Affrights like whirlwinds heave him in the air,
Swallowed at last in quicksands of despair.   270
When he looked down upon the bloodstained
      ground,
His trembling legs unfirm their station found,
Dreading that under him the earth should rive[178]
And in her dire jaws swallow him alive.
He shivered when he felt the sportful air,
Fancying his brother's pale ghost hovered there,
And while he drunk the cool refreshing flood,
Thinking it poisoned with his brother's blood,
He starts and flies from the scarce-tasted streams;
Nor is less persecuted in his dreams,   280
When grief conducts him to the House of Sleep
Where dullness doth on the tired members creep.
Then they a thousand terrors represent
And torture him in every element.
Lightning from heaven round about him flies
And sulphurous flames from the cleft mountains
      rise;
About his ears the furious tempest raves;
The sea devours him in its angry waves;

[176] share in
[177] ship
[178] split

Earth's savage brood tear him with torturing smart,
Which makes him from his frightful slumber start;   290
Whose fears being in the waking sense renewed,
He flies; but each-where by himself pursued,
In vain he roves about the world for rest,
Carrying his torturer in his guilty breast;
Thus from God's presence went.^{cccxxxviii}

                         All that do so
From light, from life, from rest and pleasure go,
And all the space they afterward survive
Keeps but their woe and misery alive
While they are dead, from God cast off; and this
Sad separation only true death is;   300
Nor need they go into a lower hell
Who in those everlasting burnings dwell
That are enkindled by the Lord's just ire
When from their due subjection men retire.
If men the reigning power of sin admit,
Hell enters them, and they abide in it.[179]

    The Lord from Paradise did Adam chase,
Yet suffered him to come before his face.
He was from transitory joys estranged,
His forfeited inheritance was changed,   310
A pilgrim he on earth became; but yet
Ps. 39[180]   With God he was a sojourner in it,
Allowed its low refreshment as he passed
Heb. 11[181]   And a most glorious home to fix at last.
Thus, to God's blessèd favour reconciled,
He rather was removèd than exiled.
But Cain a wretched vagabond did roam;
He had no quiet inn, nor blessèd home,
But by God's severe sentence driven out,

---

^{cccxxxviii} went *MS* driv'n *MSC*

[179] Cf. *PL* 4.75: 'Which way I fly is hell; myself am hell'.
[180] 'I am a stranger with thee, and a sojourner, as all my fathers were', Ps. 39.12; cited at 5.316.
[181] 'they were strangers and pilgrims on the earth ... now they desire a better country, that is, an heavenly: wherefore God is not ashamed to be called their God: for he hath prepared for them a city', Heb. 11.13, 16; cited at 1.217, 5.316.

A guilty conscience lashed him round about   320
Like whirligigs which in some spacious court
Boys with their restless scourges drive for sport:
Such pastime do the hellish Furies find
When sinners are into their power resigned.
Out of his father's house and God's church thrown,

Ps. 1[182]   Like light chaff by the blustering wind is blown,
Cain had no proper station nor no rest,
Neither in Earth nor Heaven had interest.
    As husks a while cleave to the solid grain
Till they are severed by the winnowing fan,   330
So for a while the formal hypocrite[183]
Lies in the Church till he be found too light
God's strict and various siftings to endure
When he comes in to separate th'impure
Which from the heap the Holy Spirit drives.
But Satan watches for those fugitives,
And makes himself their most pernicious guide
Who must no more in God's safe courts abide.
Then they who first walked down now headlong
    fall;
Who kept some duties up, now leave off all;   340
Who were restrained by some religious awe
Now own no curb, contemning[184] every law.
First they cast off his fear, then slight his grace,
Then impudently brave him to his face,
The Devil's badge with impious triumph wear
And hate of God maliciously declare.
Deplorable and horrid is the state
Of such a cursèd excommunicate.

[Genesis 4.16]   Such was poor Cain, who in the land of Nod
Yet found a wife who left for him her God.   350
Both founders of the Worldly State became,
And had a son whom they did Enoch name,
After whose birth their family increased
(Oft are they multiplied who are not blessed:

---

[182] Ps. 1.4: 'The ungodly ... are like the chaff which the wind driveth away'.
[183] Cf. *T* 332: Cain 'is made the ringleader and primitive patterne of all succeeding hipocrites,
from the beginning of the church to the end of the world'.
[184] despising

Thus did the numerous family advance)
Who,[185] hardened in his pride and arrogance
Raised him a city with aspiring walls
Which he Enochia[cccxxxix] by his son's name calls;
And probably in his contemptuous pride
Might say, 'Here shall the fugitive abide.   360
The favoured saints with whom we must not mix
May heaven ascend, here we on earth will fix.
Let them a trade of contemplation drive,
While we conveniencies for life contrive'.
Accordingly his sons their wits applied
To various arts, following the various guide
Of each man's genius; Jabal found out tents;
Jubal devised harmonious instruments;
Tubal-Cain[cccxl] forges iron, pliant wrought,
And brass into its various uses brought;   370
Others in other things ingenious were;
His female issue, excellently fair.
Invention, beauty, wit and art of small
Advantage are where God's grace crowns not all.
Rich talents do but make the debt more vast.
The wealth and glory which they gain at last
Proves but a fatally unhappy freight,
Sinking the vessel with its cursèd weight.
Such glittering sinners, trained in Hell's decoy,
More easily simple wandering souls destroy   380
Than th'absolute foul ugly wretches could,
Were not sin mixed with something seeming good.
Yet did not this accursèd brood alone
On useful arts employ invention:
They did as well devise new modes of sin.

Lamech, who had Here first did lustful bigamy begin;
two wives, and
boasted to them of Here impudence first choked up virtuous shame;
the man he had Here murder first a glorious boast became.
slain[186]
Lust and Revenge here from Hell's womb did rise,

cccxxxix Henochia
cccxl Tuball In

[185] i.e. Cain
[186] Genesis 4.19, 23–4.

Marching in Love's and Honour's fair disguise.   390
    Hell's oft-defeated Monarch once again
In spite of God attempted here to reign,
Nor difficultly did admission find.
They to his sceptre all their power resigned,
But with harsh tyranny he them repaid,
Uneasy[187] all their yokes and bondage made,
Allowed them not one moment's soft release.
The very images of love and peace,
Throughout his realm they were all kicked and
    torn,
Not one poor glance towards Heaven's fair
    offspring borne.   400
Though Cain got[188] sons and did a city build,
These no relief to his sad soul could yield.
Amidst his children, his renown and state,
He yet continued cursed and desolate.
God's piercing arrow stuck fast in his heart:
No worldly glory can allay that smart.
Guilt made him mad, suspicious, unsecure.
Who knows the tortures jealous breasts endure:
Still hating whom they fear, not loved by those
Whose hatred from their causeless hatred grows.   410
Far are those worldlings from life's joys removed
Who neither love nor think themselves beloved.
Such the bright slaves of Satan's empire be,
'Mongst whom there often is conspiracy
While lust or interest them in leagues combines,
But holy love or friendship never joins.[189]
Yet that they call by love's and friendship's name
Which is a wild fire and unhallowed flame.
Love is the cément of the Holy State,
Nor hath it place or fellowship with hate,   420
Hate that is sovereign in the breasts of those
Who God, the fountain of all love, oppose.
    Thus far the Lord permitted Satan's pride,

---

[187] difficult
[188] begot
[189] Pronounced to rhyme with 'combines'.

Who thought exultingly when Abel died
The holy seed extinguished by his death;
But God revived it in succeeding Seth,[190]
Born after Cain was excommunicate
To be the founder of the Holy State.
The holy seed still with advantage dies
That it in new and glorious form might rise.   430
So still th'Almighty draws life from the tomb:
Thus did the first light out of darkness come.
As single grains spring up in ears of corn,
So in one martyr's bed a church is born.
Though Abel childless died, yet God's house stood
Soon glorious up, sown in his precious blood
And bearing in his front[191] his happy name[192]
Which thus illustrious to all time became,
Allowed a martyr's crown by God's rich grace
And emulated by the next pure race   440
Who sought no safety but in innocence.
No cities built for God was their defence;
No arts, no sensual pleasures did invent,
Only with bare necessities content;
Left to the world terrestrial low delight
While their more noble spirits did unite
In the pursuit of high and heavenly things,
Rising together on prayer's dove-like wings.[193]
    In Enos' days their faculties increased,
[Genesis 4.26] First publicly the name of God professed,[194]   450
And while the world in civil leagues combined
Their souls in pious exercises joined.
This spring of godliness hell's state alarms.
Old envious Satan calls his mates to arms,
Consults how to disturb the Church's peace

---

[190] The third son of Adam and Eve, Genesis 4.25.
[191] forehead
[192] Seth was linked with a Hebrew word for 'setting'.
[193] Cf. *R* 118: prayers 'are the dove-like wings of the soule, by which it ascends to God'.
[194] Owen (*T* 338–43) interprets Genesis 4.26 as referring to Enos, whose 'second reformation' followed the 'first reformation' of the ejection of Cain and prefigured the separatist congregations in his own time: 'There is then no way left for the godly but a secession and collection into seperate assemblies' (343).

And to prevent its menacing increase.
''Tis not enough,' said he, 'that we command
The first and largest city; that we stand
On our defence against that feeble state
With whom we can no more associate   460
Except[195] they by some stratagem be caught
And under our more large dominion brought.
Woman, entangled once by our deceit,
Became for man our more successful bait.
Let us again throw out that pleasant lure:
He is not flesh and blood that can endure
The sweet attraction of their sparkling eyes
And fortify his soul against surprise.
Let us take stand amongst these murdering faces
And as our darts employ their artful graces: 470
Let us the golden shafts in poison steep;
Of pleasure's charmèd floods let them drink deep
And[cccxli] there, infected with the cheating vice,
Exchange their heaven for the fool's paradise.'
    These counsels Hell's malicious court applaud,
And all the lustful devils went abroad,
Some blowing up the young men's appetite
With the vain fancy of a false delight;
Some in the blazing females did inspire
As vain ambition human hearts to fire.   480
Then an imperious beauty thinks she reigns
When many captives languish in her chains;
Then she believes her bright cheeks richly shine
When her wan lovers all grow sick and pine.
Inhuman is their pride that can endure
To give more rankling wounds than they must
    cure.
When men's desires receive a check at first
And are not by vainglorious wantons nursed,
Their stifled hope is such a counter-charm
That love thus starved can never do men harm.   490
But this would throw the female empire down:

[cccxli] An

[195] unless

'Tis many victims gives a face renown,
Which virtuous beauties seek not, but despise
Poor glory that in one sick moment dies,
Preferring more to wither unadmired
Than cause their hurt by whom they are desired.
Proud wantons have far other thoughts, from
    whence
Poor mankind from the first and ever since
A thousand woes and troubles have derived,
By their ambitious mistresses contrived,   500
Who first from God seduce their charmèd hearts
Then keep them captives by those subtle arts
The Devil taught them, then their slaves engage
In horrid wars through jealousies and rage,
In toils and dangers both by sea and land
All undertaken at a whore's command.[196]
For these have many in fierce duel died,
Close murder and unnatural parricide.
These are the authors of all tragedies,
Adding to human arts all sorceries   510
Which rage and madness by Hell's aid inspire:
Their fatal blazes set the world on fire
When nature's force is helped by art and wit,
And all the Devils are employed in it,
Who taught them first their dresses to dispose,
Part of th'alluring members[197] to disclose;
To shade the rest with garments light and thin
Through which they are with more advantage
    seen;
To weave their tresses into a fine net;
Their curls in well-becoming order set;   520
Nature's defects, and time's wastes to repair
With false complexions, eyebrows, teeth and hair;
To soften hearts with music's charming sound,
In all the grace of motion to abound;

---

[196] Possibly a reference to the king's mistress Louise de Kéroualle, Duchess of Portsmouth, who exercised her influence in support of war with the Netherlands and close alliance with Louis XIV.
[197] limbs

Wanton among the lighter youth to be,
Nice[198] and severe with men of gravity;
To govern and conceal their own desires
That lovers might augment their ardent fires;
To counterfeit repentance, rage, tears, smiles,
Kindness and jealousy, with all the wiles   530
Of well-dissembled innocence and truth,
And modest looks that snare the simple youth.
   Cain's lovely daughters, exercising these
Too fatally, the Sons of God did please,
Who all the greater ends of marriage slight,
Conducted by their sensual appetite;
With profane wives defiling that pure bed
Which God to holy use determinèd,
To be a seminary for his plants
And fill his city with inhabitants.   540
But these mixed marriages produced a brood
That stained the earth with violence and blood:
Men of prodigious valour, strength and size
Whose monstrous crimes were no less prodigies;
Oppression, cruelty, lust, rapine, rage
Abounding everywhere in that lewd age,
Where sincere worship was no more allowed
But driven out by the tumultuous crowd
Who new ways of invoking God begin,
Bringing vain pomp and men's inventions in.   550
Nor did their tyrant, the great Prince of Hell,
Forbid this worship, for it pleased him well,
Who thus what he aspired to be became:
God of the World, under the True God's name.
God hates proud rebels' pompous sacrifice,
Nor unrevenged will bear their mockeries.
   Yet though more generally among mankind
False worship was advanced and truth declined,
There were a few that yet continued pure
Nor these polluted mixtures would endure,   560
But God in his own ordinances sought
And men his undefilèd precepts taught.

[198] coy

Enoch,^{cccxlii} descended of Seth's holy race,

Jude 14 Sprung up from Adam in the seventh place,

Is principally numbered amongst these

Heb. 11.5 Whose conversation did th'Almighty please,

For he in faith did purely God adore,

Against that wicked world his witness bore;

Encouragèd the saints of his own times

Jude 15 That when God came to judge the lewd world's
crimes   570

They who obedient in the faith remain

Shall come with him and fill his glorious train;

Warned and rebuked those reprobates of old

To whom he God's ensuing vengeance told.

 'Poor men,' said he, 'attend while yet you may.

The Lord hath set his battles in array

And with ten thousand of his saints will come

To execute on sinners his just doom.

No one vile deed, no one vile sinner shall

His inquisition[199] 'scape, who takes in all   580

The most concealèd sins; black deeds of night

Heb. 4.13 That even now are naked in his sight

Then shall be set before the sinner's eyes.

Nor shall they hide as now in bold-faced lies,

Nor find evasions by their subtle wit,

Nor will he them to any place admit.

All wicked deeds shall all apparent be;

All men his justice shall in judgement see;

Their godless speeches too, whereby they oft

Blasphemed his spirit, and his sure threats scoffed,   590

His people and his service did deride,

His Knowledge, Justice, Providence, denied,

His holy laws as harsh commands did blame;

Presumptuous invocations of his name;

Their frequent, false and blasphemous abuse;

Their careless, light, profane, irreverent use;[200]

Shall all be into open judgement brought,

cccxlii Henoch

[199] scrutiny
[200] custom, behaviour

And full conviction on the sinners wrought
How great that goodness was they did offend;
To what degrees their lewdness did extend;   600
How much the manner did exceed the act
And was an aggravation of the fact;
How their despite,[201] ingratitude, contempt,
Doth them even from the least excuse exempt
And God's long-threatened judgement justify,
Which must extend to all eternity,
To all the sad and torturing extremes
Conceivable in everlasting flames'.
     Thus he that wicked world warned and reproved
But they, hard as the rocks, were still unmoved,   610
Still in their own pernicious, lewd paths trod,
Which he declining walked up close with God.
As fires more fervent are when frosts congeal
The circumfusèd[202] air, such was his zeal:
So much more ardent as those wicked times
Did more abound in irreligious crimes.
Nor sullied it the lustre of his life
That he conducted[203] a chaste pious wife
And out of her a holy offspring raised,
Building a house which in that dark age blazed.   620
Like heaven's bright lamps that nightly wanderers
    guide
When muffling clouds day's vanquished glory hide,
So did his fair example brightly shine,
So was his conversation all divine,
Till God did him to his high court translate,
Nor would his soul and body separate;
But by his living, whole assumption gave
His saints assurance the concealing grave
Shall not their flesh for ever prisoner keep
But yield them fresher after death's long sleep;   630
And that there is a blessèd place above
To which our wakened body shall remove.
     How graciously, after that great offence

---

[201] malice
[202] surrounding
[203] led

Which all mankind involved, did God dispense
His mercies to the world, their hope renewed,
And in dark shades a light of comfort showed.
For this the devout patriarchs sung his praise
And blessèd angels joyed to see him raise
Men to their fellowship; but bad ones pined
To see the place possessed where once they shined.   640

Canto 7

[*Genesis 5.4–32*] Although Seth's offspring did God's ways decline,
Mixed with Cain's impious brood, yet of that line
In every age some few with pure hearts sought
The Lord of Life and to their children taught.
Seth was the founder of the Holy State;
Enos his son; and Cainan^{cccxliii} he begat,
Whose true but melancholy names imply
Frail Man's lamenting imbecility;[204]
The sense of which produceth God's just praise,
Who by th'infirm can his firm structure raise.   10
This, intimated in Mahaleel's name,
The monument of Cainan's faith became.
Mahaleel Jared got; he Enoch's^{cccxliv} sire,
Whose holy life, not suffered to expire,
Is yet continued in high Heaven above.
He left Methuselah at his remove,
Whose stay was longer than all others' here,
Stretched t'his six hundredth, ninety and ninth year.
From his son Lamech, pious Noah came,
Carrying his father's glad hope in his name.[205]   20

^{cccxliii} Kenam
^{cccxliv} Henochs

[204] Cainan could be linked with a word for 'smith' or 'artificer', Mahaleel could mean 'God shines forth'.

[205] 'As of old they gave *significant names* unto their children, so therein they had respect unto their present condition, or some prospect they had given them by the Spirit of God of things future, wherein they or theirs should be concerned. So have we reasons given us of the names … of Noah, chap. v.29': Owen, *Works*, XVIII.450. Noah was traced to Hebrew words for 'rest' and 'comfort'.

In ten successions thus the first world passed;
But all we know is that their lives did last
Longer than ours; no memory remained
By what such great experience they had gained.
Their deaths, their wars and all the arts they found
Were in the Deluge and oblivion drowned.
We think the world's young vigour made them strong
And that plain food preserved their lives so long,
For they on fruits, herbs, milk and honey fed;
No beasts to satiate their hunger bled;   30
No fowl were into hidden nets betrayed;
No snares for the unwary creatures laid;
No fishes caught in rivers or in brooks
With treacherous baits upon their unseen hooks;
No seas, no shores were searched for new delights
To recreate their wanton appetites.[206]
  Yet though luxurious sins were then unknown,
That world did under other vices groan.
Rapine, lust, murder, cruelty and rage,
With impious blasphemies, defiled that age.   40
For when the sons of God his sweet curb broke,
Polluted by the world's unequal yoke,
They cast off all pure reverential awe
And broke the fence of matrimonial law.
His neighbour's wife each potent lecher took,
Each wild adulterer his own forsook;
No more could modest flight secure from rape;
Chaste virgins could not ravishers escape.
Promiscuous lust polluted every bed,
Children were to uncertain fathers bred   50
Whose vices as their bodies vastly grew:
Each giant's strength the only bound he knew,
Whereby he kept the weaker vulgar down
And got his wicked greatness a renown.
As by impunity these hardened were,
At last they God no more than man did fear,
Scoff at his worshippers, his threats disdained,

---

[206] Belief that meat was not eaten before the Flood was common though not universal (Calvin I.291 disagrees).

And in contempt of him their crimes maintained;
Who yet his prophets to those lewd men sent

Gen. 6[207]   And gave them gracious warnings to repent.   60
   'By me,' said he, 'men live and move; when I

Job 27.3[208]   Call back th'inspirèd souls, the bodies die.
Their sins are grown up to that full height now
That I no longer will their lives allow,
But will command away their quickening breath,
Leave them like empty scabbards at their death.
They shall not evermore stand in my sight,
Which cannot in their impure flesh delight.
[2] No longer shall my waking Providence
Act for their sustenance or their defence;   70
Whose mighty operation ceasing, all
Confounded natures will to ruin fall.
[3] My Spirit, sent t'inhabit human kind,
Whom for myself a temple I designed,
I will retract,[209] nor shall it still remain
With those who do my holy seat profane.
I will desert their vile polluted race;
No longer will I offer them my grace.
[4] I will at last draw forth my glittering sword;
My strokes shall follow my despisèd word;   80
Nor shall the quiver still my arrows keep:
My sure revenge shall not forever sleep.
[5] No longer shall my injured spirit plead,
No more shall it this stubborn race persuade.
(i) For they are flesh, exalting fleshly will,
Which sets itself against my Spirit still;
(ii) For they are flesh: not Cain's lewd sons alone,
But my sons too; they all are fleshly grown,
And all flesh now shall in destruction end,
My spirit shall no more with flesh contend.   90
Yet the condemned have six-score years' reprieve:
So long will I permit them yet to live.'
   No sadder, worse-presaging judgement can

---

[207] God's warning comes in Genesis 6.3.
[208] 'All the while my breath is in me, and the spirit of God is in my nostrils.'
[209] withdraw

Fall on th'unhappy race of sinful man
Than when God's holy Spirit in just ire
From the polluted temple doth retire.
When God forsakes the house defiled by sin,
All the whole crew of ugly fiends throng in,
Rendering that soul which drunk in sin's first stain
Uncapable of being cleansed again.   100
As when the spirit Heaven did inspire
Retracts from the cold members'[210] quickening fire,
Corruption soon dissolves the rotten frame
Which at the first out of corruption came;
As, when the sun is set, night creeps on fast
Till blackness have involvèd all at last;
Such dark, quick dissolution follows when
The long-grieved spirit leaves rebellious men,
Who in that dead state lose all sight and sense
And motion, stiffened by impenitence;   110
Their pureness changed into an ugly hue
And carrion stinking where sweet roses grew.
Such were th'old world, when God would strive no
      more
By those kind checks he exercised before.
Angry indulgence rendered them secure,
The searèd[211] conscience could all threats endure.
They thought themselves from pupillage now free;
Their guardian gone, joyed in their liberty,
Through which their sure and swift destruction
      came.
Yet triumph they in their obdurate frame   120
As if their stout sins had caused God to yield
And leave them masters of the quitted field.
As madmen who their friendly chains had broke,
So raged they, gotten out of that safe yoke
Which was a curb to their licentious will
While waking conscience checked them in their ill.
While heaven shined and rich fruits crowned the
      earth

---

[210] limbs'
[211] dried up

They wholly gave themselves to feasts and mirth,
Ate, drunk, built piles,[212] got children and new
   wives,
As if no danger threatened their lewd lives   130
And their first natural impressions were
Vain superstitions and a childish fear;
Boasting they had attainèd to be wise
When they with manly courage could despise
Fictions of God and Hell that did control
A vulgar,[213] weak, deluded, pious soul.
So run[214] the old world then, so do they now
Who none but atheists for wise men allow:
Such as no awe of th'unseen God doth curb,
No thoughts of any future state disturb;   140
Who valiantly have conscience overcome
And feel no pain when that is once made numb.
   Meanwhile the Lord his goodness did pursue
To these ill men: their seasons did renew;
Allowed them common blessings, air and light,
Restored calm days, expelled the stormy night,
A table for his rebels daily spread
Whereat themselves they fat for slaughter fed;
His watchful providence for them employed,
Nor left the wretched world without a guide,   150
But wisely led and turned their violent streams
To ends that were not in their thoughts nor aims;
Wrought their deliverance, danger did prevent,
When they miscalled his high help accident,[215]
Nor owned nor blessed that unseen powerful hand
By whose support Nature's loose frame did stand:
Happy when mercies lie in Judgement's womb,
But sad when mercies in a Judgement come.[cccxlv]

[cccxlv] Happy ... come] *marked as a sententia or maxim in MS*

[212] castles
[213] As at 7.53, LH parodies the social snobbery of courtly atheists.
[214] ran
[215] Cf. LH's condemnation of materialists in the Lucretius preface: 'leaving all things here, to Accident and Chance, deniing that determinate wise Councell and Order of things they could not dive into, and deriding Heaven and Hell, Eternall Rewards and Punishments, as fictions' (*L* 25).

For by indulgences that store grows vast
Which will be all exacted at the last.   160
   Though God had long foreseen the cursed
     abuse
Of his abounding grace, that no excuse
To th'impenitent sinners might remain,[216]
Before he struck he searched the world again,
And did a total depravation find
In all the thoughts and actions of mankind.
Corrupted in the whole and every part,
All the imaginations of the heart
Not only evil were but only ill,
Not mixed nor intermitted evil still.   170
No signs, no admonitions, no wise fear
Had stopped the violence of their career,
Nor God's approach: before his face they yet
Held on, and him in high rebellion met.
Thus sin not only sinful seems, but mad.
No other power deserted Nature had.
Man's universal Fall left nothing good:
Nothing is pure that springs from flesh and blood.
In natural and moral actions, then,
Is there no goodness left to fallen men?   180
No, nothing's good, all ill by ill men done.[217]
Pure waters[cccxlvi] which through stinking channels
   run
Become corrupt in their declining stream:
Such all good actions are, performed by them.
If acts derive their goodness from their end,
Whate'er they do they sinfully intend.
If we would seek their goodness in the spring,
Who from impurity can pureness bring?
Though we are cheated with fair-looking fruit,
All baneful are upon a poisoned root.   190
Such are the virtues of all human race
Till fallen nature be renewed by grace.

cccxlvi water

[216] Cf. Romans 1.20.
[217] A strong assertion of Calvinist orthodoxy.

The Holy Spirit drew the old world thus
To be our emblem that, ourselves to us
In our polluted births most truly shown,
Might in ourselves no goodness seek nor own
But to the first eternal spring repair,
Carrying and seeking all our goodness there;
Dreading to drive away that Spirit whence
All that is virtuous hath its influence.   200
But if that too unhappily retire,
As when the salt floods quench day's radiant fire,
Wild beasts break from their dens and range about;
So savage crimes come^{cccxlvii} in where God goes out.
The long space given the old world to repent
Did but their provocations more augment.
Impiety at monstrous height was found
And violence did throughout the earth abound.
No dread, no soft remorse, did sin abate
Even when vengeance knocked at every gate.   210
    Love, seeing this, did into pity melt
And deeply grieved for those who no grief felt,
Repenting it had mankind made to be
Subjects of such eternal^{cccxlviii} misery.
Yet did not Mercy all to Judgement yield,
But kept one quarter of the bloody field,
Sweetly itself with severe justice mixed,
Its gracious view on pious Noah fixed:
Who^{cccxlix} when all others did degenerate
Is yet preserved in an unblemished state   220
And in his upright soul its own work crowned,
For which he grace before th'Almighty found.
Then said the Lord: 'I will all men destroy,
With all th'abusèd creatures they enjoy;
Whatever walks on earth, all creeping things,
All that divide the air with outstretched wings,
Shall in that general deluge be involved
Which I to punish sinners have resolved.

---

^{cccxlvii} comes
^{cccxlviii} Eterall
^{cccxlix} Whom

For I repent that I for mankind's sake
Did the fair world and all its dwellers make   230
To be by man's polluting use defiled
And by myself destroyed when by them spoiled'.
    After those threats looking again, the Lord
Saw th'earth still foul and more to be abhorred;
No longer now to them his summons sends,
Sad sign that he no more their care intends;
His holy prophets who the warnings gave
Calls home into the quiet of the grave,
That death's insensible and misty night
Might hide th'approaching horrors from their
    sight.   240
The Church alone in Noah's house remained,
Who to the last his uprightness retained.
To him the Lord his latest speech addressed,
Disdaining to take notice of the rest.
'The fatal period[218] of all human seed,'
Said God, 'approaches now; it is decreed
Never to be recalled, since all my grace
Is but contemned even before my face,
And violence doth in the earth abound
Which I will with its wicked dwellers drownd.   250
But thou shalt for thyself an ark provide
Of gopher wood, and pitch it on each side.
The length shall to three hundred cubits stretch;
Fifty the height; thirty the breadth shall reach.
Above, a window of a cubit square,
And in the side thou shalt a door prepare,
Into three stories shalt the room divide,
That creatures there distinctly may reside.
And now behold: I that have long endured
Men's horrid crimes, whose patience scoffs
    procured;   260
I that by threats endeavoured to prevent
The fatal stroke; allowed time to repent;
That sent so many messengers in vain
That long contest with sinners did maintain;

[218] end

At last in my just judgement gave them o'er
When my abusèd grace enflamed their store.
I that long-suffering was, to vengeance slow;
I that so oft bewailed their overthrow;
I, even I, a flood of waters bring
Whose greedy waves shall swallow everything   270
That doth in living breath respire the air,
Nor shall it any of the creatures spare
That move beneath the bright all-covering sky.
Whatever Earth contains at once shall die.
Only to thee I will indulgence grant,
With thee confirm the gracing Covenant,
Renewed to man when I of human seed
A conqueror over Hell and Death decreed.
In the preparèd ark thou shalt survive,
Thy wife and children kept with thee alive.   280
Of all the creatures thou shalt bring in two
Of every kind, that species to renew.
Thou also shalt all sorts of food provide
Whereby thyself and they may be supplied.'
   Noah without dispute the Lord obeyed;
Nor faithless, staggering objections made
Which in a scrupulous,[219] carnal soul might rise,
But with full confidence on God relies.
Flesh might have said, 'What will this ark avail
When there's no shore to which the boat can sail?   290
Why should we choose this nasty sepulchre
And lingering death before quick ease prefer?
What matters it whether, choked in the flood,
We soon expire, or when th'exhausted food
Is spent, in hunger's dry jaws slowly waste,
In vain preserved for a worse death at last?
Is life desirable, drawn out in woe
When horrid threatening storms on all hands blow?
When panthers, tigers, bears, still in our sight
Present us dread, outliving all delight?   300
While we in an unclean, hot stable dwell
Half poisoned with the various stinks we smell,

---

[219] legalistic

And difficultly our sad lives maintain
With dry, unpleasant fruits and parchèd grain;
Called from our quiet slumbers and short rest
To wait on every hungry bird and beast?
Our painèd limbs in drudgeries thus employed,
What can we hope when all else are destroyed?
What will it boot[220] us to survive a while
In constant sorrow, misery and toil,   310
When the worst death is a far happier thing
Than that sad life which can no pleasure bring?'
 But upright Noah's firmer faith kept out
Such sinful murmurs and such carnal doubt.
He did with faith the means of life embrace,
As thankful for the precept as the grace;
Slighted the mocks of the ungodly crew
And with obedience did his work pursue;
Finished the ark and laid in all the store,
When God before his entrance yet once more   320
To Noah said, 'Thy wife and children take
And now at last this wicked world forsake.
In this lewd generation there is none
Upright before me but thyself alone.
Thou shalt their plagues escape who shund'st[cccl]
  their sin.
Go therefore now and take the creatures in,
Seven of each clean bird and each clean beast,
One single male and female of the rest.
For but seven days there doth remain before
Thick clouds on earth shall their black burdens
  pour,   330
All the productions of the fields destroy
And everything that doth a life enjoy.'
 Noah, who only for the word had stayed,
Commanded once, no hesitation made,
Confirmed in his obedience when he found
The ark with animals encompassed round,
Th'assembled fowls all hovering in the air

[cccl] sund'st

[220] avail

Waiting for orderly admission there,
Who haply[221] chosen out of every kind
By the same power that them for life designed   340
Unto the house of life were freely brought,
Neither by huntsmen nor by fowlers caught,
But led by secret sweet impulse which still
Governs the inclination of the will:
Much more in those who have intelligence
Than those who rise not above corporal sense,
And only at this time were acted thus
To shadow out a greater work to us,
Whereby th'elect, to eternal life ordained,
Are wholly led by God yet unconstrained;   350
Nor wrought like stocks, by his sure fixed decree,
But by his free grace set at liberty
From Hell's mists, which benight the natural mind,
And lust's strong fetters, which the free will bind,
And are, as here, by soft impulses led,
Where he intends they should be saved and fed
And brought into a happy peaceful state
While the world perishes by mutual hate.
Peace life's chief joy, and safest guardian is;
Nor 'scape they woe and death that find not this.   360
    In vain the shelter of the ark had been
If mortal discord had not ceased within.
But gently thither the wild creatures came:
Doves, haggards,[222] lions, lambs, alike were tame.
The various animals all entering here
Forsook their natural fury and their fear.
Bears, tigers, panthers, fierce gulls, did not fight,
Nor with slain creatures gorged their appetite.
Safe by the greedy hounds the swift deer stayed;
The wolf and wanton kid together played;   370
The fox his craft forgot, the horse his speed;
Wild asses did among the tame beasts feed;
Hawks perched among the fowl and did not seize
Upon the trembling doves nor partridges;

[221] by chance (though this meaning is immediately qualified)
[222] female hawks

All else such peaceful, pleasant lives enjoyed
As once they had, before man's sin destroyed
The lovely concord of the universe
And discord sins did everywhere disperse.
   Six hundred times since Noah's birth the sun
Had now through heaven its annual circle run.   380
In that same year once had the moon her wane
Recovered, and renewed, was filled again,
And seventeen nights were seen since her last birth
Projecting silver rays upon the earth,
When in that very day at the high noon
Wet clouds first veiled the sun and then the moon.
That day the world's last seven did complete,
And Noah entered into that retreat.
He by divine appointment did prepare
To save himself and all the creatures there.   390
Then God the coffin closed, as a vast womb
Whence he intended the next world should come.
Thus the best way to draw out living breath
Is willing resignation unto death.
These did their coffin at God's word provide
And found life there when all the living died,
Whose stately piles, raised to immortalize
Their airy names, approached the archèd skies,
But in th'issuing deluge only were
The foolish builders' buried sepulchre.   400
   Meanwhile, at the first hour, the storm begun.
Black threatening clouds obscured the noonday sun
And added double horror to the night
Wherein no friendly star gave forth its light,
Those cataracts which from angry Heaven came
Seeming to have quenched out all its radiant flame
Except that whirling, cloud-engendering fire
That doth even in its dreadful birth expire.
Thick did these flames break thorough all the sky,
Where rattling south winds as their ushers fly.   410
Prodigious thunders followed the dire blaze,
Filling all hearts with terror and amaze
While they the rocks, the oaks and mountains rent,
Nor with less fury tore the firmament.

These fragors[223] thus unjointing the whole frame,
Heav'n and Earth Chaos once again became.
At once the fountains which like cisterns keep
Earth's drainèd waters to supply the deep,
Whither they through secret channels flow,
With fierce eruptions all burst out below   420
And Heaven's upper windows, open thrown,
As violently poured their waters down.
While the rude tempest thus the high roofs shook,
The crystal casements were to shivers broke
And the world's solid walls like ice did melt
When they the heats of divine vengeance felt;[224]
But though dissolved in tears, yet could not they
The fervour of that burning wrath allay,
Which made the seas like boiling cauldrons roar
And every flood devour[cccli] its neighbour shore.   430
The winds above in furious battles were
And those below did earth's fair coverings tear,
Conspiring all to make the breaches wide
And to exalt the conquering waters' pride,
Which forty days and nights advancèd still
Till every stately spire and every hill
Did fifteen cubits under water lie,
And nothing now appeared but sea and sky.
But Noah's ark above the waves did float,
They that bore all else down kept up that boat.   440
    Its trembling sailors heard sick Nature's groans
Which shattered into atoms the firm stones,
And men's more flinty hearts with terror struck
Who now like trembling leaves in autumn[225] shook
While they inevitable death beheld
With spirits sinking as the waters swelled,
And the great King of Terrors on the waves
In triumph sat, hemmed round with yawning
    graves

cccli devouring

223 crashes
224 Cf. 2.27–32.
225 Cf. *PL* 1.300–4.

Which not for the conducted[226] corpses stayed
But fierce approaches to the living made: 450
On whom rushing with fury, they did so
At once both death and sepulture bestow.
  Nor did the wretches single deaths endure,
Not less distracted now than late secure,
Struck with dire apprehension, which is still
The most tormenting plague in every ill.
Though sudden the surprise, their death was slow,
That terror might by the protraction grow.
Some run from the ascending floods in vain,
By falling torrents hurried back again;   460
Some climbed up the high hills but only there
Longer in death's sad expectation[227] were,
At last as certainly destroyed as those
Whom the first rising billows did enclose.
Some from high towers the desolation viewed,
Whom thither the triumphing flood pursued
And made them know, the walls that most aspire
Yield small defence against th'Almighty's ire.
Some unto Heaven would have raised their cries
But only Hell and Death rolled in their eyes.   470
Warnings from Heaven they did once contemn,
And Heaven in their distress despisèd them.
Some vessels got, but could not then provide
Food to sustain their lives, and starving died.
Some pushed the billows back, but with those oars
Could not convey themselves to any shores;
Their strength they did in vain endeavours spend
And fainting could no more with fate contend.
The frighted beasts themselves with swimming tired
But, swallowed in vast whirlpits,[228] there expired.   480
The wet birds flew about but no rest found,
Their food, their groves, their nests, their perches
    drowned.
Awhile in th'air their dabbled[229] wings they plied,

[226] floated along
[227] awaiting
[228] whirlpools
[229] splashed

But wearied out, fell on the seas and died.
　　Thought cannot reach this universal rack.[230]
With chokèd carcasses the seas grew black.
Dead shepherds floated with their drownèd sheep
And larger herds with those that did them keep.
The winds awhile with lighter things did play
Till ruder storms carried them all away.   490
The gallants' scarves and feathers, soldiers' tents,
The poor man's rags and princes' ornaments,
The silken curtains and the women's veils,
Themselves too borne up with light robes like sails,
Bandied in sport awhile, at last did all
Equally lost into the hazard fall.
　　Thus did the flood its victory complete.
No living soul was left, no fixèd seat,
No relics did of the late world remain.
For the ascending seas and falling rain,   500
Assaulting earth with their united powers,
As well beat down her high as lower towers
And the same waters that destroy the beasts
In their green beds, choked birds in cloudy nests,
Carrying with the rich spoils of the low fields
Those of the eyrie where the eagle builds.
Mountains and tall trees which their proud heads
　　crowned
As much were hid as all the level ground.
No mark remained of what had been before:
All turned to sea, sea bounded with no shore,   510
Which three half-hundred days maintained its pride
And did the vanquished earth in darkness hide.
　　This the malicious devils had beheld
With joyful triumph as their conquered field,
But that in it they saw with powerless spite
One chest preserved, which choked their dire
　　delight.
For from this little hold they sadly knew
A holy seed the battle should renew
And make them pay with endless plagues and woe

[230] wreck, ruin

Their impious glory in this overthrow.   520
Though God awhile do raging pride permit
Till his just judgement be fulfilled by it,
Yet violent empires but a small time last
And having climbed their heights, decline as fast.
Change in a moment comes to every state,
Both the triumphant and the desperate.
Thus God remembered Noah and all those
Whom he with him did in the ark enclose.
When God supports if he deliver not,
Wretches in misery think themselves forgot,   530
While they forget, through their distracted sense,
God's ever-active waking Providence,
Which, till he wholly out of trouble draws,
Preserves alive even in death's greedy jaws,
Conducts men's wanderings in the pathless deep,
Doth their faint heads above the proud waves keep,
Shows them strong anchor-hold against all fears,
Into his bottle gathers all their tears,
Registers all their patience, all their grief,
To which he may proportion their relief.   540
Nor is mankind, though chief, the Lord's sole care,
By whom th'afflicted beasts regarded are,
Though faint souls think he heeds not their distress
Till he put forth his power for their redress.
   Noah indeed did the old world survive,
Yet were his mates and he buried alive
In the decaying ark, nor to their sense
Appeared continuance there, or issue thence.
But faith through all the clouds saw God their
    guide
And on his wisdom for th'event[231] relied,   550
Urging his promise did their frail hearts stay,
Assured they should be saved, though not which
    way.
At last, after five months were fully spent,
The Lord, pitying their tedious languishment,
Suddenly did their staggering hopes erect

---

[231] outcome

And at their height the raging billows checked.
Whether immediately, as he before
Ruach[232]   Had framed, the sacred spirit did restore
The ruined world, or purposely, a wind
Whereof we can no cause in nature find,   560
Created as the means whereby he wrought
A miracle of mercy; each way brought
Mankind relief, checked the exulting flood,
Which at his great rebuke now patient stood
And, guilty of its late exorbitance,
Shrunk in as fast as it did first advance.
The upper windows were fast closed again
And stopped the issues of continued rain.
Th'attenuated waters, hastily
Rising in mists, sought their first place on high,   570
And some, condensed above, formed dark clouds
    there;
Others, more rarefied, resolved to air.
The same almighty breath drove the wild waves
Of raging floods back to their native caves,
Again unclosed the doors of Earth's drained womb,
Whose issues did not late more fiercely come
From thence, than now thither again they fled
In thronging crowds, driven by th'Almighty's dread.
That powerful breath that did their pride reprove
At the same time the ark to firm rest drove.   580
On Ararat's high mountains, yet o'ertopped
With swollen waters, she her voyage stopped,
And thus, her wanderings finished, she no more
Floated in deeps, but on the fixèd shore
Took up her rest, and felt the solid ground
Though circling waters yet begirt her round,
And Earth, concealed behind that fluid screen,
On the great theatre was yet unseen.
But God had turned destruction's furious tide
And every hour bore down its conquering pride.   590

232 Hebrew for, literally, 'wind, breath'.

Canto 8

Next day, after the Lord revealed his grace,
All things appeared with a new cheerful face.
The sun no more its radiant lustre shrouds,
Muffled in dismal, black and weeping clouds,
Which seemed to have extinguished his bright fire
While Heaven mourned under its Maker's ire.
No more did watery fogs the air condense,
Shutting out all superior brightness thence,
While thick black did the dying world enfold.
Now, the veil thinner drawn, azure and gold   10
With paler flames, carnation, sky, and white,
Vary the sweet reflections of the light.
No more did seas, disordered as before,
Swell up like mountains and with fury roar,
But calm as peace in a broad level lay
Where the winds' rage turned all to sportive play;
One while in rings the fluid waters twirls,
With the next breath varies the latest curls.
As women, with their proud fantastic care
Ne'er satisfied, set and unset their hair   20
A thousand times ere they themselves can please:
So played the soft gales on the varied seas,
Now crisped, now marbled the successive streams,
Now weaved them into bredes[233] with glittering
    beams
Whose penetrations changed their sullen hue
While gold appeared through the transparent blue.
    What will full Restoration[234] be, if this
But the first daybreak of God's favour is?
[Genesis 8.5]   Through which as Heaven still benignly shines,
So still the late insulting[235] flood declines,   30
Till after forty days' continued waste
The mountains' long-hid heads emerged at last.

---

[233] plaits
[234] 'The order of nature destroyed by the flood is restored by God's promise': Geneva Bible annotation to Genesis 8.22.
[235] arrogantly triumphing

And now a pleasant difference was seen
Betwixt the sea and Earth's more perfect green.
Yet as a prince who, long in prison bound,
Comes squalid forth at first, untrimmed,[236]
    uncrowned:
So rose the mountains from th'imprisoning flood,
Their faces slimed, their standards dropping mud,
When Heaven's compassionate, kind, refreshing
    eye
With its all-clearing glances looked them dry.   40
More gently washed with night's descending dew,
Again they fair, again they stately grew,
Again looked down on the sunk realm where they
So long space late captived and vanquished lay.
    But curb, fair hills;[237] O curb your growing pride:
He who above your covering clouds doth ride,
Whose pity drew you from your low estate,
When you insult will cast down your proud height.
If humbled waters must no more ascend,
Thunders will fall which shall your bosoms rend.   50
Your new-restorèd glory shall expire,
To ashes turned in the world's funeral fire.
And you, great Lords, who on the mountains reign,
With them shall once more be destroyed again.
When you through horror run into the caves
The Almighty's voice shall open all your graves,
And draw you trembling out to see them high
To whom your pride did sepulture deny.[238]
But while you think his threatened day far off,
Like the old world you these predictions scoff,   60
With blindness cursed; not to recover sight
Till your own dreadful flames be your first light.
    But let's not glance at judgements due to you
While we old miracles of grace review:
Grace which did not confound with violence

---

[236] unprepared, unadorned
[237] Cf. Isaiah 2.12–19.
[238] Revelation 11.7–10 describes two witnesses to the truth whose martyred bodies remain unburied; possibly a glance at the disinterment of republicans from Westminster Abbey in 1661.

But, gently issuing, feasted human sense
With such variety of sweet delight
As fed at once and bred new appetite.
Safe are those precious joys which so distil,
Endangering not the vessels they would fill.   70
   The ark which Noah through the wild waves
      bore,
Left on firm ground where seas could come no
     more,
Did like a fortress on the mountains stand,
The only habitation in the land;
Which having brought him thither, Noah yet
Did not with rash precipitation quit,
But from the mountain's first appearance stays
In quiet expectation forty days;
Then did the window of the ark unclose,
And for his messenger a raven chose,   80
Whom he into the new world sends to see
If yet there any food or firm rest be.
The melancholy bird no towerings made
But, hovering all about the ark, there stayed
Until the sun had dried the earth's wet face,
Then for herself sought out her natural place.
   So in the church that's figured by this ark,[239]
Impure and pure together may embark,
While showers of vengeance blacken in the skies,
Threatening a deluge of calamities   90
To the polluted world; which if they fly,
A while concealed they in its bosom lie,
But issuing thence, though for a little space
Not quit[240] of dread, they hang about the place
Until they find their earthly joys renewed;
Yet then they seek again their carrion food
And foul delights, and utterly forsake
What in distress they did their shelter make;
Nor that alone, but turn to open hate
Of those with whom they did associate.   100

[239] Cf. Williams 236–7.
[240] free

And as when a weak sheep expiring lies
These ravenous birds alive pick out her eyes,
So doth a late church-fostered hypocrite
Watch to put out a sick saint's dying light.
We from this ill-presaging bird may draw
A parallel of the death-denouncing caw[241]
Who, sent forth the soul's comfort to explore,
No restoration finds but, evermore
Ingeminating[242] curses, with hoarse cries
About the secure roofs and windows flies.[243]   110
   After he sent the raven forth seven days,
Hoping the sun had with his drying rays
Exhaled the wet, Noah, ill satisfied
With that first messenger, a dove employed,
Who with high mounting wings the soft air cleaves
And a long tract of skies behind her leaves.
But when her curious search, because the ground
Was yet undried, no firm clean footing found,
With tired pinions to the ark again
She came for succour and was taken in.   120
Endeavours, though they want success, are still
Acceptable, with the same cheerful will
Performed as those which happier issues gain,
Nor do just lords such services disdain.
   When seven days more had with time's current
     run
The dove, sent forth again, her flight begun,
Cutting her passage through the spacious skies,
Where, keeping on her wing, she bent her eyes
On th'underlying world, discovers there
An olive, whose fresh boughs new flourished were.   130
Here she descends, awhile her journey stops
And one of the fair sprouting branches crops,
Wherewith again she mounts her outstretched
     wings
And in her mouth the happy ensign brings,

---

[241] raven's cry
[242] repeating
[243] For LH's – unusual – allegorization of the raven and dove in terms of godly and ungodly
church members, cf. Bunyan 229–31, 439n.

A pledge of peace; implying that love once more
Renewed the world which it produced before.
   In memory of this, the olive tree
Was after sacred to posterity,
So that in embassies where peace was sought
The humble suppliants still those branches brought.   140
But this dove's olive was th'effect and sign
Of a pacification more divine.
Peace, which all other blessings comprehends,
Springs not from th'earth, though^{ccclii} it to earth
   descends.
Its pure untroubled fountain is above
In the fair bosom of eternal love.
The pledges here, types, hopes, effects, are all
But various streams from that original.
Earth's restoration did from thence proceed,
When peace in heaven was for men agreed   150
After sin had averted God's first grace
And brought a flood of wrath on human race,
That gracious Providence might so prepare
The Prince of Peace a proper theatre,
Where, to confirm the heavenly sanction, he
Awhile might conversant with mortals be.
   This dove emblems the spirit which, in prayer
Ascending Heaven, is directed there
To make a stoop[244] on that late leafless tree[245]
Where dying Love destroyed the enmity   160
And caused new peace, life, pleasure, health to
   sprout,
Sending the Everlasting Gospel out
Which in its mouth the active spirit brings,
The sight of whose returning radiant wings
With the glad pledge a firm hope reassures
To those whom mercy's dark womb yet obscures.
   Of all the plants that spring up from the ground,
With more or richer blessings none are crowned

---

^{ccclii} thoug

[244] bird's sudden descent: usually on prey
[245] the cross

Than is[cccliii] the olive, which still feeds that light
That makes the altar and the temple bright,   170
Gives lustre to the face, poisons expels,
All rankling wounds, all venomous bitings heals,
Produceth softness, smoothness, suppless,[246] ease,
Fattening all food, allaying all disease.
Such are the blessed effects the gospel hath
On sinners wounded with the sense of wrath,
By fiery serpents stung; it cures their smart,
Rough nature smoothes, softens th'obdurate heart,
Feeds the internal temple's lamps of grace
And sets sweet lustre on th'exterior face.   180
But where these glorious great effects are wrought
The olive must in the dove's mouth be brought,
For fruitless is the gospel remedy
Except the spirit do the cure apply.
    But to proceed: yet six days had the light
To shades resigned; a seventh chased the night
When Noah sent his dove out as before,
Who after that third flight returned no more.
    Great father, when my soul shall fly away
Out of this flesh, when thou this house of clay   190
Shalt with thy breath dissolve, O let me then
The swift wings of thy sacred dove obtain,
Which may bear up my soul through empty air
To thy celestial court and fix it there.
    Noah, thus knowing that the world was dry,
Laid his ark open to the cheerful sky
And from the decks his glad eyes recreates
While he th'Almighty's farther order waits;
Nor stayed he long but, licensed by command,
Opens the door and sets the freight on land.   200
Gladly the creatures their long prison leave,
Their old minds with their liberties receive,
And now no more observe[cccliv] the loving truce
Which their late common danger did produce.

[cccliii] are
[cccliv] obscure *MS* observ *MSC*

[246] suppleness

All, led by Nature's secret guide, soon find
The habitations proper to each kind.
Again the gentle amorous turtle-doves
Single their mates in solitary groves;
The greedy kites and murderous beasts of prey
Their wings like standards in the skies display,   210
Threatening the weaker and the gentler brood
Who seek again the shelter of the wood;
The owl herself in hollow trees conceals,
The light no more her ugly looks reveals;
Geese, poultry, ducks, all turn to their old haunts,
Swans to the streams, to rocks the cormorants;
In cloud-wrapped trees, eagles their eyries build,
Partridges make their beds in the green field;[ccclv]
Sweet nightingales and the small sylvan choir
To solitary thickets all retire;   220
The reptiles to their various dwellings creep;
Unlovely things themselves in dark holes keep;
Cruel wild beasts seek coverts from the light,
Waiting in deserts for the treacherous night;
Serpents conceal themselves in rushy fens
And other monsters lurk in secret dens;
Foxes to their well-guarded holes resort;
Lions make hollow caves their mountain fort.
Some melancholy creatures, urged with dread,
Into concealing solitudes are led,   230
And while they waste their lives in musings there
They almost starve themselves to feed their fear.
Whose[247] hearts plot mischieves, murders, stealths
     and fraud,
Muffled in darkness only walk abroad;
But all that's hurtless, kind and lovely play
In open fields, nor shun the cheerful day.
So generous horses in the valleys feed
And beauteous kine[248] in the green meadows breed;
The gentle sheep in open pastures graze,

ccclv fields

247 i.e. those whose
248 cows

And fly not from the sun's discerning rays.   240
   All creatures else thus to their places sent,
Noah himself, his wife and children went
Last forth, with solemn pace and reverent dread,
Heaving his eyes and bowing down his head
While he th'Almighty God did there adore
Who had conducted them to the dry shore;
Where he, before he his own house projects,
An altar to the Lord of Life erects,
So consecrating the restorèd ground;
Which first he did for holy service wound,   250
Then on it the long-destined victims slays
And as they burned, with fervent prayer and praise
His heart he for a living sacrifice

Gen. 8.21–[2] Presents unto th'Almighty's well-pleased eyes;
Wherefore, delighted in the perfumed smoke,
Jehovah thus his gracious purpose spoke:
   'Although man's nature be corrupted still
And all his thoughts even from his childhood ill,
I will not yet for his unpurgèd stain
Inflict my curse upon the earth again.   260
An universal deluge shall no more
Destroy all lives as it hath done before.
While the world stands in its vicissitude
The various seasons shall be still renewed:
Moist springs, when seed into the earth is thrown;
Fair weather when those seeds are ripe fruits grown;
Successive cold shall temper the hot air
And due heat shall expel the cold frosts there;
Rough winters shall in their just course prevail
And after pleasant summers shall not fail;   270
Night shall succeed the day and day again
Shall never cease to'imploy th'alternate reign'.

Gen. 9.1,15 And that they might not be too much oppressed
With sad discouragements, th'Almighty blessed
Noah and his sons with the same word of grace
He used before to th'first founder of man's race:[249]
'Increase,' said he, 'and multiply, until

[249] 3.419–32

Your numerous offspring shall the whole earth fill.
My delegated power to you I give
Over the whole creation, those that live   280
I'the watery element, in moist air fly,
Walk on the earth or in her crannies lie:
To your dominion I subject them all.
Let them under your awful[250] terror fall,
Dispose them as you please: their flesh is meat
As free as growing fruits for you to eat.
But, eating flesh, you shall from blood abstain
For blood the quickening spirits[251] do contain.
Your blood, wherein your human lives reside
I will require of every homicide.   290
No one unpunished shall commit that fact:[252]
Even of beasts I will your blood exact,
Much more those men who violators prove
Of human rites and of fraternal love
No favour in their bloody guilt shall find,
But men shall slay the murderers of mankind
Because they thereby God himself contemn,
For in his image he created them.
But be you fruitful, cherish those you breed
And multiply a numerous spreading seed.   300
From you let diverse nations take their birth
And reinhabit the unpeopled earth.'
      The world's great Sovereign, to man's fallen
            state
Suiting his laws, doth here subordinate
Inferior substitutes armed with his sword
To punish such as disobey his word.
These his commands the transcripts are
Of his pure nature and paternal care,
Its testimonies 'gainst rebellious fools
Who, not directed by his saving rules,   310
Guilt of their ruin on their own souls draw,

---

[250] inspiring reverential fear
[251] Vital spirits in Renaissance physiology were one of a series of fine fluids mediating between blood and brain; 'inasmuch as the vital spirits chiefly reside in the blood, it is, as far as
our feeling is concerned, a token which represents life' (Calvin I.293).
[252] deed

Their safety being provided by his law:
A law that doth to holy concord bind,
Wherein th'obedient their chief blessing find,
And proud contemners, then when they commit
The sin, even in the acting punish it.
Yet burning lust and the wild thirst of blood,
Not quenched with all the waters of the flood,
In man's polluted nature lay concealed,
Which the sad crimes of every age revealed;   320
When those whom God did institute to curb
The world's disorders, did the world disturb,
To murder and to slaughter led whole hosts
Till searèd conscience made their crimes their boast:
Which long since had extinguished human race
But that God, by his wise and powerful grace
Bounding and turning man's fierce rage, did raise
Eternal trophies to his own just praise.

Gen. 9.8   To Noah and his sons God further spake:
'Lo, I an everlasting Covenant make   330
With you and with your offspring and all those
Whose lives I spared, whom th'ark did late enclose;
Who issued thence with you as they did share
This mercy and your preservation there.
So shall the grace of this my Covenant too
Imparted be to all that live with you:
All earthly animals, birds of the air,
Tame and wild beasts, even Earth itself shall share
This universal mercy whereto I
Myself by this most stable Covenant tie: 340
That waters never more on Earth shall drownd,[253]
Nor in one ruin man and beast confound:
And to confirm the promise of my grace
To th'Earth, to you, and your succeeding race,
I'll add a sign that shall my word assure:
Confirming you, when black clouds heaven
    obscure,
My bow will I then in the dark skies place
Whose wondrous arch a thousand colours grace;

---

[253] variant form of 'drown'

And it to you perpetually shall be
A sign as a remembrancer[254] to me   350
That I have promised you the threatened rain
Shall not the drenchèd earth destroy again.
This give I as the pledge of my free grant,
The signal of a lasting covenant.'
    The Hebrews say, while God was speaking so
Th'obedient skies presented their fair bow
With varied shades of yellow, blue, and green,
In stronger and in fainter mixtures seen,
According to those condensations which
The penetrating beams did so enrich: 360
That emeralds, rubies, sapphires, jacinths were
Outshined in beauty and in lustre there,
Though all the loveliness and glory was
But a wet cloud reflecting the sun's rays.
Thus the most sad lamenting soul and face,
Receiving beams of God's transforming grace,
May an illustrious admiration grow
While amiable splendour shines through woe.
These Jews, to superstition still inclined,
Would in the several colours mystery find:[255]   370
The blues, they say, present those swelling waves
Wherein the old world's sinners found their graves;
The flaming colours show that latest fire
In which the outworn fabric shall expire;
The green emblems[ccclvi] the present state of things
And that firm hope which from the promise springs.
When, therefore, these appear in the moist skies,
They God adore and bend their guilty eyes,
Acknowledging they merit not his grace
But those plagues which destroy the former race;   380
Their humble thanks for his indulgence pay
And chase their fears when showers obscure the day.
    This fine enamelled arch the pagans too

[ccclvi] Emblem

[254] reminder
[255] Contrast Du Bartas, *DWW* II.2.1.480–94; such explanations, often found in rabbinical commentaries, were disparaged by Calvin and many other Christian commentators.

Not without wonder did and reverence view;
Feined it a female deity, the child
Of ravishing Thaumantis, Iris styled,
Great Juno's herald sent forth to declare
The approaching war that threatens the calm air.
   But to pass by their fictions, even we
When this amidst the blackened clouds we see   390
With humble gratitude should call to mind
God's past and present mercies to mankind,^{ccclvii}
Whose guilt might make us fear that every rain
Should drown the earth which our pollutions stain,
But that this sign of the approaching shower
Is given to teach us that almighty power
Alone doth all inferior threatenings bound,
Nor can high heaven afflict the humble ground
Farther than the supremest Lord permits,
Who above all as moderator sits,   400
Restoring clearness to the darkened skies
And pleasant smiles to the late-weeping eyes.
Nor rules he only in the elements
But orders all our human accidents,
And hath himself by Covenant tied to those
Whom his ordainèd ark did once enclose,
That universal misery as before
Shall not distress or seize them any more,
Yet trouble shall arrive as rains descend,
Not to destroy but fruitful moisture lend.   420

Canto 9

[Genesis 9.20]   Noah and his sons gladly God's promise heard
And, in the hopes of their successors cheered,
Those dreadful horrors from their thoughts
    expelled
Which seized their frighted souls when they beheld
The old world's ruin; that sad sight forgot,
The dead they now vainly lamented not,

---

ccclvii *This is the final line written by the first scribe; the second scribe continues immediately*

Applying all their thoughts and busy cares
To plant and build for their succeeding heirs.
Now were the sunny hills covered with vines
And from the swelling grapes they pressed forth
    wines.   10
Then Noah of the sparkling juice drunk deep
And, stupefied with liquor, fell asleep,
Whom Ham, his scoffing son, in lewd plight found
Immodestly incovered on the ground.[256]
    Of all the generous and useful plants
Earth nourisheth for her inhabitants,
None more abounds with blessings than the vine
In whose fair arms numberless bottles shine,
All filled with precious, noble, powerful juice
Which doth a thousand miracles produce.   20
It reinflames sick nature's dying fires,
New vigour adds to those whom labour tires,
Revives sad hearts oppressed with loads of grief,
To low dejected spirits gives relief;
It valour animates, dispels cold fears,
Vigour of youth recalls to wasted years,
Conquers that dull, that poor unmanly shame
That in faint breasts smothers a glorious flame;
Raises dull fancy to its noblest flights,
Quickens the dead and languid appetites.   30
The baths of it cold palsied limbs restore.
For these and many sovereign virtues more,
The after-ages held those men divine
Who taught the nations the first use of wine:
Wine which they did to sacred altars bring
As the most rich and precious offering
They could elect[257] among those various fruits

---

[256] For royalists Noah was the first post-Flood monarch and a pattern for all later government, and this episode was mainly interpreted as a rebuke of irreverence towards the mysteries
of state. (For a Cromwellian variant see Andrew Marvell, *The First Anniversary*, lines 289–
92.) LH instead concentrates on the moral abuse of Noah's drunkenness, with relevance for
the notorious drunkenness of the Restoration court, and lays primary blame for rebellion on
the sins of governors (9.218–21). There may be specific glances at LH's brother, Sir Allen
Apsley, who caused scandal by appearing drunk in the House of Commons, and at John
Wilmot, Earl of Rochester.
[257] choose

Heaven's bounty by the kind Earth contributes.
　But whate'er most excels in its right use
Is most pernicious in its vile abuse.   40
Wine which, drunk moderately, doth mortals bless
So many various ways, by its excess
As many various mischiefs doth produce,
And turns a poisonous and bewitching juice,
Whose operation by the effects is shown
When it doth sovereign reason disenthrone,
Reason that ruled as monarch in the breast,
The great distinction between man and beast,
Which, charmed by it, hath no force to control
The transportation[258] of the feeble soul   50
Whose lustful and whose raging appetite
The too-inflaming liquor doth excite.
According to the rate that it prevails,
The understanding and the memory fails.
Forgotten are friendship's and nature's ties,
All obligation and all injuries.
There rivals bury for a while their hate
And wretches drown the sense of their sad state;
Princes forget their ranks and great affairs,
Cast off their kingdoms' necessary cares   60
And revel in their drunken jollities
Till unwatched foes the silly beasts surprise.
So was Belshazzar[259] cut off in his sin
When the besieging Persians suddenly broke in;
So have great conquerors oft met sudden falls
And drunk themselves into their funerals,
While the Lethean cups sealed up their eyes,
Forgetting all the dangers of surprise.
Oft so, forgetful of eternity,
The vulgar drunkards in their surfeits die   70
Who wine adore, because it will not let them think
A serious thought of Heaven, till into Hell they
　sink.
To it they sacrifice their glorious days,

---

[258] rapture, ecstasy
[259] Daniel 5: a favourite image of idolatrous tyranny.

Racking their wits to celebrate its praise,
Nor give tired Nature the relief of sleep
Till they their brains in their crowned goblets steep,
When the wine, working with wild fancy, makes
False dreams of pleasure, horrid sad mistakes
Which, waking, too unhappily they find.
Yet, the infection rooted in the mind,   80
They violently court their plague again,
Run into brutishness and thirst for pain:
For where the force of conquering drink prevails,
The sight grows dim, the active vigour fails,
The weak legs cannot bear the members' weight
But march with an uncertain staggering gait;
Th'eyes, deeper sunk, no liveliness retain,
Black misty vapours fume up to the brain;
Trembling the hands, numbness the joints invades,
Sickness the stomach; the fresh colour fades;   90
All o'er cold sweats and ghastly paleness creep
Till the faint spirits yield to death-like sleep
Which lays all down in their transformèd shapes:
Some wanton and ridiculous like apes,
Some roaring with more senseless furious wrath
Than the fierce mastiff or the lion hath;
Some acting goats whose bloods hot lust doth fire;
Some nasty swine that wallow in foul mire;
Some filthy dogs by loathsome vomits made;
The stupid ass the sottish drunkard played.   100
Nor from the form of man alone estranged,
But in their proper inclinations changed:
The powerful charm makes cowards brave and
    bold,
Makes misers cast away their hoarded gold,
The silent talk, the talkative sit dumb,
The froward[260] kind, the patient quarrelsome,
Base minds to high and haughty thoughts erecting,
And to mean actions noble souls dejecting.[261]
It makes the cold and chaste burn with wild fires;

---

[260] difficult, refractory
[261] abasing

In the hot lover drowns all fierce desires;   110
Th'effeminate to manly acts excites;
The bold and brave inclines to soft delights;
Makes sly dissemblers hidden truth reveal
And th'open-hearted everything conceal.
Nor doth it always work by contraries,
By horrid transformation and disguise;
As oft it doth men's inclinations draw
Without regard of any bound or awe
To the extremest acting of their powers
Which all their merit and their praise devours,   120
Rendering them monstrous who exceed all rules,
Exposing wise men to the scorn of fools.
   Yet though the greatest drunkards this confess,
There is that witchery in drunkenness
That, wheresoe'er it is indulged at first,
Th'infection causes an unquenchèd thirst
Which makes them still pursue the sin although
They all the cursèd consequences know,
And their own follies in all else despise;
Which when they cannot conquer, they devise   130
Extenuating pretences for't and say
They drink to drive their anxious cares away,
To entertain the melancholy night,
Which, did they not soft slumbers thus invite,
Would vainly be consumed in waking grief.
Wine is the only sovereign relief
For that inevitable woe that waits
On human life, perplexing all estates,
Which drowns the memory of ills that are
Already past and future fears doth bar,   140
Which stifles sorrow and gives Hope new birth,
Glad Hope, the nurse of life-prolonging mirth.
   Dull impious argument, foolish pretence,
Sad aggravation of the great offence,
By ignorant fools and vicious cowards sought,
By the voluptuous, cheating devils taught!
Should silly mortals, shunning dread and woe,
Their refuge seek in that from whence they flow?
Intemperance with disobedience joined

Began the fatal ruin of mankind.   150
Are long-renewed experiences so scant,
Or can we an unhappy instance want
How vain, how contrary is that delight
Propounded by the brutish appetite?
Is frenzy, sickness, torture, impotence,
Hot bloods, cold sweats, faint powers, disordered
    sense,
A happy cure of grief, a pleasant ease,
Adding ten plagues to drive out one disease?
Which yet is but confounded, not expelled,
Like the poor infants' cries which Moloch[262] held   160
Frying in his arms, which with the various sound
Of barbarous instruments they strove to drownd.
Were there no God, no future heaven, no hell
As those fools dream who thus would cares expel,
Yet were it but unmanly cowardice
So to decline short-lived calamities
And fly to vices rather than oppose
With virtuous courage fortune's hurtless blows.[263]
But neither could they be evaded so:
Their arms in fight the drunkards from them throw   170
When in their flowing cups they drown their sense,
Fame, wit, strength, virtue, health, their chief
    defence
Against whatever can man's life invade,
All which by this enchantment are betrayed.
No lot is so unfortunate but may
Admit a change; black nights[ccclviii] must yield to day,
But small advantage will he have of light
Who digged out his own eyes because 'twas night,
His understanding quenched lest he should be
Too sensible of his calamity.   180
Most other sins are punished in the event,[264]
But this draws with it its own punishment;

[ccclviii] the blackest night *MS* blacke nights *MSC*

[262] Cf. 2 Kings 23.10, *PL* 1.392–9.
[263] Cf. Shakespeare, *Hamlet* 3.1.60–88 (see also 18.7).
[264] outcome

Especially in princes, who thereby
Make themselves cheap, profane their majesty,
Expose their shame unto their subjects' eyes,
Who, seeing their impotence, their rule despise.
   Noah, the new world's monarch, here lies drunk,
His awful dread[265] is with his temperance sunk;
And Ham, finding him naked on the earth,
Dares make him thus the subject of his mirth,   190
Fears not to publish his indecent shame
And to his brethren doth the news proclaim.
But they, more pious, hating to deride
A father's frailty, did contrive to hide
Even from their own eyes the sin-tempting view,
And with averted steps and faces drew
A covering on their naked sire till he
At his awaking found their piety
And the miscarriage of that lewder son
That would not spare him from derision.   200
This knowledge did impress a various sense
Of the kind[266] duty and th'unkind offence
Which to[267] a prophet and a magistrate
Thus did he sentence, thus remunerate:
'Cursèd be Canaan, vassalage his doom,
His brothers' servants' servant to become.
Blessed be the God of Shem: by special grace
He shall be lord of Canaan's servile race.
God shall enlarge Japhet's still growing stem,
He shall inhabit in the tents of Shem   210
And Canaan shall be servant unto him'.[ccclix]
   Here Hell's malicious chief again renews
The fatal war and his old hate pursues
Against the new foundation of mankind
Late in God's blessing laid; this undermined,
He at the fatal breach of one frail sin

---

ccclix "God shall perswade Japhetts compliant race / "To come and dwell in Shems deserted place] *MS after line 21: apparently an alternate version of lines 209–11*

265 the reverence that he would expect for his majesty
266 natural
267 i.e. which being performed against

Leads a large train of woes and curses in.
A prince and father yielding to his sense
Divests himself of awe and reverence,
Gives the more pious children cause to mourn   220
And yields occasion to the rebels' scorn;
That scorn a father's dreadful wrath provokes
Whose tender hand still smarts with its own
    strokes.
Sad is a parent's curse, however given,
And very seldom unconfirmed in heaven,
Which when on the devoted[268] head it falls
At once it punisheth two criminals.
Were not the governors first guilty by
Foolish remissness or harsh tyranny,[ccclx]
Or weak vice which betrays their impotence   230
And gives occasion to the next offence
Of those who formal majesty despise
When sin's base slave struts in the great disguise,
Pride and rebellion under their wise curb
Would not start out and the whole state disturb.[269]
Who sentences his sons his own sins dooms
And his own executioner becomes,
Cutting those rotten limbs off that were fed
With corrupt influence from the unsound head.
Yet when a father is a judge, he must   240
Impartially discharge his sacred trust.
When guilty grace favours one criminal,
Injustice draws down vengeance upon all.
Those who the reins of government remit
Because they've sinned must not persist in it,
Lest, finding a slack curb, the headstrong beast[270]
In its loose fury run down all the rest.
This remiss David found: unpunished rape
Murder provokes; the murderers' escape

[ccclx] or Tyranny *MS* or harsh Tyranny *MSC*

[268] doomed
[269] Ham's sin was equated by royalists with republican irreverence for kingship, an interpretation LH here turns against kings.
[270] The many-headed monster, the multitude.

Rebellion did produce; for where the law   250
Unexecuted is, reverence and awe
Sink in contempt and untamed hearts no more
The empty name of royalty adore.[271]
God's pure laws are with such firm sanctions made
That, howe'er broke, the forfeit must be paid.
Though men indulge each other's crimes, yet he
Will not a partial judge to any be.
Eternal wisdom so brought Mercy in
That there is no impunity for sin,
Especially their bold presumption who   260
To flatter lust make God nor just nor true,
Nor steadfast in his holy fixed decrees
Who all sin with most just abhorrence sees.[272]
    But why on Canaan doth the curse descend,
Since 'twas his father, Ham, that did offend?[273]
Blessings once given God would not recall,
Yet can he add unto the manna gall
When secure[274] wantonness from that grace springs
That should engage men's hearts to better things.
Ham's personal miseries with himself had died,   270
But slavery on his successors tied
Must needs afflict him more than all the woe
That he himself could singly undergo.
Envy, remorse, disdain, anguish and spite
Ulcerate his rankling, proud heart day and night,
When he revolves[275] that by his aweless scorn
His children, equal to his brothers' born,
Excluded from the special blessing were
And all the common mercies they did share
But little would avail a hapless race   280
Still multiplied to sorrow and disgrace.
So heinous, so degenerate a crime
Deserved a brand to all succeeding time.

[271] 2 Samuel 13–19.
[272] With possible undertones of criticism of the Anglican clergy who both abandoned Calvinist theology and failed to speak out against Charles II's sins.
[273] The explanation here given is close to the *Westminster Annotations*.
[274] over-confident
[275] considers

Who love to scoff at others' frailties shall
Themselves at last into abjection fall.
Ham's proud, irreverent derision
Cut his whole offspring off, although but one
Was by God's sovereign will designed to be
The special instance of his just severity,
Whose issue, thus preventing[276] grace denied,   290
Pursued their father's disobedient pride
Till their own sins were ripe for vengeance grown
And justified the execution,
Which, though nine hundred years reprieved, was
    not
In all that space remitted or forgot.
When threatenings are delayed the wicked grow
Secure in ill, but vengeance that is slow
By daily aggravations gathers strength
And with more dreadful fury strikes at length.
God's truth is firm in promises and threats.   300
Where either faith and humble awe begets
The promised grace and blessing shall prevail;
Where both are slighted, vengeance shall not fail.
Who sows iniquity must curses reap:
Indulgence but augments the fatal heap.

Canto 10[ccclxi]

Now several sons were born to Noah's sons
And those sons fathers of great[ccclxii] nations.
Seven sons Japhet, the eldest brother, had,
By whom plantations in the isles were made,
And from their several offsprings did arise
The spreading European colonies,
The cursèd Canaanites from Ham descended,
And the Assyrian kings, whose realms extended

[ccclxi] *Marginal note:* There were taken out of the old notes after they were dead.
[ccclxii] the *MS* great *MSC*

[276] predisposing to repentance

Canto 10.th

Now severall Sons were borne to Noahs Sons
And these Sons fathers of of the great Nations
Seven Sons Japhett the eldest brother had
By whome plantations in the Ysles were made
And from their severall offsprings did arise
The spreading European Collonies
The Cursed Canaanites from Ham descended
And the Assirian Kings, whose realmes extended
Through all the east with spice & balme perfum'd
Nimrod the regall title first assum'd
In Babilon did he his throne erect
And all the neighbours by his powers subject
Which spread abroad the terror of his name
That he a Proverb in the earth became
Three cities more he founded in the plaine
Ashur his Son in Ninevek did reigne
Who Resen, Rehoboth and Calah built
Three populous cities where his subjects dwelt
Thus the first mightie Monarchs of the earth
From Noahs gracelesse Son deriv'd their birth
His race the land of Canaan first possest
His Colonies first planted in the east
From Shem the other Son Arphaxad came
Hee Heber got whence Hebrews have their name

Plate 4 The opening of canto 10: New Haven, Yale University, Osborn Collection fb 100, p. 190. (Original size 303 × 188 mm.) Reproduced by permission of the James Marshall and Marie-Louise Osborn Collection, Beinecke Rare Book and Manuscript Library, Yale University.

Through all the east with spice and balm perfumed.
Nimrod the regal title first assumed.   10
In Babylon did he his throne erect
And all the neighbours by his powers subject,
Which spread abroad the terror of his name,
That he a proverb in the earth became.
Three cities more he founded in the plain.
Ashur, his son, in Nineveh did reign,
Who Resen, Rehoboth and Calah built,
Three populous cities where his subjects dwelt.
Thus the first mighty monarchs of the earth
From Noah's graceless son derived their birth.   20
His race the land of Canaan first possessed,
His colonies first planted in the east.
From Shem, the other son, Arphaxad came.
He Eber^ccclxiii got, whence Hebrews have their
    name.
Peleg was Eber's^ccclxiv son, whose name implied
That men in his days did the earth divide.[277]
Four other sons were born to pious Shem
And many branches more sprung out of them,
From whom the Lydians[278] and the Persians came,
And whom the Indians for their father claim.[279]   30

[Genesis 11.1–9]   Hell's chief, envying that God should man
    restore,
Employs his cursèd spirits and once more
Attempts their ruin by his sly deceit:
First representing the deplorèd[280] state
Of the old world, declaring God severe
Whose cruelty might justly cause their fear
That if his wrath were once provoked he would

---

ccclxiii Heber
ccclxiv Hebers

---

[277] Peleg is associated with a Hebrew word for 'divided'. Genesis offers two genealogies of Shem, each of which makes Eber the grandson, not the son, of Arphaxad (Genesis 10.24, 11.12–14).
[278] Lydia: territory in the west of Asia Minor.
[279] The genealogical table in the Authorized Version showed these nations stemming from Shem.
[280] given up as hopeless

Again destroy them with another flood;
That better was to make their own defence
Than in God's mercy place their confidence;   40
That they might raise a tower up to the skies
Which should all future storms and waves despise.
Upon the fearful minds these motives wrought;
Other persuasions for the proud he sought:
'O wretched men,' said he, 'escaped in vain
The tempest's rage, if you must not attain
Some certain seat to fix your own great name
And leave a mention whence your children came.
A short time will destroy your house of clay
And from the earth sweep all this race away;   50
But if you build a cloud-ascending Tower,
No time your glorious memory shall devour.
So strong a fortress now you may erect
As shall your sons from Heaven's ire protect;
Who, reigning there in every age, will strive
To make your honourable names survive.
For all your present strength and beauty must
Extinguish, soon forgotten, in the dust.'
    Thus the ambitious and the coward, inspired
With equal ardour, both one thing desired.   60
'Come,' said they, 'let us build a noble place
Which may continue to our following race,
That mankind here together may converse,
Lest God should them throughout the world
    disperse.'
With these vain hopes the sons of men grew bold,
And set upon the work: some carried mould,[281]
Some levelled ground, some the foundation laid,
Some framed the doors and some the pillars made,
Some burned the clamps and some prepared the
    bricks,
Others with sand and slime the mortar mix.   70
So when the bees a colony send out,
The new swarms soon disperse themselves about
And several labours busy every one:

[281] earth

Some search for honey, some expel the drone,
Some suck the flowers, some carry their loads
    home,
Some take what they bring in, some work the comb:
All various toils with diligence intend,[282]
Yet in one public work their labours spend.[283]
So did these builders, who with blasphemies
Extolled the pile which now began to rise.   80
    'While we,' said they, 'inhabit this high tower,
We need not fear th'Almighty's threatening power.
By this we may to his own Heaven ascend
And with the ireful Thunderer[284] contend.'
But the great Lord, whose all-surveying eyes
Behold the secret'st thought which in man's bosom
    lies,
Saw and derided all their vain intent,
Then, wrapped in mists from the arched firmament,
Amongst the sons of men came down to view
Their growing walls. 'Fond mortals,' then said he,   90
'Imagine now with a vain arrogance
They can their structures unto heaven advance;
But I will presently chastise their pride,
And them with several languages divide.
Nor shall they any more together stay,
But every language lead a several way.'
Forthwith what God decreed was done, and all
The builders did into confusion fall.
Such then who could each other understand
Together flocked, and every several band   100
To several regions went: accursèd Ham
Into the scorchèd sands of Libya came;
Among the godly then reigned pious Shem,
And fixed his palace in Jerusalem;
Yet in Chaldea stayèd his third[ccclxv] son,

[ccclxv] his son *MS* his third son *MSC*

[282] attend to
[283] These lines are a paraphrase of Virgil, *Aeneid* 1.430–6. The bee simile was traditionally associated with monarchy; LH's republican revision parallels *PL* 1.768–75.
[284] The name euphemistically applied to God by Satan, *PL* 2.28.

And there the Hebrew family begun.
Nimrod made Babylon his royal seat,
Where his successors long continued great;
But could not with their own remaining power
Further advance the late-designèd tower.   110
Yet did they there their ample realm extend,
And other kings to their dominion bend.

Canto 11

The sons of Shem, with other nations mixed,
In Ur, a city of Chaldea, fixed,
Where unto Peleg, sprung of Heber's breed,
Reu, Serug, Nahor, Terah did succeed,
Terah the father of great Abraham
Who founder of the faithful state became.
[Genesis 12.1] Him God called forth of his own native soil
And thus excites[285] to undergo the toil:
'Come, leave these shores: I'll lead thee to a place
Where thou, engendering an illustrious race,   10
Shalt be a blessing to the earth. In time
Thy glorious nephews by my grace shall climb
To starry seats. Delay not then, nor fear
To quit thy country and relations here.
A holy seed out of thy loins shall rise;
In thee shall all the whole earth's families
Their happiness find; thou shalt a blessing be,
For I will bless whoever blesseth thee,
And such as curse thee shall themselves fare worse,
For I will lay on them my heaviest curse.'   20
     Abraham, thus called forth by the Lord's
          command,
Immediately left the Chaldean land,
His brethren and his kindred there forsook,
Only his wife and Lot his nephew took.
With these he many unknown cities passed
And to the land of Canaan came at last,

---

[285] stirs up

Where then the cursèd nations dwelt again.
The Lord appeared to him in the large plain
Of Moreh where the Sichemites^{ccclxvi} did live
And promised he would all that country give   30
To Abraham's seed; who, with a grateful sense,
There to the Lord an altar raised, and thence
To mountains on the east of Bethel went,
And on those hills, before he pitched his tent,
Another altar unto God did raise,
Invoking his great name with prayer and praise;
Soon after which that land yielded no grain
Which could his family with bread sustain.
Famine drove him to Egypt, whose fat soil
Needs not heaven's showers, watered with his^{ccclxvii}
     own Nile.   40
But there his former resolution failed,
And fear of death above his faith prevailed,
Who thus to Sarah spoke: 'O thou my wife
And sister, now have mercy on my life,
Nor here the first of those dear titles own
But let the sister's name be only known.
For these are lustful men and thou art fair.
If thy known marriage put them in despair
When they enamoured of thy beauties be,
I shall be killed that they may seize on thee.'   50
Sarah agreed and both the marriage hide,
Professed the sister but the wife denied.²⁸⁶
     And now her sparkling eyes dispersed the flame
And Egypt's king heard of her beauty's fame.
Then he himself with eagerness desired
To see that face his courtiers so admired,
And sent for her. Then those youths who before
Hoped for themselves did only then adore
The excellencies of their future queen
Whom Pharaoh with such ravishment had seen.   60

^{ccclxvi} Shechemites
^{ccclxvii} his *MS* their *MSC*

---

²⁸⁶ See note to 14.30; and compare the episode in *M* 89–90, where LH colludes in deceiving
the royalists into confusing her husband with his brother (I owe this point to Bryan Love).

Upon her looks he feasted his glad sight
And drunk down love's infection with delight.
The more she saw him burn, the more she blazed,
For blushes which her guilty fear had raised
The lustre of her beauty did augment
And more attractions to his eyes present.
Then in the court her lodgings were assigned,
But there she did not any pleasure find,
Her thoughts still fixed on her dear husband kept
And for the want of his loved presence wept;   70
But yet in private vents her griefs lest they
The secret of her marriage should betray.
For as her brother kind to him they were,
And largely he did Pharaoh's bounties share.
Presents he had of asses, camels, kine,
Servants, and sheep, for then there was no coin
And quick[287] goods were the riches of those days.
   But God his curse on Pharaoh's kingdom lays,
Who, seeking why those heavy plagues so reigned,
Found he unjustly Abraham's wife detained,   80
Whom he with grief to her own lord returned,
And now with rage as erst[288] with love he burned.
'What madness,' said he, 'did thy thoughts inspire
To kindle in me this unquenched desire?
Whilst thou thy wife didst for thy sister own
I might myself have married her unknown.
My guiltless land now suffers for thy sake.
Wherefore thy wife with all thy[ccclxviii] substance take,
And wholly from my injured sight remove
The lovely object of my lawless love.'[ccclxix]   90

[Genesis 13.1]   The king dismissed them thus, and gave command
They should receive safe conduct through the land.
From Egypt then back to the south he went,
And once again in Bethel pitched his tent,

---

ccclxviii with thy *MS* with all thy *MSC*
ccclxix *MS adds after this line* The faire enticer of forbidden love *and a bracket marks this with lines 89–90 as a triplet; but this line reads like an alternative draft*

[287] living
[288] formerly

And on the altar built when first he came
Into those parts again invoked God's name.
His riches in his travels were increased,
Silver and gold he plenteously possessed.
Both he and Lot had much improved their stocks,
Abounding with large herds and bleating flocks,   100
Which every day so multiplied their breed
They could no longer in one pasture feed.
For then they sojourned with the Canaanite
And in that country had no proper right;
Wherefore their herdmen, straitened in the ground,
So brawled that they forced Abram to propound
A separation from his kinsman. See
What inconveniences in riches be!
Their servants' frequent quarrels now destroyed
That quiet they in meaner states enjoyed.   110
Rich men drive all their dearest friends away
To make their own room large; yet cannot they
Assure themselves that they at last shall have
More of the earth than what serves for a grave.[289]
    When Abram saw contention still increased,
To Lot his kinsman he this speech addressed:
'We brethren are, and linked by many ties:
Betwixt us, therefore, let no quarrels rise,
But to remove the cause, divide our stocks
And choose out several pastures for our flocks.   120
Make thy election[290] what part of the land
Thou lik'st to inhabit:[ccclxx] if on the right hand,
I will the left my habitation make;
If thou choose that, I will the right hand take.'
Then from the hills of Bethel Lot surveyed
The country round and for his dwelling made
Choice of a pleasant vale through which did glide
Jordan's clear stream, and all the riverside,
Adorned with trees which various fruits did bear,

ccclxx likest if *MS* likest t'inhabite if *MSC*

[289] Geneva annotation: 'This incommodity came by their riches, which brake friendship, and as it were, the bond of nature'.
[290] choice

Made the rich plain a paradise appear.   130
There for his flocks fresh pastures did abound,
And silver currents watered all the ground.
There saw he groves and cities, all the grace
That could give ornament to any place.
But lewd men did this pleasant land possess,
For plenty oft occasions sinfulness.
In prosperous fortunes men neglect their God,
Nor think on him but when they feel his rod.
Those only to celestial seats aspire
Whom pressures in their earthly dwellings tire.   140
None willingly part with the things that please
Or wish a change before they feel disease.²⁹¹
    Then God to Abram once again appeared
And in his solitude his sad heart cheered.
'On all this land,' said he, 'now cast thine eyes.
Whatever on the north or south side lies,
From the eastern hills where first the sun displays
The purple splendour of his early rays
To the western sea in which his car is drowned:
All that long, spacious tract of fruitful ground   150
I on thy future offspring will bestow,
Whose families to such multitudes shall grow
That sands on the sea-shore and all those bright
Ethereal flames which grace the silent night
Shall be as easily numbered as thy race,
To whom I have decreed this ample space.
Wherefore arise now, the whole land survey,
Pass through all the countries every way,
And when thou dost those pleasant regions see,
Know they're reserved for thy posterity.'   160
Abram obeyed the Lord, from Bethel went
And in the plain of Mamre pitched his tent,
There to the Lord another altar rears.
[*Genesis 14.13*]   Soon after, breathless at his tent appears
A man whose staring eyes full of affright
Expressed ill news before he could recite:
How war had ruined Sodom's glorious state

²⁹¹ discomfort

And Lot in it had shared a captive fate.
This sad report the patriarch heard with grief,
And while his household armed for Lot's relief   170
He bade the messenger at large declare
The cause and the proceedings of the war.[292]
'I'the vale,' said he, 'watered with Jordan's flood,
On those green banks five goodly cities stood:
Luxurious Sodom with strong walls girt round,
Stately Gomorrah with high turrets crowned,
Admah and Zeboiim, both well fortified,
And little Bela placed on the hillside:
These cities, built by Syrian colonies,
While as their yet unperfect[293] walls did rise,   180
For twelve years served that king, but at the length
When now they were confirmed in their own
     strength,
His tribute they denied, his fetters broke,
And scorned to wear a foreign prince's yoke.
But Chedorlaomer, who in Elam reigned,
With three kings more yet under his command,
Even Arioch, Amraphel, and Tidal, made
All warlike preparations to invade
His late-revolted subjects; they again
With no less care their liberties maintain.   190
All love of culture[294] ceased; some were employed
To cast up trenches, others to provide
The magazines with victuals and with arms.
     'While this is doing, daily new alarms[ccclxxi]
Spur on their diligence, for fame brings news
How Chedorlaomer's conquering host subdues
The neighbour realms, the countries of the vale

[ccclxxi] aarmes

[292] The messenger's speech amounts to a mini-epic following the conventions of classical poetry – note the concentration of epic similes. This framing device reflects LH's perception that this section of Genesis (chapter 14) departs from the manner of the rest of the book; it is thought by modern scholars to represent later material, though it is still one of the earliest surviving narratives of warfare. Du Bartas treats the battle at greater length and with more extended similes, *DWW* II.3.1.251–910.
[293] unfinished
[294] agriculture

Already vanquished, that he did assail
The castles and strong^{ccclxxii} places of Mount Seir
And in the hilly countries spread his fear,   200
Chasing his foes into the wilderness;
That his victorious troops, proud with success
And full of threats, were marching back again.
Like to a furious torrent swelled with rain,
Which in its violent passage overthrows
Whatever doth the rapid stream oppose,
And falling down the hills, with horrid noise
All the plantations, vines and corn destroys,
Carrying away the oxen-stalls and fruits,
Resisting banks and trees torn from their roots:[295]   210
So came these proud, insulting[296] enemies,
Encouraged by their conquests to chastise
The late-revolted towns; in whom despair
Prevailed not yet, but with more prudent care
They endeavoured to make good their own
     defence,
Encouraged by a noble confidence
That th'enemy's triumphs would renown the field
And glory to their fall or victory yield.
     'Each of these cities had a several king,
Yet did not they small scattered armies bring   220
To encounter such a foe, but all unite
And in the conduct[297] of one general fight
The royal Bera that command obtained,
For he in Sodom, the chief city, reigned.
He then a council of the captains calls
And there thus spoke: "No more within these
     walls,"
Said he, "let us expect[298] the coming foes,
But in the field our fearless lives expose
Unto the chance of war. If we must die,

---

ccclxxii the *MS* strong *MSC*

[295] The simile is very close in phrasing to *L* 1.287–96.
[296] inrushing
[297] leadership
[298] wait for

Let us not basely yield the victory,   230
But sell our noble blood at such a rate
As shall leave all the blame upon our fate,
And us[ccclxxiii] more fame in death than conquest
    gain.
Yet let us not too easily entertain
Despair of victory: though we may fall,
It is not therefore certain that we shall.
All worldly things have a vicissitude:
Who often conquers is at last subdued.
Although their numbers ours exceed, yet may
Valour as much into our balance lay.   240
If motives could great courages excite,
We for our country, wives and children fight;
If victory incline to us, the spoils
Of vanquished nations shall reward our toils
And all the glories which they have acquired
Shall heighten ours, who, with this thought
    inspired,
Can be content to make a bare defence,
And will not strive for such a recompense.
Let feeble women, men of wasted age,
Keep fortresses, but let brave youths engage   250
In open fields and not to bulwarks owe
Their preservation from th'invading foe."
    'This speech their eager valours did inflame
And the brave youth out of the cities came.
As bees which from the hive send forth new swarms,
So their thick troops march out with glittering arms.
In Siddim's slimy vale their camp they made,
Nor there long idle in the trenches stayed:
For clouds of rising dust obscured the skies
And ushered their approaching enemies.   260
Then all the soldiers in battalia stood,
When with the fury of a violent flood
The adverse host marched down the shady hills
And all the plain with horrid clamour fills.
Now the hoarse trumpets give the fatal sign;

[ccclxxiii] us *MS* wee *MSC*

All run up to the charge; both battles join;
On every side they close with horrid cries,
And grapple rending heaven with loud noise.
Clashing of steel did dying groans confound,
And mangled limbs lay scattered on the ground   270
Falling as thick from men's redoubled strokes
As riper acorns from the shaken oaks.
The air grew dark with steams of reeking[299] blood,
Whose crimson streams discoloured Jordan's flood.
The showers of darts obscured Heaven's shining
    light
And hid their glorious deeds in horrid night.
Against the assaulting Syrians' furious shocks
The Sodomites at first stood like firm rocks
Amongst the raging waves; but, oft assailed,
Numbers above their vain-spent strength prevailed.   280
Breathless and fainting, they at last gave ground:
Which great advantage when the Syrian found,
They with more eagerness renewed the fight,
Slaughtered the valiantest, put the rest to flight
And, being now sole masters of the place,
Did like faint herds the flying cowards chase.
    'The fugitives, possessed with fear and shame,
Some to their towns, some to their trenches came;
Hurried with dread, some in the slimepits fall;
Some in the rocks their wretched lives conceal;   290
Some seek the shelter of a well-known cave;
Some the thick woods and some the steep hills
    save;
Some in the reeds, some in the sedge did hide.
But brave Gomorrah's king in battle died.
Th'insulting[300] foes, revived with their success,
After the slaughter felt no weariness
But marched up to the cities, where they met
A weak resistance, for their minds were yet
Lost in amazement which their sad souls filled
When from the stately turret they beheld   300

[299] warm
[300] attacking

The battle's loss, their vanquished friends, some
    dying,
Some prisoners, some from fierce pursuers flying.
The fearful matrons fill the streets with cries
And poured forth prayers to heedless deities.
But now their vows[301] were offered up too late:
The proud triumphing victor brought their fate,
Sacked all the towns and took their wealthy spoils
To recompense the soldiers' glorious toils.
No house nor temple 'scaped the victor's rage,
No mercy showed to any sex or age,   310
To innocent virgins or the hoary head.
Into a sad captivity they led
All the inhabitants, nor strangers spared,
But Lot the prisoners' wretched fortunes shared.
And now, triumphing in their victories,
They march secure nor think of a surprise,
So that if any force arrived with speed
The miserable captive might be freed
And the rich spoil redeemed.' 'No more let's
    waste,'
Said Abram, 'time in story which our haste   320
Will not allow.' Eshcol and Mamre then,
And Aner's troops, joined to three hundred men,
All lightly armed and in his own house bred,
He swiftly to this expedition led.
The sun's tired steeds bathed[ccclxxiv] in th'Iberian
    deep,
Night's treacherous shade had brought a fatal sleep
Upon the conquering host when Abraham
Into their undefended quarters came,
There all things in a vast confusion found:
Weapons dispersed, men stretched upon the
    ground,   330
Chariots unharnessed while the cattle grazed,
And all the waking guards so much amazed,
By th'unexpectedness so terrified

[ccclxxiv] bath

[301] prayers

That even they without resistance died.
Thus fell the conquering kings in this surprise,
Where death gave period to their victories.
Some, whose vain valour did the camp maintain,
Were there by the prevailing Hebrews slain,
The rest were slaughtered in their flight, and dead
Strewed all the ways which to Damascus led.   340
    Thus from one easy conquest Abram reaped
All the rich spoils which diverse victors heaped,
At liberty the hopeless captives set,
And marching back, in joyful triumph met
Melchizedek, God's priest and Salem's king,
Who bread and wine did to his army bring
And with prophetic zeal the patriarch blessed;
For which he reverent gratitude expressed
And to the holy man a present made,
Tithed out of all the booty that he had.[302]   350
Then came forth Sodom's king and did implore
That Abram only would to him restore
The late-freed captives for the other spoil:
He thought 'twas just it should reward their toil.
To whom the generous Abram thus replied:
'The men are yours, and all the prey beside,
What the young men have eaten and the share
Of my three friends which helped me in this[ccclxxv]
    war.
But I'll have none, nor shall it e'er be said
That I by others' goods am wealthy made;   360
Not prey but my dear kinsman's liberty
I sought, and that my recompense shall be.'
Thus, Sodom's sons and goods restored again,
He only brought home his own conquering men.

[ccclxxv] the *MS* this *MSC*

[302] Abraham's gift to Melchizedek was interpreted by Catholic commentators as foreshadowing tithes paid to the church; Protestants denied this, reading Melchizedek as a type of Christ (Williams 252–4). LH follows the text closely without further elaboration.

Canto 12

[*Genesis 15.1*]   Abram, returned victorious from the fight,
Had cause to fear the envious Canaanite
Might, by disturbing him, strive to suppress
A stranger's power augmenting with success.
Amidst these doubts, in visions God appeared
And with such gracious words his servant cheered:
'Abraham,' said he, 'let not thy spirits yield
To fear's intrusions, for I am thy shield:
Therefore in me build up thy confidence,
And I will be thy ample recompense.'   10
'Ah! gracious Lord,' the patriarch then replied,
'What canst thou give to me, who am denied
Children, of all thy temporal gifts the best?
Behold, thou hast not me with issue blessed.
Eliezer of Damascus takes the care
As steward of my substance, and my heir
Must be a son born in my family,[303]
Since I myself have no posterity.'
'Then,' said the Lord, 'this man shall not succeed
In thy inheritance. I have decreed   20
An heir to be of thine own bowels[304] bred.'
Then God out of the tent his servant led,
Saying, 'To Heaven now advance thine eyes:
Tell,[305] if thou canst, those stars which grace the
    skies:
For to an equal, infinite, account
The number of thy children shall amount.'
Abram the promise of the Lord believed,
And God his faith for righteousness received,
Then further said, 'It was by my command
That thou wert brought from the Chaldean land,   30
And I, to recompense thy place of birth,
To thee and thine will give this fruitful earth
For an inheritance.' 'Ah, by what sign,'

[303] I.e. household (Authorized Version 'one born in my house'); for the usage cf. *M* 267.
[304] interior of body (the Authorized Version wording, Genesis 15.4)
[305] count

Said Abram, 'Lord, wilt thou confirm it mine?'
'A female goat,' said God, 'before me here,
A ram and heifer, all of the third year,
A turtle-dove and a young pigeon bring,
And of all these make me an offering.'
Abram immediately the Lord obeyed,
Killed and dissected all the beasts, then laid   40
Half of each sacrifice on either side,
But the two lifeless birds did not divide.
Then down he sat and drove the fowls away,
Which stooped to make those carcasses their prey.
    Now day resigned th'alternate throne to night,
Which with black mists extinguished heaven's light.
No radiant star broke thorough that thick shade.
Horror did Abram's anxious mind invade
Till God cast him into a sleep profound,
Whose charming power his active senses bound.   50
All vital motion ceased in this dull state,
And then the Lord declared his future fate.
'Thou,' said he, 'in a good old age shalt have
A quiet death and honourable grave.
To thy posterity all that rich soil
Which lies between Euphrates and the Nile
I for a sure inheritance will give.
But first they shall in a strange country live,
And great afflictions for long time sustain.
Then will I bring them to this place again,   60
Their wealth with their late master's spoils increased,
And judge the land in which they were oppressed.
But ere they their own heritage acquire,
Four hundred years of bondage shall expire.
Then shall they be restored at those just times
When the Amorites have filled their unripe crimes.'
    Now was all light departed from the skies
When there appeared amidst the sacrifice
A fiery lamp which did bright flames disclose
And clouds of smoke which from a furnace rose.   70
These unperceived came where the bodies lay,
And only passing through, vanished away:
Which Abram as a joyful sign received.

[Genesis 16.1] But Sarah, at her own misfortune grieved,
No longer would prevent her husband's heirs,
But she herself his concubine prepares:
Hagar, a young Egyptian, her own maid,
Whom kindly she in his warm bosom laid.
Nor was it long before the damsel knew
That in her pregnant womb the wished fruit grew.   80
Hence did her pride, thence Sarah's anger, rise,
Which the insulting[306] Hagar did despise.
In vulgar breasts such base thoughts ever dwell
That they against their raisers first rebel.
No obligations can mean[ccclxxvi] spirits bind:
Favours are lost upon a servile mind.
Sarah, afflicted with her handmaid's scorn,
For slaves' contempt is most uneasily borne,
With harsh reproach to Abram represents
The grievous story of her discontents.   90
    Frail is the state of all our earthly joys:
What comforts one hour brings, the next destroys.
The trouble of this female strife allays
That pleasure which the hope of heirs did raise:
A haughty minion and a froward wife
Disturbing all the quiet of his life.
Then said he thus: 'If Hagar give offence,
Complain not, but suppress her insolence.
Why am I troubled with those injuries
Which thou thyself hast power to chastise?'   100
Sarah, encouraged thus against her slave,
Harsh usage to the poor Egyptian gave,
Who fled the terror of her mistress' frown
And, in a desert wandering up and down,
Found out a spring by which she sat, and first
Borrowed a few cool drops to quench her thirst;
But twice as many from her eyes returned.
    The gracious Lord above saw how she mourned.
A wingèd messenger from the arched skies

---

ccclxxvi base *MS* meane *MSC*

306 scornfully triumphing

To the afflicted woman he employs,   110
Whose joyful errand in his face did shine
And made her wavering thoughts to hope incline,
When thus the Angel spoke: 'Hagar, who art
Great Sarah's handmaid, whence dost thou depart
Or whither wilt thou go?' 'Alas,' said she,
'I only fly my mistress' cruelty.'
'Go back,' the sacred messenger replied,
'And towards thy mistress bend thy stubborn pride.
 I with glad fruit will comfort thy distress
And raise from thee a people numberless.   120
Within thy womb thou hast conceived a child
Whose disposition shall be rude and wild.
All men that dwell near him shall be his foes
And he again shall every man oppose,
And prosper so by his prevailing might
That he shall still dwell in his brethren's sight.
Ishmael shall be the name thy son shall bear,
Because the Lord did thy affliction hear.'[307]
Then, rising up, she said: 'Thou, Lord, dost see
Such as invoke thee in calamity.   130
Here have my fervent prayers successful been:
In woes I looked to God and I was seen.'
Returning then, she God's command obeyed,
And Abram was a joyful father made.
[Genesis 17.1]   When after Ishmael's birth the glorious sun
Had thirteen races through the zodiac run,
And now Abram ninety-nine birthdays told,
When God again appeared and said: 'Behold,
I am the Lord, whose power is unconfined.
Walk thou before me with a perfect mind   140
And I will make a covenant with thee.
Father of many nations shalt thou be
To Abraham, which doth imply the same:
From henceforth thou shalt change thy former
        name.[308]

---

[307] Ishmael could be read as 'God has heard'.
[308] 'This name of "an high father" … [was given] by the designing, holy, wise providence of God': Owen, *Works* XVIII.450, discussing the change of names from Abram to Abraham.

Thy seed shall be abundantly increased
And spread their families in the spicy east.
Princes thy noble lineage shall renown,
The sacred mitre and the regal crown
The heads of thy great nephews shall adorn
And it shall be a blessing to be born   150
Out of thy holy stock. To thee will I assure
A lasting covenant, which shall endure
For evermore to thy posterity:
I will their God, they shall my people be.
They in their land of sojourning shall reign
And henceforth in their flesh my seal retain,
The seal of circumcision, by which sign
I will distinguish all thy holy line.
Wherefore, now circumcise thou all thy males,
For whosoever of this duty fails   160
My wrath with death shall punish his contempt.
Neither the child nor stranger is exempt:
Whoever in your congregations live
Must this perpetual ordinance receive,
And circumcise his males at eight days old,
That I in them my covenant may behold.
And now my promises shall take effect,
Nor shalt thou long the blessèd seed expect.[309]
Yet not from Hagar's but from Sarah's womb
The children of the covenant shall come,   170
And ere twelve moons have compassèd the earth
Her ripe fruit shall receive a happy birth.'
　　These words in Abraham's heart did laughter
　　　　raise:
'Ah,' said he, 'shall such joys crown my old days?
Shall I have sons who count a hundred year,
And Sarah in her ninetieth summer bear?
O God, how great a blessing wouldst thou give
If Ishmael too might in thy presence live.'
The Lord replied, 'I will thy Sarah bless
And her son shall the promised land possess,   180
And mighty nations out of her shall grow.

[309] await

Upon her nephews I will thrones bestow,
My covenant establish with her seed,
In which I the world's blessing have decreed.
Yet Ishmael in my favour shall have place
And I will multiply his prosperous race.
His twelve sons shall twelve princes be and reign;
But Sarah's shall my covenant retain.'
After these words, from Abraham God withdrew.
Then he, the Lord's commandment to pursue,   190
With all his males and Ishmael his son
Received the seal of circumcision.

[*Genesis 18.1*]   Soon after, when at noon the scorching heat
Made every creature seek a cool retreat,
As Abraham sat in the tent door, he spied
Three men[310] which seemed to stand by the wayside.
To these he, running forth, himself addressed
And with a courteous invitation pressed
That till the sun his fervour had allayed
They would accept repose beneath that shade.   200
'Let us,' said he, 'fetch water for your feet
And your faint spirits here revive with meat.
Only afford your servant this short stay,
And, thus refreshed, keep your intended way.'
The men assented to his kind requests
And then,[ccclxxvii] acquainting Sarah with his guests
While she prepares the meal and kneads the cakes,
Which, moulded, she upon the hot hearth bakes,
In diligence he to the next herd goes,
There a young calf out of the fatlings[311] chose,   210
This recommended to a servant's care,
Who did with speed the tender flesh prepare,

---

ccclxxvii And *MS* And then *MSC*

[310] Christian commentators often linked these men with the three persons of the Trinity; Abraham becomes aware during the visit that he is receiving a divine visitation. Owen, *Works* XVIII.222, concludes: 'There is therefore in this place an appearance of God in a human shape, and that of one distinct person in the Godhead, who now represented himself unto Abraham in the form and shape wherein he would dwell amongst men, when of his seed he would be "made flesh"'. The variant at 12.243 seems to suggest hesitation about the interpretation of this episode.
[311] animals fattened for slaughter

Which to his guests with milk and butter set,
Himself stood waiting while the strangers eat.
　How happy times that primitive age enjoyed!
Nature was not with strange excesses cloyed.
Firm was their health then when their food was
　　plain;
By surfeits caused, diseases did not reign.
O how sweet peace doth relish these plain
　　fruits[ccclxxviii]
Which the poor rural garden contributes.　　　　　220
This is not served up at the splendid feast:[ccclxxix]
All there with salt and vinegar is dressed.
Proud scorners turn all the sweetness sour
And whet their teeth each other to devour.
Something disgusted[312] chokes the appetite
Or makes them vomit up their first delight.
Great women were not delicate and nice,[313]
Bred up in idleness, the nurse of vice.
Luxurious diet made them not unchaste,
Nor did the stock of living creatures waste.　　　230
Queens their own hands to housewifery applied,
They spun the wool and they the scarlet dyed.[314]
They with the honourable ladies wrought,
And by example the mean damsels taught.
They did not flattering courtships then attend,
Nor did the men their hours so vainly spend.
Great ones lived not like slothful drones as now,
But kings fed flocks and councillors[ccclxxx] served the
　　plough.
　Thus Sarah, though a noble dame, made bread;
Abraham, who four great kings had vanquishèd　　240

---

ccclxxviii *lines 219–26 are found in the manuscript at the end of the canto, but as a later annotation points out, 'What is at the end of this Canto seems to belong to this place', and the lines have been numbered accordingly*
ccclxxix feasts
ccclxxx councells *MS* Counc'llers *MSC*

[312] offensive
[313] over-refined
[314] For Sarah as a type of female modesty and simplicity cf. 1 Peter 3.5–6.

And from their slaughter in such triumph late
Returned, now on three travellers did wait:[315]
Not knowing that they, from heaven's high courts
    employed,[ccclxxxi]
In human shapes did angels' natures hide
Till, after the conclusion of the meal,
Th'ambassadors their message did reveal,
Assuring Abraham ere the year had run
His circle round, Sarah should bear a son.
    She then by chance[316] within the tent door stood,
And hearing this, laughed at the unlikelihood: 250
'My Lord and I', said she, 'are old: can we
After a barren youth, hope age should be
With children blessed?' They who her thoughts
    descried
To Abraham said, 'Why doth thy wife deride
Our gracious words, as if they were not true?
Is anything too hard for God to do?
Though she cannot our promises believe,
Yet thou th'expected blessing shalt receive.
I will revisit thee at the fixed term
And by performances my words confirm.'   260
    When Sarah did this reprehension hear,
Her heart was seized with a cold trembling fear.
She by denial thought[ccclxxxii] t'evade th'offence,
But they convict her guilty conscience,
Then, rising up, their steps towards Sodom bent,
And Abraham onwards with the angels went;
To whom the Lord did thus his grace reveal:
'Shall I,' said he, 'from Abraham conceal
The vengeance which I now on earth intend,
Since from him mighty nations shall descend   270
And all the families of the world shall be
Hereafter blessed in his posterity?

[ccclxxxi] In human ... hide] Divinitie in humane forme did hide *MS after line 243, deleted*
[ccclxxxii] though

[315] For the situation and sentiment cf. *PL* 5.298–505.
[316] Some commentators rebuked Sarah for the allegedly typical female vice of eavesdropping; LH emphasizes that her position was an accident.

I know he will instruct his sons the way
Of godliness, commanding them t'obey
My righteous precepts and prepare his seed
For those great blessings which I have decreed.'
Then further said the Lord, 'Lewd Sodom's pride
And proud Gomorrah's lust for vengeance cried.
The urgent clamour heard in Heaven's high court,
I thence descended to examine the report: 280
And if I find their crimes to ripeness grown,
I will by vengeance make my knowledge known.'
   This said, to Sodom th'angels took their way
And Abram with the Lord alone did stay;
Whom reverently approaching, thus he prayed:
'Lord, let there be a just distinction made.
On good and bad let not one mischief light,
Shall not the Judge of all the earth do right?
If with the rebels thou the faithful slay,
Who will thy name adore, thy laws obey?   290
Shall pure souls lose the promisèd reward
And piety in Heaven find no regard?
Lewd men will scoff, seeing one punishment
Involve the guilty and the innocent,
And will ascribe to the blind rule of chance
The dire effects of thy just vengeance.
Rather let sinners the saints' mercies share,
And for the godly the lewd city spare.
If it but fifty righteous ones include,
For their sakes save a wicked multitude.'   300
The Lord replied: 'For fifty I will save
If Sodom fifty righteous persons have.'
Then Abraham said, 'Let it not cause thine ire,
Great Lord, that dust and ashes dares aspire
After one grant to make a new request:
Though five of fifty fail, let not the rest
For want of five amongst the wicked fall,
But rather for their sakes reprieve them all'.
Again the Lord replied, 'For forty-five
The wicked people shall be saved alive.'   310
Still as God granted, Abraham begged the more:
For forty, thirty, twenty, did implore,

And having gained exemption for those few
At last for ten did his request pursue.
'Ah, Lord,' said he, 'since my bold prayer
Hath been received with such a gracious care,
Let me once speak again and not incense,
For thus encroaching on thy patience,
Thy just, deservèd wrath; but this one time
Will I thine anger tempt: if Sodom's crime   320
Be so infectious that of all those men
Who dwell within her lewd walls only ten
Be found unstained whose righteous souls have not
The infection of her spreading evil got,
Shall not those ten, though all the rest should fail,
More than ten thousand wicked ones prevail
And have a greater power by thy kind grace
To save, than sinners to destroy the place?
The Lord replied, 'Ten shall the city save';
Nor more converse would then with Abram have,   330
But in a shining cloud made his ascent
And Abram back to his own household went.

[223]

Canto 13

[Genesis 19.1]   Heaven's flaming coursers now did steep
Their fiery fetlocks in th'Iberian^{ccclxxxiii} deep³¹⁷
When Sodom's children, who with day begun
Their works, conclude them with the setting sun
And to the circumjacent fields repair
For the refreshment of the evening air.
Here th'active youths to several games addressed.
In manly exercises some contest,
Run, wrestle, pitch the bar;³¹⁸ in Jordan's streams
Some swim with art, some cool their sweaty limbs;   10

ccclxxxiii Isberian

³¹⁷ 'steep ... deep': borrowed from Sandys 30.
³¹⁸ game in which an iron or wooden bar was thrown as far as possible

All several ways to one conclusion move:
Tempting or tempted to lascivious love.
The elder sort, sitting without[319] the gate,
Seem gravely to discourse affairs of weight;
Meanwhile among the sportful youth their eyes
Are searching to find out a lustful prize.
　　With these sat Lot, by a far different thought
Into the highway of the city brought.
He searched out guests to save from Sodom's sins,
For then great cities had no common inns   20
And the lewd Sodomites, in the disguise
Of hospitality, used to surprise
Passengers who, to their houses trained,[320]
Had their chaste bodies with their foul lust stained.
This pious Lot endeavouring to prevent
Unto the city gates each evening went
And, if abroad he any strangers saw,
Did them into his own protection draw.
Thus the two angels whom the Lord had sent
To inflict the lustful cities' punishment   30
Disguised in human shapes the good man meets
And with a courteous invitation greets;
Which they at first as modestly deny,
But, vanquished with his importunity,
Entering the courteous house, became his guests;
Whom while he with plain food and free heart
　　feasts,
A great disturbance at his gates arose.
The furious Sodomites his house enclose
And with loud clamour his two guests require
To quench the rage of their unnatural fire.   40
　　He, stepping forth, employed his eloquence
To turn their thoughts from such a foul offence;
But they, like a strong flood whose rapid course,
A little stopped, gathers more violent force,
Demand the strangers with more instant rage.
And though he freely offered, to assuage

[319] outside
[320] enticed

Their burning lust, two daughters of his own
Who, virgins, never yet had mankind known,
This yielding rather their desire increased
And with rude threats upon his house they pressed.   50
'Dost thou,' said they, 'who only sojournst here
Believe we will thy contradiction bear?
Darest thou to make thyself a judging prince?
We shall chastise thy saucy insolence,
And what reproach we only for thy guests did aim,
Since thy denial hath increased our flame,
Thou shalt from us receive both that and more.'
Then they all rudely rushed upon the door,
Whenas the angels thought it now was time
To use their power against so bold a crime.   60
Pulling back Lot, they struck the others blind,
Who, groping long for what they could not find,
Perceived they were involved in double night
And had the want of sense as well as light,
Which to their eyes, where lust so lately burned,
No more but in their funeral flames returned.
    Lot with astonishment these things beheld,
But terror his first wonder soon expelled
When the two angels Sodom's doom declared.
'This place,' said they, 'will not be longer spared.   70
Loud have their sins to heaven for vengeance cried,
And we now are by the just Lord employed
To manifest his wrath with such a power
As shall the wicked and their seats devour.
Only for thee the storms of vengeance stay,
Which until thou art safe God will delay.
But hasten then to leave this impious town,
That God's long-urgèd vengeance may fall down.
Fly quickly with thy daughters and thy wife,
Thy sons and those to whom thou wishest life;   80
Nor grieve thy house and all thy wealth to leave:
It is enough thou dost thy life receive.'
    Two bridegrooms for his daughters Lot designed,
To whom his friendship was so firm and kind
That for their safeties he did his expose,
Venturing once more amongst his furious foes.

His future sons in every place he sought
To tell them what sad threats the angels brought;
But they God's warning scoffed, which unto them
Seemed only as a melancholy[321] dream.   90
Then, Lot returning full of grief and doubt,
The wingèd angels earnestly called out:
'Were not God's mercy very great,' said they,
'Thou hadst already perished by thy delay.
Too long these wicked walls have thee confined;
Forsake them now, nor cast thine eyes behind.
Those that the warnings of the Lord reject,
'Tis just they perish by their own neglect,
And 'twill be sin in thee to mourn for them
Who the late proffered mercy did contemn.'   100
Yet Lot still lingered till day's infant light
Deposed the sickly tapers of the night.
Unwillingly his thoughts to flight he bends,
Grieved to forsake his house, his wealth, his friends.
Such frailty reigns in every mortal breast:
Outward enjoyments scarcely by the best
At God's command are willingly resigned;
So wealth's temptations captivate the mind.
Men cannot from their golden fetters 'scape
Till their coy souls endure a holy rape   110
Which to himself the Lord by violence draws
Even as they enter hell's extended jaws.
    Thus Lot was thought obediently slow
And had not of himself a power to go
Till his, and his wife's[ccclxxxiv] hand one angel caught,
Th'other his daughters out of Sodom brought;
Whom now, with gracious violence snatched from death,
The angel thus again admonisheth:
'Fly for your lives, haste from this cursèd plain,
With speed the top of yonder mountain gain,   120
Nor this way evermore revert your eye,

ccclxxxiv wives

321 Excessive melancholy was a familiar theme of anti-Puritan writing; Sylvester has the Sodomites term Lot a '*Puritan*', *DWW* II.3.1.1191.

For in the moment you look back you die.
Haste, haste you to the hills: vengeance comes fast,
And only stops her rage till you are past.'
Then Lot replied: 'Since God hath shown his grace
In drawing me forth of this cursèd place,
Let me not be so long a flight enjoined,
Lest there I meet[ccclxxxv] death of another kind.
What will it boot me swifter plagues to shun
If I into the mouth of famine run?   130
That monster's slow jaws will as sure devour
As the quick flame from whose more vehement
    power
I strive to fly; wherefore, if now the Lord
Will mercy to his servant's soul afford,
Let us our lives in little Zoar save
And that small town for us exemption have.
'Tis far to the hill-foot and steep th'ascent;
Our strengths will be in such a long flight spent,
And we shall find nor food nor shelter there.
Perhaps wild beasts our tired limbs will tear,   140
Or should we not their ravenous stomachs cloy,
Consuming famine might our lives destroy.
Wherefore, O Lord, this little city spare.'
The angel then replied: 'I grant thy prayer,
For thy sake will that little place reprieve.
Make hast then to it that thy soul may live.
The time requires thou shouldst increase thy speed;
Till thou art safe, vengeance cannot proceed.'
    These words did Lot's dull lingering sense
        excite
And made him hasten his commanded flight.   150
His daughters, winged with fear, outstripped the
    wind;
Yet his grieved wife came tardily behind:
Ill could her covetous heart such losses brook,
But, to her wealth reverting[322] one sad look,

[ccclxxxv] meet with *MS* meet *MSC*

[322] turning back

While she with tears the glittering spires beheld,
A sudden horror all her blood congealed.
Her lips and cheeks their lively colours lost;
Her members hardened with death's chilling frost;
Her hands grew stiff, her feet stuck to the ground;
Striving to cry, her voice no passage found.   160
She would have turned her looks away from thence,
But, to inform us what was her offence,
Her neck stiff as the other parts was grown,
Her disobedience in her posture shown.
Thus she, a lasting statue of hard salt,
Became the monument of her own fault,
And God's just punishment of that fond[323] love
Which she from that lewd place could not remove.
Well suited, therefore, was her severe doom,
There to remain her own long-lasting tomb,   170
Which, underneath Engaddis' high hill placed,
For many ages suffered not time's waste,
But for example to her sex remained,
Teaching how curious minds should be restrained
And kept within the Lord's prescribèd bound,
Which none e'er passed but swift destruction
     found.[324]
She longed to see how Sodom was o'erthrown
And, looking for its ruin, found her own.
Lot and his daughters into Zoar came
Just as the sun disclosed his radiant flame;   180
And then, with eyes in floods of sorrows
     drowned,
First his unhappy consort's loss he found,
Which so augmented all his former fears
As stopped the current of his pious tears.
     Meanwhile the angels for his safety sent,
That work performed, back into heaven went,

---

[323] foolish
[324] Cf. LH's concluding remarks on her husband's death: 'God had removed me that I might not tempt him [to] look back upon this world as a flaming Sodom while the angels [were] carrying him to the mountains of rest and safety' (*M* 337), and her apology in the Lucretius dedication for 'the defects and errors of my vainly curious youth' (*L* 27).

Where Divine Vengeance had her troops arrayed
And ready for quick execution made.[325]
That day she in a fiery chariot sate
On whom the armèd elements did wait,   190
Each in the head of their own furious bands
Attending to receive her dire commands.
In Fire's brigade under red ensigns fought
Rage, famine, thunder, pestilence and drought;
Whirlwinds, hail, frosts and tempests did repair
Unto the standards of the shining Air;
Frogs, monsters and fierce inundations went
With black flags under the third element;[326]
Her russet banners then the Earth displayed,
Wild beasts and scorpions filled up her brigade.   200
The goddess' scarlet robes in blood were dyed.
Dreadful portents before her chariot ride:
Pale Horror, wild Amazement, ghastly Fear,
Despair and Sorrow her attendants were;
Her weapons flame, darts, savage teeth, keen
    swords,
Whatever plagues heaven, earth, or sea affords.
Ruin and Desolation followed her.
Pale Death, like a triumphant conqueror
With funeral blazes crowned, marched in the rear,
And fatal shafts did in her quiver[ccclxxxvi] bear.[327]   210
As her solicitor at heaven-gate
The cries of the oppressèd world did wait,
And, when the angel brought in their report,
Obtained a full commission from that court.

---

ccclxxxvi in quiver *MS* in her quiver *MSC*

[325] Genesis 19.24 declares that 'the Lord rained upon Sodom and upon Gomorrah brimstone and fire from the Lord', and commentators ascribe the agency directly to God, or occasionally to Christ; the allegory is LH's invention. The figure of Divine Vengeance recalls the triumphal chariot of God, *PL* 6.750ff., which borrows from Ezekiel 1.4–28; Ezekiel's four-faced, four-winged figures were often allegorized as the four elements. The evils invoked by LH parallel Dissenting literature, which catalogued portents and prodigies of divine judgement against the idolatrous Restoration regime (McKeon); Divine Vengeance may particularly evoke the Great Plague in 1665 and the Fire of London in 1666.
[326] water
[327] Cf. Milton's regal (though masculine) Death, *PL* 2.672–3.

The word now given, flames and sulphurous
   showers
Made a fierce onset on the lustful towers,
Converting suddenly to dismal night
The morning which had risen so gay and bright.
Mists filled their eyes, terror their minds amazed,
When light worse than that horrid darkness
   blazed,[328]   220
By which they saw their palaces consume
In dreadful splendour mixed with noisome fume.
At first distractedly they run about,
But, quenching one, a thousand fires broke out.
Heaven's inevitable[329] darts struck down
The frighted sinners first, and then the town.
The stately palaces and temples burned;
Whatever the flame seized, to flame was turned.
Each turret had a blazing coronet
Where fiery floods which fell from heaven met   230
The flames that did from burning beams aspire
And raised their unopposèd triumphs higher;
Yet were they but like sacrifices crowned:
Their fatal splendour burned them to the ground.
Like men who honours still accumulate
Till they consume in a too-glorious state,
Those who before did Heaven's threats deride
To Heaven at last in vain for succour cried;
Their loud shrieks louder thunder did confound,
And crackling flames their dying clamours
   drowned.   240
Ugly Despair in their last moments rose
And to their hopeless souls worse terror shows.
Death might the tortures of those burnings cure,
But those of Hell would evermore endure;
There would they wish for these now-dreaded falls
To be concealed in heaps of ruined walls.
But death would vainly be implored to close

---

[328] Cf. *PL* 1.61–3: Hell 'on all sides round / As one great furnace burned, yet from those flames / No light, but rather darkness visible'.
[329] unavoidable

The endless term[330] of their uneasèd woes,
When they too late would their lewd crimes repent
Not for the sin but for the punishment.   250
   O how much earthly glory in one hour
Did this outrageous element devour!
The garden of the world, the chequered fields,
The pride of Nature to the conqueror yields.
Gomorrah's gilded roofs fed greedy flames;
Wild fire now burnt up the unmelting dames;
Unnatural heat unnatural lust did quench:
Perfumèd courtiers were choked up with stench.
This sea of wrath flowed over all the plain
Where poor beasts for their masters' sins were slain.   260
The fair groves perished, burnt up to the roots;
The earth itself with all her shining fruits,
From its first native beauty much estranged,
Into a killing, noisome lake was changed,
Bounded with slime and noisome poisonous weeds,
Where no fish lives, nor any fowl e'er breeds.
If any luckless birds by chance here fly,
They with the infection of the foul air die,
The waters such unsavoury vapours make,
Whence Heber's brood surnamed it the Dead Lake.   270
   O how are men bewitched with sensual love
Whom neither judgements nor sweet mercies move:
Mercies held out in sinners' punishments,
By which the Lord frail mankind's crimes prevents,
And such whose hard hearts love-cords will not
   draw
He by severer justice strives to awe.
Yet those examples no impressions make,
Nor will the wicked their lewd ways forsake.
These lustful cities to prevent their crimes
Had the example of those impious times   280
When God, incensed with all of human birth,
Washed the bold sinners from the stainèd earth
In that great deluge which the whole world
   drowned

[330] end

And with the wicked did their seats confound.
Yet that prevailed not and themselves, now made
As great examples, are as little weighed.
Such ruin as theirs the whole world shall endure
When Earth's dark mists shall Heaven's high arch
          obscure
And mounting flames set th'elements on fire
In which the whole world's glory shall expire.   290
[Genesis 19.29–38]   But how should we have sense of this, when Lot,
Who saw the judgement, had so soon forgot
That he could his unguarded soul resign
To the allurements of the sparkling wine.
For he in Zoar heard the thunder's roar,
Saw the transformèd land, and had no more
Desire or courage to abide so near,
But climbed the mountains, full of urging fear;
There in a cave by night his lodging made,
By day reposed under some spreading shade.   300
His girls their bread beneath the broad oaks
          sought.
Some wine they had perhaps from Zoar brought,
But their most usual drink the next spring gave.
Yet hot lust found the entrance of their cave.
The coldest springs, no, not the icy flood,
Could quench the wildfire of their youthful blood.
The bashful red did from their cheeks retire,
The white was sullied with their foul desire.
Awhile they were restrained with modest shame,
Not knowing their thoughts and lusts were both
          the same,   310
But when concealing did their pain augment
The eldest thus first gave her passions vent:
     'My dearest sister, sole companion,
Sad is our doom thus to survive alone
Like wild beasts in this melancholy den
Where we shall never know the joys of men,
Nor those sweet comforts of this mortal life
Exchanged betwixt the husband and the wife.
Happier who did in Sodom's flames expire
Than we who languish with unquenched desire.   320

Ah, fairest rose, unfortunately blown,
Where thy fresh beauty never can be known;
Where thou no fruits of love shalt ever taste
While time the glories of thy youth doth waste,
Leading sad age into thy desert cave
Which, living, is thy house and, dead, thy grave.
I could my own misfortunes overcome
Might I but hope successors from thy womb,
But vainly we in this dark solitude
Protract our lives if one death must conclude   330
All our whole race and no sweet babes survive,
When we are gone, to keep our names alive.
Wherefore, though daughters are prohibited
To be their fathers' wives, yet since that bed
Is all we can expect, let's not be nice:[331]
Necessity excuses it from vice.
This crime will be a piety in us,
Who seek our father's preservation thus.
Wherefore, if you will add your help to mine,
We will inflame his agèd blood with wine,   340
And as he gave us being, so shall he give
Posterity which after us may live.'
    The younger girl was glad her sister broke
The fence of shame and her own wishes spoke.
They both, agreed, their wicked plot designed
And did[ccclxxxvii] a husband of their father find.
Though he, by wine's strong charms deprived of
    sense,
Unknowingly committed the offence,
Yet see how fortunate ill actions prove:
The fruit oft-times denied to a chaste love   350
The lust of these incestuous daughters blessed
And each of them a longèd son possessed:
Moab and Ammi, whose incestuous birth
Some ages flourished in the fruitful earth
Where they two prosperous spreading nations grew

ccclxxxvii And a *MS* And did a *MSC*

[331] over-scrupulous

Till Jacob's sons their kingdom overthrew.
For though the Lord spare sinners a long time
[Genesis 19.27-8] Yet judgement will at last meet every crime.
 The evening which did Sodom's day conclude,
As Abraham from the hills that region viewed   360
It seemed a furnace whence he might behold
Black clouds of smoke which towards heaven rolled
Their sable[332] waves and darkened the bright air
Who for the ruined Earth did mourning wear.

Canto 14

[Genesis 20] Abraham from his own dwelling now no more
Beheld that goodly prospect which, before
The lustful cities were with fire destroyed,
He in his pleasant evening walks enjoyed.
The beauteous plain, with fire and brimstone
  burned,
Into a stinking and dead lake was turned
Whose noisome waters poisoned everything.
Here no fish lived nor no fowl stretched her[ccclxxxviii]
  wing.
If luckless chance did any thither guide
They soon, infected with those vapours, died.[333]   10
All overhead was dark and gloomy there,
Unwholesome mists corrupted the whole air.
Hence desolate the neighbouring mountains grew,
Which, having lost the pleasure of that view
And the commodities they had from thence,
No more afforded life's convenience,
For the inhabitants' corn, which the vale
Before had still[334] supplied, begun to fail.
No travellers did now those ways frequent
By which the merchants late to Sodom went.   20

[ccclxxxviii] stretched wing *MS* stretched her wing *MSC*

[332] black
[333] For this detail cf. *L* 6.795-6.
[334] always

Now, Abraham's habitation rendered thus
Neither delightful nor commodious,
He into Palestine removed; but there,
Again fearing his wife, who yet was fair
And had escaped the injuries of age,
Lest that her beauty should his life engage,
He as before did her his sister call,
By which more hopefully desired of all,
The king himself, enflamed with her report,
Commanded that she should be brought to court.[335]   30
Thither she came and there she was admired.
Abimelech the king her beauty fired:
But not a common love within him burned,
The excess of this into a fever turned.
The queen herself and every concubine
Did at this passion with such envy pine
That the disturbance violent sickness bred,
Which suddenly surprised the court with dread,
And the late much-expected triumphs so
Converted to a face of general woe.   40
Skilful physicians tried their art in vain,
The king still languished with uneasèd pain.
    At length, when earthly succours were denied,
He to the Lord of Heaven his prayer applied,
Who, always gracious to poor mortals' cries,
A wingèd messenger from Heaven employs
Unto the gloomy mansion of dull Sleep.[336]

---

[335] The episode LH proceeds to versify, Genesis 20, is very close to Genesis 12.10–20 and 26.6–11; in the first episode Abraham pretends to Pharaoh that Sarah is his sister, here he performs the same deceit on Abimelech, and in the final episode Isaac deceives the same Abimelech. Modern scholarship resolves these incongruities by taking the first and third episodes to belong to the Yahwist narrative and the second to be a telescoped version by the Elohist, who tries to offer ethical justifications for Abraham's and Abimelech's behaviour and distances God by having him appear in a dream. LH's elaborate allegorical treatment of the dream seems to be a way of distinguishing this episode clearly from the other two, which she versifies at 11.41–90 and 17.249–66; she further distinguishes them by distinguishing between two Abimelechs (see 17.313 and note).

[336] This allegorical episode down to 14.85 is a close imitation, at points a literal translation, of Ovid, *Metamorphoses* 11.592–625. A fragment of a translation by LH of *Metamorphoses* 1.89–103 is preserved in Nottinghamshire Archives, DD/HU3, p. 277. Du Bartas uses a comparable imitation (*DWW* II.3.1.521–606).

Sleep in a valley dwelt hemmed round with steep
And craggy rocks, whose overhanging brows
No passage for the sun's bright beams allows,   50
Perpetually excluding all light's cheerful rays.
In this dark shade no lowing cattle graze,
No barking dogs live there, no bleating flocks,
No wakeful geese nor day-exciting cocks;
All jarring tongues and sounds are banished thence
But such as bring a dullness on the sense,
Soft, gently-running springs and whispering gales.
The humid earth thick vapours still exhales
That evermore in misty waves arise
And interpose between the radiant skies   60
And the moist ground, which no glad issue breeds
But poppy and those stupefying weeds
From whence the night that drowsy juice collects
Wherewith she every creature's eyes infects.
One rock there was hung like a canopy
Under whose shelter did the dull Power lie
Upon a couch with sable coverings spread.
Fantastic dreams hovered about his bed,
To which the angel coming, with his bright
Appearance for a while suspended night.   70
The lazy god thrice for his rest he calls,
Whose head thrice reared, thrice on his bosom falls,
Which he at last supporting on his hands,^{ccclxxxix}
With half-closed lids attends the Lord's commands;
Which thus the glorious messenger declares:
    'O Sleep, thou sweet release of anxious cares,
Life's best refreshment, in whose sacred reign
Mortals forget all grief and torturing pain,
Restorer of the tired limbs and mind,
Thy pleasing charms the vexèd senses bind,   80
Thou calm'st the rages of unquenched desires.
Remembrance from thy presence still retires
And gives the agitated thoughts repose;
From thee man's pleasant'st consolation flows.
Haste with thy leaden mace to Gerar's king

ccclxxxix hand

And stupefaction on his senses bring;
Then to his fancy in a dream present
The unknown cause of his sad languishment
Which I, assisting,[337] clearly will expound
When thy dull charms have his quick senses bound.'   90
　　Sleep, thus commanded, lazily did rise
And in Night's chariot through the gloomy skies,
Ushered by Silence, passed along like death,
Poisoning the air with his contagious breath;
At whose approach all living things fell down
And did their busy cares in stillness drown.
Sad Philomel[338] abruptly ceased her songs
And,[cccxc] sleeping, lost the memory of her wrongs;
The larger herd, benumbed with stupid[339] night,
No more could keep their drowsy limbs upright   100
But stretched their heavy members on the ground;
The silent rivers to their banks seemed bound;
The new-blown flowers shut up their gaudy leaves;
The violet droops while it night's juice receives
And like a bashful virgin hangs her head;
Even the fish rest in their watery bed;
The birds, perched on the boughs, their lids fast
　　close,
And stupefaction into all things flows.
The student can no more with wakeful eyes
Pursue his search in learnèd mysteries;   110
Upon his open book his head declines,
And sleep the vastness of his thought confines.
Giddy with sleep the toilèd servants reel;
Industrious matrons drop down at the wheel;
The watchful dogs lie stretched out by the fire
And drowsiness gives pause to all desire.
Sleep doth the fair one at her glass surprise
And shuts the eager gazing lover's eyes.
All passions which each creature doth possess

cccxc An

337 being present
338 the nightingale
339 lethargic

As he passed by gave way to stupidness.[340]   120
Oblivion did in the same chariot ride.
All various kinds of dreams marched on each side,
Who, when the first two had performed their
     charms,
Entered the easeful head in numerous swarms
And strange fantastic apparitions made,
Suiting the brains where they reception had.
Deformèd Sloth and nasty Poverty
Among the crowd of his attendants be;
But in the rear there marched a handsome pair,
The Cure of Weariness and the Release of Care.   130
Most tardy is the monarch's natural pace,
But several active troops his slow steps chase,
By swift and powerful commanders brought
To dispossess him of the agile thought.
Restless Ambition, Care, and Unfilled Love
In the first rank of his pursuers move;
Then follow Industry and strong Desire,
Melting his chains with youth's still active fire.
But now a greater power their force controlled
And made him long that night his empire hold   140
When he into the sick king's palace went,
Whose fever want of quiet did augment,
Till at the undiscerned approach of sleep
A dullness did through all his members creep,
And so his tortured wearied sense benumbs;
In whose still rest the sacred herald comes
And thus his heavenly embassy declares:
     'The Lord,' said he, 'invokèd by thy prayers,
Wherein as guiltless thou pourst forth complaints,
Thee with the cause of thy disease acquaints: 150
For 'tis thy sin prevails against thy life
While lewdly thou retain'st another's wife:
Wherefore thou art but dead for this offence.'
'Ah, Lord,' said he, 'shall then my innocence
Suffer like guilt? wilt thou with me include
In general ruin a just multitude?

---

[340] unconsciousness

Did not her husband her his sister name,
And did not she herself affirm the same
With innocent hands and with integrity?
In my whole heart thou knowst, O Lord, that I   160
This fatal unknown error did commit,
Nor is her chastity polluted yet.'
The Lord replied,[341] 'I know thy heart was free
From foul intent; 'twas I restrainèd thee
From such an unknown crime, and by my grace
Thou hast been yet withheld from her embrace.
Wherefore restore the man again his wife
And his prayer shall restore thy threatened life,
For he's a prophet and his favoured zeal
Shall the distempers of thy household heal.   170
But if thou still pursue his injury,
Quick death shall swallow up thy family,
And thou thyself shalt in their ruin fall
Unless thy quick repentance save them all.'
   With this the king awaked full of affright,
When now the morn disclosed her purple light.
His terror had surmounted his disease,[342]
Anguish did more his mind than members seize;
When early he his whole court congregates
And the sad threatenings of the Lord relates.   180
Which when they had with wild amazement heard
Their courage failed, nor were they less affeared
Than when poor men in a besiegèd town
See part of their strong rampires[343] tumble down
And make a breach for death to enter in:
So did they look on this destructive sin.
The fatal cause of this they durst not curse,
Fearing to make their dreaded ruin worse.
Prayer they thought a safer way, and ran
To crave th'assistance of the holy man,   190

---

[341] Calvin I.523 comments that God showed himself 'so that [Abimelech] might clearly
perceive himself to be divinely reproved, and not deluded with a vain spectre'; LH's fiction
moves rather abruptly from the vision to God.
[342] unease
[343] rampart

Whom when the king beheld, struck with the
   sense
Of God's late threats, 'Ah,' said he, 'what offence
In me or mine can have provoked thee thus
To bring this desperate ruin upon us?
What have I or my guiltless people done
To merit from thee this destruction?
Our fault proceeded from our ignorance,
But thou didst wilfully our sins advance;
And sure, though I bear all th'affliction,
Yet thou hast done what ought not to be done.'   200
   Abraham, whom justly thus the king accused,
Without reply stood silent and confused,
When still the king urged on: 'What didst thou
   see?
What could thy motive to this action be?'
Abraham, who found no fair excuse to hide
A fault so manifest, at length replied:
'I do confess, though that cause be not just,
I have offended you by my distrust.
I in my heart had said when I came here:
"Perhaps these men do not th'Almighty fear,   210
And if they know this beauty be my wife,
To obtain her they may attempt my life."
Yet when I said she is my sister, I
Did but affirm the truth: our nuptial tie
Is added to our natural bond, for she
And I the children of one father be,
Though we our births from several mothers took.
Wherefore, when I my native earth forsook,
Informed by angels of the Lord's command
Which made me wander in an unknown land,   220
I from my beauteous wife implored this grace,
That whensoe'er we came to any place
She would the sister's title only own
Nor let our marriage be to strangers known.
This our concealment, though unlucky here,
Proceeded not from malice but from fear.'
   The gentle King would urge his shame no more
But unpolluted did his wife restore,

Adding a royal gift[cccxci] and gracious words.
'Behold,' said he, 'where'er my land affords   230
Thee best convenience, choose thyself a seat,
There with thy wife and family retreat
And amongst us in perfect freedom live.
These oxen, sheep, and slaves from me receive.'
To Sarah next the king his speeches bent:
'A thousand silver pieces with thee sent
My kindness to thy brother testifies.
Let him still be the covering of thy eyes.
Let not this accident procure thee shame,
Yet never more endanger thus thy fame,   240
For fear, though thou preserve thy chastity,
Rash-grounded censures may dishonour thee.
Let him for thee and for thy maids provide
Such modest veils as may from all men hide
The flames which may beget unlawful fire:
'Tis easier to prevent than quench desire.
All would not, as I do, return thee pure.'
    This just reproof did their frail fear procure.
Then Abraham prayed to God with fervent zeal,
And, by his prayer moved, the Lord did heal   250
The king with all his concubines whom he
For Sarah's sake plagued with sterility.

[Genesis 21]   To comfort their disgrace, now Sarah's[cccxcii] womb
Grew pregnant with that promised fruit in whom
A blessing was designed for the whole earth,
And the ninth moon disclosed the joyful birth.
Isaac they call their son, whose name implies
Their gladness,[344] him th'eighth day circumcise.
Then grew the child, fed at his mother's breast,
Whose weaning, celebrated with a feast,   260
Bred envy in the proud Egyptian's boy,
Whom Sarah found scoffing their solemn joy,
Nor a just anger at these flouts[345] refrained

[cccxci] guilt *MS* gift *MSC*
[cccxcii] Sarah

[344] Hebrew
[345] insults

But to her Lord with bitterness complained.[346]
    'This slave,' said she, 'in her own insolent pride
Hath bred her brat who did my son deride;
Wherefore no more will I sustain their scorn,
Nor shall a slave's proud son, so basely born,
A share of Isaac's heritage expect:
Wherefore this Hagar and her son eject.'   270
Much did these words poor Abraham's thoughts
    disturb.
Hardly[347] could he a stepdame's fury curb,
Nor bring his heart to yield that his own child
Should for one scoff be evermore exiled.
Grieved both at Ishmael's scorn and Sarah's spite,
Feeding his sorrows in the silent night,
The Lord, descending from the firmament,
Thus said: 'No more pursue thy discontent,
Nor cherish the disturbance of thy life,
But yield to the harsh instance of thy wife;   280
Nor let it more afflict thee to fulfil
The jealous bent of her obdurate will.
Consent to cast thy son and servant out,
Nor vex thy soul with a perplexing doubt[348]
What evil chance may unto them betide;
For I their future fortunes will provide,
Direct their wandering steps to a safe seat[349]
Where I will make his glorious issue great.
Twelve princes shall spring from his fruitful loins,
And, prospering in all their brave designs,   290
Shall their strong enemies before them chase
And conquer for themselves a pleasant place
Wherein they shall in power and glory reign
And still invincibly their realm maintain.

---

[346] The second dispute between Sarah and Hagar, Genesis 21.9–21, is probably an Elohist reworking of Genesis 16.
[347] with difficulty
[348] fear
[349] The conjunction of 'wandering steps' (here and at 14.333 below) and 'happy seat' (14.338) recalls *PL* 12.642, 646–9: 'Paradise, so late their happy seat … The world was all before them, where to choose / Their place of rest, and providence their guide: / They hand in hand with wandering steps and slow, / Through Eden took their solitary way'.

Fear not t'expose them then whom for thy sake
I henceforth into my protection take.
But though this son my outward blessings share,
The other to my promises is heir.
It is in Isaac that I have decreed
A glorious name unto thy holy seed.   300
From him the godly nations shall descend,
His sons their eastern conquests shall extend,
And from a race of kings at last shall rise
That glorious Monarch whose great victories
Shall overthrow the powers of Death and Hell
And them from their usurpèd realm expel.
Then all mankind, whom they did captivate,
Shall by his grace attain a blessèd state.
Redeemed out of the^{cccxciii} dark unpleasant grave,
He shall their lives in sacred dwellings save.   310
But first a long and various tract of time
Must be expired before thy nephews climb
To these last glories; yet here steadfast rest
Thy faith: the world shall be in Isaac blessed.
Then let not longer thy affections flow
In a divided channel, but bestow
It whole on him who is ordained thy heir,
And trust thy other child unto my care.'³⁵⁰
      This said, the Lord that spoke it disappeared,
And Abraham's sad soul with this comfort cheered.   320
His wavering thoughts at length grew resolute,
Nor did he more in his fond heart dispute
But when the cheerful morning did disclose
Her first red beams, he with the daylight rose,
Then Hagar and her scoffing son dismissed,
Whom as he with a fruitless fondness kissed,
'Enforced,' said he, 'by your own insolence,
God knows 'tis with much grief I send you hence.

---

cccxciii out the *MS* out of the *MSC*

350 Calvin I.541–7, following Paul in Galatians 4.22–31, sees the rejection of Ishmael as part of the process by which God inverts the expected order of the world to elevate the elect, and identifies the presumption of Hagar and Ishmael with the Roman church's pride in its ancestry compared with the Protestants.

He doth this exile for your pride inflict,
And I must not his pleasure contradict.   330
If this just punishment correct your sin
And you an humbler course of life begin,
He will your wandering steps to safe paths guide
And an establishment for you provide.
Wherefore I you unto his grace commend,
Who never leaves such as on him depend.'
Then, loading Hagar with some drink and meat,
'God,' said he, 'guide you to a happy seat.'
    Thus he his son and concubine exiled;
Who, wandering in a desert waste and wild,   340
When all the water they brought forth was spent
Under a tree she left the child and went
Some distance from him, that she might not see
His life brought to the last extremity.
Again she searched the woods but no springs
      found,
Then, desperate, flung herself upon the ground.
Vanquished with weariness, thirsty and faint,
Abandoning herself to sad complaint,
The horrid wilderness she vainly cursed:
'Ah, must we here,' said she, 'expire with thirst?   350
Must Abraham's son for want of water die
By his injurious stepdame's cruelty,
Who, ever since she did my low state lift
Above my fellows, envied her own gift?
O how malicious was her first design
In making me my master's concubine,
Who could not with such horrid woes have died
Had she not given occasion to my pride.
Though she her marriage-privilege dispute,
'Twas I that bore her husband the first fruit.   360
But ah! in vain do I recount that joy:
Perhaps this moment doth his life destroy,
He perisheth, he dies with parching thirst.'
At this the tears did from her full eyes burst.
'O that I could,' said she, 'thaw to a spring
Which might my Ishmael some refreshment bring!
With what content should I my life resign

Could I prolong his day with losing mine.
But vainly I express my fond desire:
We both at once must wretchedly expire.   370
Neither will death a quick deliverance bring:
We must endure a tedious languishing,
And while he doth in wretched torture pine,
His death augments the bitterness of mine.
O that I never had conceived this child!
Is mercy both from heaven and earth exiled?
Will not the Lord employ his gracious power,
Either relieve us with a gentle shower
Or cause a spring to rise whereat we may
Our thirst before death seize us yet allay?   380
No,^{cccxciv} we must surely die, nor shall we have
In these wild woods the honour of a grave.
Vultures and wild beasts may perhaps become
To our torn, mangled corpse[351] a living tomb,
But we more misery in death sustain.
Let us invoke him, then, to end our pain.
Ah, cruel! he comes not at wretches' cries,
Nor makes much haste to close the weeping eyes.'
    A thousand things thus in her thoughts revolved,
She lay as in a flood of grief dissolved   390
When, at the height of all her bitter woes,
The Lord a seasonable mercy shows.
An angel's voice she out of heaven hears:
'Hagar,' said he, 'why melt'st thou so in tears?
At length leave off thy unbelieving fears.
The penitent prayers of thy afflicted child
Have him to heaven's favour reconciled.
True prayer hath everywhere equal success,
As soon heard in the desolate wilderness
As in the assemblies: then no longer grieve,   400
For God will your distressèd state relieve.
Return thou where thy fainting Ishmael lies,
That he, by thee supported, may arise.
For God not only will at this time save

^{cccxciv} Ne

[351] corpses (the plural form down to the eighteenth century)

His feeble life approaching to the grave,
But will make all his future actions thrive,
And nations shall themselves from him derive.'
   At these words Hagar wiped her blearèd eyes
When from the earth a fresh spring did arise,
Which with amazement she at first beheld   410
But, ceasing wonder, straight her bottle filled,
With which unto her fainting son she hastes,
Whose strength renewed as he the liquor tastes.
'Mother,' said he, 'since God hath heard our
      prayer,
Let not our sad state drive us to despair.
He who for us produced this crystal spring
In future times may happier fortunes bring.
Meanwhile here let us make ourselves a seat.
I, hunting in these woods, will kill your meat,
And God himself, you see, hath sent us drink,   420
That we may not beneath our sorrows sink.'
These things so Hagar's troubled mind assured
That she more patiently her griefs endured,
Till prosperous days did her sad years ensue.[352]
Then Ishmael first a cunning[353] archer grew
And in the woods of Paran led his life,
By Hagar matched to an Egyptian wife
Whose fruitful issue soon his house increased,
And all his labours by the Lord were blessed.

Canto 15

[Genesis 21.22] Now Abraham great in wealth and power became.
His foretold glories were divulged by Fame,
Who the report from Isaac's nurses caught
And to the courts of neighbouring princes brought.
These prophecies in Gerar's palace known,
The king, solicitous to assure his throne,
Visits the blessèd patriarch and contracts

[352] succeed
[353] skilful

A league with him, that not by hostile acts
Nor secret practices each should invade
The other's right, and that this covenant, made   10
By them, their next successors should include,
And to their generations be renewed.
Beersheba hence received its name,[354] for there
They did with solemn rites this covenant swear.
    Near this Abram planted a grove, and paid
His vows to God beneath that sacred shade;
Though while the saints lived in their pilgrimage,
No stately temples in that infant age
Were for the worship of the great God raised
But men in woods and fields their maker praised;   20
Yet near whatever spring or shady oak
Devout assemblies did the Lord invoke,
That place holy esteem from thence obtained
And was no more with common use profaned.
But what first decently was set apart,
Men after to an idol did convert,
And did the Almighty's monarchy deride,
Making peculiar deities preside
O'er every lake and spring and greater flood,
The valleys, mountains, and each shady wood.   30
    Poor weak and silly mortals, who conceived
Too foolishly of God while they believed
That this divinity could be confined
To any of those places they assigned,
When even Heaven, which doth this globe
    embrace,
Cannot hold him who yet fills every place,
Still present in the earth, the sea, the air,
Not bounded, nor excluded anywhere.[355]
He in kings' courts and great assemblies dwells,
In private houses, and obscurèd cells.   40
His presence over the whole world extends,
And he to every single heart descends.

---

[354] One explanation of 'Beersheba' was 'well of the oath'.
[355] Cf. *PL* 11.335–8: 'Adam, thou knowst heaven his, and all the earth. / Not this rock only; his omnipresence fills / Land, sea, and air, and every kind that lives, / Fomented by his virtual power and warmed'.

Before designs to their ripe birth are brought,
He's at their first conceptions in the thought,
And when the black deeds are brought forth, not
   night
Nor darkness can obscure them from his sight.
Yet though he all men's inclinations knows,
He often makes experiment of those
Who boast his name, that when their weak holds
   fail,
They, finding mortals' best perfections frail,   50
More humbly may to the Almighty bend
And upon his, not their own strength depend.
Sometimes firm faiths are tried which, else
   concealed,
Impious bosoms could not be revealed
To the just glory of triumphant grace
And the example of the future race;
[Genesis 22]   And such a pattern is presented here,
While God again to Abraham did appear,
Saying, 'Take now Isaac, thine only son,
And offer him for a burnt oblation   60
Upon that mountain I shall lead thee to.'
   This said, the amazèd patriarch senseless grew
And trembling horror did his breast invade,
Yet without scruple he the Lord obeyed,
For faith, soon recollecting[356] his wild sense,
Prevailed and bred a prompt obedience.
No sleep that night his careful eyes did close,
But early he with the next morning rose
And calm looks did his troubled thoughts disguise
While he, preparing for the sacrifice,   70
With knives and cloven sticks his ass did lade[357]
And all provision for the voyage made;
Taking two of his servants and his son,
His journey toward Moriah's mount begun.
Two days they travelled, nor in all that space
Could he discover yet the fatal place;

---

[356] recovering
[357] load

But whenas the third morning had dissolved
Those gloomy mists which the whole earth
　involved
As she in the east her purple curtains drew,
Whence light broke forth and unto mortals' view　　80
Disclosed those regions which the expulsed[358]
　night
Before had hidden from their blinded sight,
Abraham, still marching on with heedful eyes,
Afar off the appointed place descries,
Then at the bottom of the mountain stayed
And upon Isaac the cleft fuel laid;
The knife and fire in his own hands he bore,
And to his young men said, 'I shall no more
Employ your service here: what's to be done
Must be alone by me and by my son　　90
Performed; wherefore, while he and I ascend
To worship on that hill, do you attend
And with the ass in this low place remain,
Till, having finished, we come down again.'
　Much mystery in this whole story lies;
Each part some doctrine or some type implies.
Abraham here represents the devout mind,
And the two servants which he left behind
Earthly affections,[359] human reason be.
These, when souls climb the hill of piety,　　100
By faith led up to God, must even so
As they, be left with the dull ass below;
For worldly cares retard her nimble flight,
And fleshly reasons blind her piercing sight
While they converse with earth and earthly things
And hang like clogs upon her soaring wings,
Which once shook off, the soul at liberty
Is swiftly carried up to God on high,
And there upon his holy altar pays
Her pure oblations of spiritual praise.　　110
　Now Abraham and his son climb the ascent,

---

[358] driven out
[359] emotions

Isaac not knowing to what end he went.
'My father,' said he to his thoughtful sire,
'I see the ready fuel, knives and fire:
But where's the lamb for sacrifice decreed,
Whose bleeding flesh the holy flames must feed?'
The patriarch's faith this mighty shock did stand,
He heard unmoved this innocent demand,[360]
Nor at the question by his melting tears
Betrayed his own or raised up his son's fears,   120
But with a firm untroubled look replied,
'My son, God will his offering provide.'
Now, to the mountain's top arrived, they there
An altar of erected turf prepare.
The wood in order placed, all ready made,
Abraham his son bound on the altar laid
And in obedience to the Lord's command
With an unwavering faith stretched forth his hand
Ready to strike, armed with the fatal knife,
Without remorse threatening so dear a life.   130
     O how religion changes styles[361] of things,
Making the same act diverse as it springs
From man's own nature, or obedience
To God's command to murder innocence.
To have an unrelenting father kill
His only son, guiltless of every ill:
What barbarous cruelty would this have been,
If God's command had not from impious sin
Changed it into the highest piety
Which can in any mortal bosom be.   140
For not to quit that natural tenderness
Which the kind hearts of fondest sires possess,
But whilst it is in fullest strength and height
To conquer it with faith's prevailing might,
And, where the precepts of the Lord enjoin,
The dearest pledges of our love resign,
Is such a pattern of victorious grace
As scarce can find belief in mortal race.

[360] question
[361] names

Yet those whose spirits fleshly bounds transcend
Yield all, while they on God alone depend,   150
Nor lose by what to him they freely give,
But with advantage that or better things receive.
    Now, Abraham's faith sufficiently tried,
To him an angel out of heaven cried
To stop the execution, at whose call
He stayed his heaved-up hand ready to fall
Upon the destined innocent sacrifice,
And as he listened to the angel's voice
These glad words pierced his ears: 'Abraham,
        forbear
To hurt the child. In that thou didst not spare   160
Thine only son whom I required of thee,
But freely hast resigned him up to me,
I know by this that thou dost fear the Lord.
This act thy faith shall to the world record.'
The joyful father then his son unbound,
And as he cast his eyes about they found
A thicket where a ram by his horns was caught,
Which, disentangled, he to the altar brought,
And there in stead of his late destined son
Offered it for a burnt oblation.   170
    In memory of that did here befall
The place he did Jehovah-jireh call,
Which name doth signify 'upon God's hill
It shall be seen'; and time did this fulfil,
For then the patriarch ignorantly foretold
What future glory men should there behold.
There Solomon's fair temple stood, and there
God oft appeared, invoked with zealous prayer.[362]
There Israel's devout[cccxcv] congregations joined,
The Jewish Church in her full splendour shined;   180
There princes sacred fires with whole herds fed;
Thither poor men their single offerings led,
And while the sacrifice in flames consumed

[cccxcv] devout *MS* pious *MSC*

[362] The mountain of Moriah is identified with the mountain of the Temple in Jerusalem at 2 Chronicles 3.1.

The darkened air with incense was perfumed.
This, one of the world's wonders held,
All glorious structures in that age excelled.
    But when forgetful Israel more relied
Upon the place than him who sanctified
That sacred seat, and, coming thither, stained
With their foul sins the house of God prophaned,   190
He left the place he did inhabit late
And did the dwelling-people's[cccxcvi] offerings hate;
Against them sent the Babylonish powers,
Who without mercy razed fair Zion's towers,
And in the city licensed furious rage
Which spared no sort of men, no sex nor age.
Down every channel ran a mixèd flood,
With streams of royal and of common blood.[363]
The princes were with vulgar prisoners chained,
Lords with their slaves one servitude sustained.   200
Chaste virgins, matrons, priests escaped not free.
Without regard of weakness, sanctity,
High blood or holy orders, some were led
In captive troops, some at the altar bled,
And priests the sacrifices there became
While the whole temple blazed with wasting flame.
That glorious fabric, with such reverence reared
That no noise was in the whole building heard,
Was now with horrid fragors overturned;
In crackling fires the cedar roofs were burned;   210
The ornaments became the victors' prey,
Who carried all the precious things away,
Spoiling God's house their idols to adorn,
Scourging his people with their heathenish scorn.
Level with earth thus was the temple laid,
Jerusalem a heap of ruin made.
The holy people in a barbarous land
Long time continued in a captive band
Till God at last, moved with their penitence,
In mercy brought them back again from thence   220

[cccxcvi] people

[363] The destruction of the Temple at Jerusalem by Nebuchadnezzar, 2 Kings 25.

And they anew re-edified the place,
Assisted by the Persian monarch's grace,
Who did again the holy things restore.[364]
But that ground where the temple stood before
Unbuilt without[365] the new walls did remain,
That the pure Lamb of God might there be slain
Where it so long before was typified
By all those beasts which on his altar died,
And by young Isaac's immolation.

    For Abraham, thus resigning his dear son,   230
His only heir, to death, presents that love
Which did the great eternal Father move
To give his only son for lost mankind
That by his death they might redemption find.
As Isaac, the designèd offering,
The wood which should consume himself did
    bring
Up to the place appointed for his death,
So Christ was after led sweating beneath
The burden of that cross on which he died,
And God's severest justice satisfied.   240
    Then on this mountain of the Lord was seen
That spectacle which hath in all times been
Beheld with faith's prophetic, joyful eyes:
Man's guilt purged by this guiltless sacrifice,
From whose pierced side streamed forth a
    plenteous flood
Of cleansing waters and all-healing blood.
Here dropped that balm which doth the passions
    cure,
Here sprang that fountain which makes sinners
    pure,
Here forfeit mankind's desperate debt was paid,
Here was the treasure of God's love displayed,   250
Here death's large power by dying vanquishèd;
Here hungry souls, with heavenly manna fed,
Who ever since have sick or weary been,

[364] Ezra 1.2.
[365] outside

Here have their cure, here their refreshment seen.
In all extremities who looks up here
Forever quits his sorrow and his fear.
By these stripes only mortal wounds are healed,
In this rock is the spring of life revealed.
The ceremonies of the Law, which led
All to this end, were here consummated.   260
Nor needed the Almighty now restore
That glorious temple which stood here before:
Since this perfection to mankind befell,
Th'immortal God in our frail flesh doth dwell,
Nor doth in temples built with hands reside,
But in the hearts himself hath sanctified;
Nor to one corner of the earth confines
His glory, but in all the churches shines,
Delighting more amongst them to behold
Pure worship than that splendour which of old   270
His temples did adorn,[366] and signified
The inward glory of the heavenly bride.[367]
    Yet the first fathers had but a dim sight
Of what we now enjoy in a clear light.
But in this hope they did their faiths erect,
And the revealing of the Lord expect.[368]
While he their souls with promised blessings fed,
Their lives with pious confidence they led,
Rejoicing in the Lord. Now when the ram
Was sacrificed, again to Abraham   280
An angel out of heaven appeared, and said,
'Because thou hast no difficulty made
When God required to yield him up, "Thy son,
Thine only son, for this that thou hast done,
I by my self," saith God, "have sworn that I
Thy blessings and thy seed will multiply;
Dispensing blessings I will still bless thee.
Thy enlarged seed as numberless shall be
As stars in heaven or sands on the sea-shore.

[366] Cf. *PL* 1.17–18: 'thou, o Spirit, that dost prefer / Before all temples the upright heart and pure'.
[367] Cf. 3.467ff.
[368] await

Nor shall their spreading families be more   290
In numbers than in glorious power increased.
By them their enemies' gates shall be possessed.
Because of thy obedience in thy seed,
An universal blessing is decreed
To all the nations which on earth survive.
From thee shall they their happiness derive." '
    Thus, his devotions ended, Abraham then
Returned again with Isaac to his men
And travelled home unto Beersheba, where
His wife, his dwelling, and his household were.   300
Here news arrived which his own joys increased,
Hearing his brother Nahor so was blessed
With eight sons which his wife, fair Milcah, bore,
To whom his concubine had added four.
Of Milcah's eight sons Bethuel was one,
The father of Rebecca, and his son
Laban was father of both Jacob's wives,
From whom great Israel's stock itself derives.

[Genesis 23]   But short's the date of all our our earthly joys,
Which following grief successively destroys.   310
Abram, late gladded by his nephew's birth,
With grief now went to lay his wife in earth,
Who, absent from her lord, in Hebron died;
Nor is there any of her sex beside
Whose years the sacred writings do repeat.
A hundred twenty-seven did complete
Her age, whose beauty, though it did contend
With time, and triumphed, yet death in the end,
Assaulting it with his unvanquished power,
Did her and all her loveliness devour.   320
    O boast not, fair ones, in the grace you have:
All beauty must be swallowed by the grave,
Where even the finest flesh and blood shall rot,
Its glory in a little time forgot.
But if the soul be beautiful within,
No matter then what colour is the skin.
For as the exterior fleshly house decays,
Through nature's cracks it sends forth splendid
    rays,

And, when th'earth swallows the dissolvèd^{cccxcvii}
    frame,
Mounting to heaven, leaves her immortal fame,   330
While life itself is but a speedy race
And human beauty lasts but half that space:
We well may term it a short fading^{cccxcviii} flower,
Disclosed and withering in one hasty hour,
Which only like a flash of lightning shines.
But virtue is a sun that ne'er declines:
This still preserves our memories alive,
This glory human frailty doth survive.
Wherefore here only is true beauty placed,
Which conquers Death's and Time's devouring
    waste.   340
    When Sarah's death came to her husband's ears,
He went to bathe her pale corpse in his tears,
Then, having spent the first rage of his woes,
More calmly he from the dead body rose
And to the princes of the place addressed
With complemental language this request:
'A stranger and a sojourner who have
Not earth enough to serve me for a grave
Here begs your leave that for a due price I
A sepulchre for me and mine may buy.'   350
The sons of Heth as civilly accord
His suit with this reply: 'Hear us, my Lord:
Thou a great prince amongst us art, and where
Thou pleasest choose thy self a sepulchre.
None of us shall his own to thee deny,
But in our choicest graves thy dead may lie.'
Then Abraham, bowing to the sons of Heth,
Again thus spoke: 'Since you a house of death
Allow me here, let me entreat once more
That you would speak to Ephron, son of Zohar,   360
That for the worth in money I may have
The field of Machpelah and the dark cave
At th'end of it, which having bought I may

---

^{cccxcvii} the earth ... dissolv'd *MS* th'earth ... dissolvèd *MSC*
^{cccxcviii} term it a short fading] *ed.* terme a short fading *MS* terme't a short and fading *MSC*

My dead within my own possession lay.'
Ephron stood by and at the city gates
Thus, in the audience[369] of the magistrates,
To Abraham spoke: 'The field and cave are thine,
Freely to thee my interest I resign,
And to this grant my people witness be:
Make it, my lord, a burying place for thee.'   370
Then Abraham bowed again and thus replied:
'It is enough that I am not denied
Th'inheritance, which since you're pleased t'admit,
Name too the price, that I may purchase it.'
Ephron replied: 'My lord, we hold the land
Is worth four hundred silver shekels: stand
Not on so poor a thing 'twixt thee and me,
But let it freely thy possession be.'
This spoke, Abram the silver shekels weighed
For which the field was then to him conveyed,   380
With the cave in it and the growing wood
Which in the ground and round the borders stood.
This contract before all the people made,
Abram into the cave his dead wife laid,
Whose rites performed, awhile left desolate,
He grieved till time his sorrows did abate,
[Genesis 25.1]   And then again the comforts sought of life,
And to his bosom took a second wife.

Canto 16

[Genesis 24]   Now to the patriarch age death's summons gave,
Who, when he found his life approach the grave,
Recounting how the Lord had blessed his cares
And made him prosperous in all affairs,
How he in wealth and plenty did abound,
That no room now for more desire was found,
He piously his latest thoughts employed
Successors for his family to provide
Who worthily might all his wealth possess;

[369] hearing

And since that both the parents' godliness   10
To children's education is required,
He for his son a virtuous wife desired,
And lest his unexperienced youth should be
Betrayed by fond love to idolatry,
The father's harsh prerogative doth use,
Nor leaves it in his young son's power to choose;[370]
But on a faithful servant, wise and staid,
This weighty trust with two strict cautions laid:
First, that he should not link the holy seed
To any of the Canaanitish breed,   20
And next he binds him with a strict command
That Isaac go not from the promised land
Back to his father's native soil, though he
Must only out of his own family
Elect his wife. To this the servant swore,
Cleared in some scruples he had made before:
'For,' said he, 'if the woman should deny
To come, how shall I then 'scape perjury?'
To which the faithful patriarch said: 'That God
Which took me from my father's first abode,   30
From all my kindred, and hath sworn this land
Shall be given to my offspring, will command
His angel to prepare the way for thee
And make the virgin willing; but if she
Refuse to come, thou from my oath art clear:
Strive only not to match my Isaac here.'
     Instructed thus, the prudent servant goes,
His equipage doth handsomely dispose,
Ten camels takes laden with precious things
Which he to Haran,[cccxcix] [371] Nahor's city, brings.   40
Without[372] the gates he saw a fountain where
The city maids each evening came, and there

[cccxcix] Aram

[370] LH, *M* 292, tells of her husband's anger that his eldest son married without his blessing (in fact, to a Catholic) – though they eventually became reconciled.
[371] The nomenclature here reflects inconsistencies in the Biblical narrative: cf. Genesis 11.31, 24.10.
[372] outside

Making his camels kneel, while as he stayed
For their approach, thus to Jehovah prayed:
'O thou, the God whom Abraham doth adore,
Grant him the mercy I this day implore.
'Tis evening now and the declining sun
Almost unto his journey's end is run.
Behold, I at this fountain stand, and here
Soon will the virgins of the town appear.   50
If thou thy favour to my Lord incline,
Grant that the damsel whom thou shalt design
For Isaac's wife, when I to quench my thirst
Shall water crave, may say to me, 'Drink first
Thyself, then let thy beasts their drought allay,
And I may know her by this courteous way.'
    Whilst yet he spoke, behold, Rebecca came:
Bethuel her sire's, Milcah her mother's name.
Pure were her thoughts, and beautiful her face,
Her body ne'er defiled with man's embrace.   60
Her chaster mind upon her work intent,
She with a pitcher on her shoulder went.
The honest labours of those innocent times
Kept honest women from adulterous crimes.
The pride and idleness of our loose dames
Are the lewd parents of those lustful flames
Which fire the world and make them blazing stars,
Engendering murders, hate, and civil wars.
While to the well her journey she pursues,
Her fair form then he with much wonder views.   70
As she, returning, her full pitcher brought,
He meets her and implores a little draught.
'Drink, sir,' said she, 'and when you have enough,
I'll give your beasts.' With that, into the trough
She poured the water she had drawn, and made
Haste to fetch more, till all their thirst allayed.
    The servant, wondering at this providence,
Could scarce recover his amazèd sense,
In joyful admiration lost to see
Such beauty joined with such humility,   80
Such quick and just success to his late prayer:
A damsel courteous, diligent, and fair.

'Oh,' said he to himself, 'if this might prove
My master's wife, how worthy of his love
Would such a partner be: O what a pain
My soul doth labour with, till God explain
Whether my voyage in this maid be blessed!'
Then to the virgin he himself addressed:
'Fair one,' said he, 'tell me what happy bed
Hath such a blessing to her parents bred.'   90
'Bethuel my sire, Nahor my grandsire are,'
Said she, 'and Milcah me to Bethuel bare.'
'Can you,' said he, 'at your good father's home
Afford a wandering stranger courteous room?'
'Sir,' said she, 'we can give you a retreat,
Nor shall your camels too want room or meat.'
   At this the servant, bowing low, presents
Her arms and ears with golden ornaments,
And, heaving up to heaven his pious eyes,
Adoring God, with joyful lips he cries: 100
'Blessed be Jehovah God, my master's Lord,
Who grace still to his servant doth afford:
Who, quickly granting the success I sought,
Hath me amongst my master's kindred brought.'
Meanwhile the maid ran home and these things
      told;
On whom whenas her brother did behold
The wealthy presents, he hastes forth to meet
The stranger, whom he doth thus kindly greet:
'Thou blessèd of the Lord, why stayest thou here?
Thy welcome is prepared within: draw near.'   110
With that his guests into the house he led,
And there the weary beasts refreshed and fed.
To him and his attendants for their feet
He water brought, and then prepared them meat.
But the good servant said, 'First let me crave,
Before I touch your food, that I may have
Leave to declare a certain embassy
On which I'm sent to Nahor's family.'
Laban replied, 'You freely may with us
Proceed'; to whom the licensed servant thus   120
Unfolds his errand: 'Know', said he, 'I am

The servant of your kinsman Abraham,
Whose travails[373] the Almighty so hath blessed
That plenteous fortunes are by him possessed.
Oxen and sheep, camels and asses he
With slaves and maids enjoys abundantly.
Silver and gold his treasuries afford
So amply as make him the honoured lord
Of a most potent wealth, designed to be
The inheritance of a noble son which he   130
Received in his old age from Sarah's womb:
Who now to perfect age and manhood come,
My master will not marry in that land,
But I, sent hither by his own command,
Must carry back his son a wife from hence;
For which Rebecca seems by Providence
Marked forth, for as I at the fountain stood
I begged of God that the first maid who should
Come thither and give drink to me and mine
Might be the virgin which he would assign   140
For Isaac's wife; and while as yet I prayed,
Behold, God sent[cd] this fair and noble maid,
Whose courtesy confirmed to me the sign
I asked of God: and if he now incline
Your gentle hearts to give me your accord,
I shall return successful to my lord;
If not, give me your answer soon, that I
To other courses may myself apply.'
　　When thus the servant had his message closed,
Her parents said, 'This cannot be opposed.   150
God's will herein so plainly is beheld,
We can say nothing, but obedience yield.
Behold, Rebecca here before thee stands,
Whom freely we resign into thy hands,
That she wife to thy master's son may be:
Take her, and let her now return with thee.'[374]

[cd] send *MS* sent *MSC*

[373] labours, hardships
[374] It is interesting to set LH's treatment of this episode against the Genesis narrative and
its commentators. Many commentators discussed the implications of lines 150–6 for a

The servant, hearing this, bowed down once more
And with a thankful heart did God adore,
Then to his master's lovely spouse presents
Vessels of gold and silver ornaments^{cdi}   160
Of all sorts fitting such a noble bride,
And fine robes in the richest tincture dyed;
Then to her mother and her brother brings
Presents of choice and very precious things.
Then they the late-preparèd meal increased
And turned it to a joyful bridal feast
At which in mirth much of the night expired.
The mother of the maid ten days desired
To enjoy her daughter ere she went away,
But the good man, impatient of delay,   170
A quick dismission pressed. The friends at last
Referred it to Rebecca, and she cast
It for the present voyage;[375] wherefore they,
Giving her fit attendants, the next day
With blessings to her spouse the virgin sent,
With whom a nurse and train of women went.
      How different were those virtuous days from
            ours!
Beauty and goodness then were women's dowers,
Whom pride of their own wealth did not erect
To haughty carriage, but with due respect   180
Obeying their own husbands, they became
Strangers to their first family and name.
Not want of filial love or piety
Made fair Rebecca here so soon agree
Forever from her father's house to go,
But she believed, since 'twas concluded so,
A short stay might her pious griefs augment,

---

^{cdi} onaments

---

daughter's freedom of choice in marriage; the *Dutch Annotations* come down firmly on the
side of parental authority, while Calvin and others suggest that this passage does not rule out
the need for Rebecca herself to have agreed. Modern commentators find differing views of
female autonomy in different historical stages of this story.
[375] 'And they called Rebekah, and said unto her, Wilt thou go with this man? And she said, I
will go', Genesis 24.58. This verse was often taken to imply the need for her consent to
marrying rather than, as here, to leaving at a particular time.

And make her virtuous courage[376] to relent,
Softened with her fond mother's melting tears,
Which might have filled her with such doubts and
    fears   190
As would have stopped the entrance of that love
That must the blessing of her whole life prove;
And since she must forsake her native home,
She wisely chose occasion now to come
With obligations to her future lord,
Who needs must kindly take her quick accord,
Without impeachment[377] to her modesty
So freely given, but yet not till she
Was by her parents first disposed; and then
With prudence maids incline unto those men   200
To whom their future service is designed
When it becomes their duty to be kind.
Besides, when sorrow must pierce through our
    hearts,
'Tis better to receive quick-flying darts
Than while we sit expecting[378] an ill fate
To grow more sensible of its sad weight.
Amazement dulls our sense of sudden blows,
And when they're past we seek to cure our woes.
Rebecca gave herself no time to make
Reflection on those joys she must forsake –   210
Dear parents, loving friends, her native place –
An unknown land and husband to embrace.
Had she considered this, perhaps it might
Have filled a tender virgin with affright,
Yet could not have her destiny controlled.[379]
Tedious consideration checks the bold;
Whilst cautious men deliberating be,
They oftener lose the opportunity
Which daring minds embrace than[cdii] with their
    wise

[cdii] them

[376] purpose
[377] discredit
[378] waiting for
[379] Cf. LH's account of her own fears on leaving her family on her marriage, *M* 53.

Foresight escape the threatened precipice.   220
Where choice is offered we may use the scales
Of prudence, but where destiny prevails,
Consideration then is out of date
Where courage is required to meet our fate.
    Wherefore, with her dear home the parting bride
Forsook her tender thoughts, and now applied
Herself unto her present state: in which,
Hearing her spouse was godly, honoured, rich,
Her hopes of happiness with joy she greets,
And gladly so her future blessings meets.   230
Thus, many days in travel now expired,
Her longing soul with expectation tired
More than her weary limbs, her eyes at last,
As she towards evening through a large plain
    passed,
Found out a man far off and, being inspired
With a prophetic fancy, she inquired
Of her conductor if the man in view
Were not his lord; whom soon the servant knew,
And told her 'twas her spouse, his master's son;
Whereat through all her veins a chillness run,[380]   240
Begot by virgin fears, which swiftly chase
Her lively blood out of its proper place,
And her fair cheeks with crimson blushes dyed,
Which, pulling down her veil, she strives to hide;
Then from her beast with duteous haste descends
And the encounter of her spouse attends.
    Good Isaac from a fountain came, where he
Was used to exercise his piety,
And when his lone[cdiii] thoughts had devotion raised
The name of God he there implored and praised.   250
Returning from his holy exercise,
His father's camels he afar off spies,
And his wife's train, which made him guess
The servant was come back with wished success:
Toward whom he hastes, and scarcely stays to hear

His story out when now the bride came near;
Whom he with open arms received, and led
Into his mother's tent, his glad eyes fed
On her unveilèd beauty there until
They did his soul with loving ardour fill,   260
And banished out of it that pious grief
Which since his mother's death found no relief
But in the glad arrival of his wife,
Reserved to be the comfort of his life,
At whose approach, to her such love he took
That every passion else quickly forsook
His much-enamoured breast.
                              Where Love doth come,
If it come powerfully, it leaves no room
For any other cares, while as it brings
In its own swarm too many smarting stings   270
Which where desires are unenjoyed abound.
Nor is the soul blessed with fruition found
Wholly exempt the fear of loss and change,
Making thoughts oft in wild distempers range;
But where impatience and desire prevail,
A thousand arrows at one time assail
The undefended heart and every breast
That lets in Love, for that imperious guest
Must banish joy unless he can retain
That temper[381] which makes Reason sovereign.   280
Reason, by violent desire expelled,
Good correspondence hath with chaste Love held,
And to their fellowship received delight,
Which never can with their wild fire unite
That most unjustly arrogate[cdiv] Love's name,
Due only to a pure legitimate flame,
Such as in Isaac's virtuous bosom reigned
And the pure joys of his whole life maintained.

[Genesis 25]   But ere we enter on another age,
Conclude we here great Abraham's pilgrimage,   290

[cdiv] arrogates

[381] balance

Who after the decease of his first wife,
Ill brooking the sad solitudes of life,
Received an humble virgin to his bed,
Keturah named, who in her bosom fed
No proud ambitious thoughts and did not scorn
The second offspring of her body born
Should be inferior to the first wife's race,
And she herself ranked in a lower place.
Six sons she brought the patriarch, who, lest they
Their brother should disturb, sent them away   300
While yet he lived to plant the unpeopled East;
Where so the Lord their families increased
That they to mighty nations gave a name,
And Lydian monarchs from their bowels came,
Whence also did the Arabian princes rise.
But Abraham saw them not: death closed his eyes.
Eight score and fifteen years now from his birth
Expired, his flesh returned unto the earth,
That universal mother whose vast womb
Doth all her own productions reintomb.   310
Ishmael and Isaac brought him to his grave
And lodged his corpse in Machpelah's dark cave,
Where, placed again by his dear Sarah's side,
Death now rejoins whom death did late divide.
But none the joy of these reunions share,
For after death the tenderest loving pair
No more converse, though lodged in one cold
     bed;
No more embrace when sense and life are fled.
   The brethren, having thus interred their sire,
Back to their several homes in peace retire.   320
Fraternal love had chased[382] their youthful feud,
No more after their mother's[cdv] death pursued.
With mutual kindness each rejoiced to see
The enlargement of his brother's family.
Along those pleasant banks by whose green side
Euphrates' gently-flowing waters glide,

[cdv] mother

[382] banished

Ishmael first pitched his tents, the cities built
Where he and all his sons in honour dwelt,
And as their families larger still became,
Founded new towns whereon each his own name   330
Bestowed, and reigning there with enlarged
    powers,
Erected principalities, strong towers
And splendid palaces, whose vast extent
From Havilah to Sur near Egypt went.
Then Ishmael, having seen his sons thus great,
Established in a fair and fruitful seat,
At last out of the upper world descends
To th'earth's dark entrails, where his glory ends
In dust, the period of frail humans' grace,
The certain goal of every splendid race: 340
For neither honour, wealth, nor power, can save
The destined victims from th'unpitying grave.

Canto 17

[Genesis 25.20] At forty years the patriarch Isaac wed,
For twenty more enjoyed a fruitless bed.
O the unperfect state of human bliss!
The happiest mortals still some comforts miss,[cdvi]
And such man's wayward nature is that, one
Felicity denied, all else seem none.
For it they pine, all other blessings slight,
And where 'tis offered them, refuse delight.
Great gifts enjoyed common and worthless seem,
And small ones wanted have a high esteem,   10
Which men with toil and eager thoughts pursue
But loathe them gained, and long afresh for new;
These too acquired, th'ungrateful restless mind
Will not in them a satisfaction find,
But while the world one object can present
To new desire, disdaineth all content

[cdvi] Such is my spouses beautie white and red
Fresh healthy colours in her cheekes are spred *MS after 17.4, deleted MSC*

Its own enjoyments can afford. This kills
The sweet of life, men's souls with anguish fills,
While they, preferring still what they have not
To what they have, despising their own lot,   20
Think human happiness is only found
In that wherewith their fortunes least abound.
He who is rolled in heaps of wealth repines
That his mean[cdvii] house with no great titles shines,
Thinks blessedness alone on honour waits.
The nobly-born, struggling with mean estates,
Believe none but the rich are truly blessed.
In busy courts, with throngs of clients pressed,
Men cry, 'True bliss is in dark cells immured'.
Those whom their quiet fortunes have obscured   30
Believe that none are happy lives allowed
But such as still converse among the crowd.
Merchants commend the country-dwellers' lives,
These envy their rich houses and gay wives,
Esteem themselves condemned to endless toil
While th'other pride it with the ocean's spoil,
And glad themselves with the large wealthy heap
Of what their youth could in strange countries
    reap.
Th'unlearnèd think that knowledge only can
Give true felicity to mortal man;   40
The scholar, with dull tedious study tired
When he the height of wisdom hath acquired,
In human knowledge no content can find,
Believes[cdviii] it vain disturbance of the mind
And thinks[cdix] those quiet mortals are most blessed
Whose unvexed brains no studious toils molest.
Husbands that have unhandsome, virtuous wives
Think enjoyed beauty only crowns men's lives
With true delight, th'obedient and the wise
(If they're not fair) with froward scorn despise.   50
Such as imperious beauties rule, they cry

[cdvii] meanes *MS* meane *MSC*
[cdviii] Believe
[cdix] thinke

'Tis the wife's humble carriage, modesty
And kind compliance, makes a husband blessed –
Without these, beauty adds to his unrest.
Where fruitful wedlock is with children crowned
And heirs more than the heritage abound,
There men believe themselves in bondage tied,
Oppressed with cares and sorrows to provide
For such large families, and those alone
Happy who ne'er beneath such burdens groan.   60
They that have wealth, chaste wives, and good
     repute,
What nature or kind fate can contribute,
If to all these they want a certain heir,
Amidst their store they pine with sad despair
And fathers only happy men esteem
Whose children may their flesh from death redeem,
Retain their figures and defend their fame,
Preserve their memories and a lasting name,
While others who no happy offspring have
Must wholly perish in the silent grave.   70
     Unhappy man, who knows not his true want,
Thus wastes his wretched life in sad complaint
And, neither with his own nor his God's choice
Well pleased, doth not, as creatures ought, rejoice
In his good Maker's will, his present state,
But with his murmurings alters his own fate:
For every lot which the Lord gives is good,
And only ill when not well understood.
We know not what gifts for ourselves are best,
Yet cannot in God's dispensations rest,   80
Who, to his children gracious, good, and wise,
Nothing but what is hurtful e'er denies.
Yet even the best and purest of his saints
Daily present him with their sad complaints.
     Isaac, although unanswered twenty years,
Still prays for children till th'Almighty hears
And grants his suit: his wife conceives two sons.
The fathers of two different nations,
As soon as quickened in her pregnant womb,
Begin to struggle in that narrow room: 90

Whose strife the wretched mother so torments
That she with grief her late desires repents.
'If these,' said she, 'be mothers' joys, ah why
Am I a mother made if only I
Must feel those tortures others never know?
Why yet doth God let me continue so?
Why sends he not Death to conclude my pain
But makes me more than all my sex sustain?'
Then, with impatience tired, and terrified
With her strange pains, at length to God applied.   100
Her anxious soul her help from him did crave,
Who satisfaction to her sad mind gave.[383]
Forth to the altar of the Lord she went,
There did her offerings and her prayers present.
Thence back returning through a private grove
Haunted by the devout who dark shades love,
Down by a spring she sat, repeating there
The late petitions of her anxious prayer,
When to her supplications and her tears
At last the Almighty bent his gracious ears.   110
About his throne myriads of angels stand
Ready to execute his great command;
One of these nimble spirits, then employed
To comfort the sad dame, doth swiftly glide
Through yielding air and, from th'ethereal clouds
Descending, in a human figure shrouds
His angel's form, puts on a prophet's face,
Long silvered beard and tresses, a slow pace;
So with a reverend gait and countenance
Towards the pensive matron doth advance: 120
    'Daughter,' saith he, 'resume thy joyful cheer:
The Lord, to appease thy grief and quit thy fear,
Acquaints thee whence thy sore pains come.
Two male twins struggle in thy pregnant womb:
There their dissensions in the gate of life
Are the beginnings of no private strife.
From them two mighty nations shall descend,
And with each other evermore contend.

---

[383] The angelic visitation seems to be LH's invention.

The people born of them shall be as far
From concord as the light and darkness are.[384]   130
Different their dwellings, manners, minds, shall be,
Nor shall their fates or persons more agree.
The elder people shall in might excel
The other, and in stronger places dwell,
Yet all their numerous hosts and powers shall fail:
The younger's happier destiny shall prevail.
He shall his elder brother subjugate,
Courage and strength in vain opposing fate:
Fate whose irrevocable laws decree
The eldest must the younger's servant be.'[385]   140
   This said, the angel vanished, and the dame
With comfort back unto her women came,
Expecting[386] till th'accomplished[387] time that
   showed,
When nine moons had their waning horns
   renewed,
The ripe births to the cheerful light disclose;[388]
Then, being seized with strong and painful throes,
Lo, twins were born: the first, o'ergrown with hair
All red like Tyrian[389] scarlet, did declare
His nature cruel, daring, fierce and wild:
Yet then the flattering gossips[390] gave the child   150
A name which glorious action signified,
And to his bravery these signs applied.[391]
Thus this robustious infant forced his way,
Nor did his brother long behind him stay.
He catched his heel, but his inferior might
Could not prevent him from first greeting light.

---

[384] Cf. 2 Corinthians 6.14–15.

[385] Calvin and other Protestant commentators saw the Jacob–Esau story as paralleling that of Isaac and Ishmael: the normal order of primogeniture is inverted for the sake of the elect, anticipating the belated triumph of the true church; cf. Romans 9.6–13.

[386] waiting

[387] completed

[388] open

[389] crimson or purple dye from ancient Tyre

[390] female friends present at birth

[391] Esau's other name was Edom, which echoed a word for 'red'.

For this they called him Jacob[392] as a sign
How he should still[393] his brother undermine.
   The children grew, and in their youthful age
Various employments their delights engage.   160
Esau, being strong of temper, wild and fierce,
Did not in softer companies converse,
But all the day through the thick hilly wood
With nimble feet and darts wild beasts pursued,
And when black night her sable shadows spread
O'er heaven's dark vault, made the hard earth his
   bed,
There did till day his weary limbs repose
And with the morning to his hunting rose.
By daily exercise[394] he cunning[395] grew:
The red and fallow deer sometimes he slew,   170
Now badgers, tuskèd boars, and timorous hares
Fall by his shafts, or tangled in his snares
Are seized alive: he finds out all the arts
Of murdering beasts, pits, nets, and well-aimed
   darts
Which to the fairest head carry slight wounds,
Then runs down the hurt deer with nimble
   hounds;
Thus oft-times tender hunted venison caught,
The dainty flesh to his old father brought
Makes this young vigorous son his chief delight,
His love being governed by his appetite.   180
   Jacob, of a complexion not so tough,
As gentle as his elder brother rough,
At home still near his tender mother stayed
And her commands with diligence obeyed.
His weakness first made him her darling prove,
And then his duty gained upon her love.
One day as Jacob walked i'the neighbouring
   ground,

[392] 'Jacob' was linked with words for 'supplant' and 'heel'.
[393] always
[394] practice
[395] skilful

He there certain red-coloured lentils found,
Of these a savoury pottage made, which boiled,
Lo, Esau, from the chase returning, toiled   190
And faint for hunger, begs his brother's mess.
Jacob, prevailing on his greediness,
'Thy birthright,' says he, 'shall my pottage buy.'
Then answered Esau: 'If I faint and die,
What boot[396] my vain pretensions in the grave?
Give me the broth, thou shalt the birthright have.'
'Confirm it with an oath,' Jacob replies.
Esau swears, eats, and goes; thus did despise
God's favour in his birth, and for a slight
Vile mess of pottage, sold that native right.   200

[Genesis 26]   Now after Abraham's death no showers of rain
Had moistened Canaan's field; the buried grain,
By the hard clods stifled in its new birth,
Abortive died, and caused a general dearth.
Throughout the land grass parched upon the
     ground,
No food for either man or beast was found.
The withered herbs and plants, with hot suns
     burned,
Crumbled to dust; russet[397] the green leaves
     turned,
As before autumn, dropped off from the boughs.
No cattle could on any fresh trees browse.   210
The fountains deep into the earth did shrink
And left no cool streams for the herd to drink.
Good Isaac, in this general plague involved,
By famine chased, to leave that land resolved.
He only now deliberates to what stage
He next should carry on his pilgrimage,
And all the neighbouring lands poised[398] in his
     mind.
His thoughts to Egypt at the last inclined.
Heaven's bounty is not needful to that soil,
Which only owes her plenty to the Nile.   220

[396] avail
[397] reddish-brown
[398] weighed

Fixed upon this remove,[399] his breast finds ease
And gentle sleep doth his dull eyelids seize.
His senses charmed, his soul, which ever wakes,
Now undisturbed a free reflection makes
On the Almighty's will, who to his sight
Presents a vision in the dead of night,
Forbidding him the voyage he designed.
'Quit Egypt,' saith the Lord, 'and thou shalt find,
Following the tracks where I thy footsteps guide,
All life's convenience by my grace supplied.   230
Thou shalt not leave this land, by me decreed
To be th'inheritance of thy blessed seed,
Which I will make more numerous than those
     bright
Ethereal flames that guide the silent night.
The covenant I with faithful Abraham made,
Because that my commandments he obeyed,
I will to thee confirm; all nations shall
Thy happy offspring their chief blessing call.
Hell's conqueror shall spring out of thy stem,
The regal and the priestly diadem   240
Shall thy illustrious nephew's temples crown.
Spreading in power, riches, and renown,
They shall become a mighty glorious state
And the neighbouring regions subjugate.
Stay in this land, then, given unto thy line,
And believe every place thou dwell'st is thine.'
     Then Isaac did a just obedience yield,
Assured these promises would be fulfilled.
At Gerar, where Philistia's monarch reigned,
He as a sojourner was entertained.   250
But when the men Rebecca's form admired
And after her more curiously inquired,
He said she was his sister, not his wife,
Fearing her beauty might betray his life.
A long while there he lived in this disguise,
Till from a window Gerar's king descries[400]

399 departure
400 sees

Such sportive fond behaviour as revealed
The marriage their denial had concealed;
Which, when chance in this manner did detect,
The king for his dissembling Isaac checked;[401]   260
Who, to excuse though not to justify
The action, said he[cdx] was afraid to die.
The king then charged his subjects to forbear
Attempting any wrong to him or her:
'Whoever dare this warning disobey,
His head the forfeit of his faults shall pay.'
   Now Isaac, quiet, from his fear released,
Began to hope fortune her malice ceased,
Since in his favour thus the king declared,
And his successful labours well repaired   270
His substance, which the famine had before
Consumed; and sense of poverty no more
Perplexed his thoughts, for even that hungry year
The ground he sowed a hundredfold did bear,
His flocks and herds abundantly increased
And he a numerous family possessed.
Thriving thus quickly by God's special grace,
He grew the admiration of the place.
   But perfect bliss in any mortal state
Is not to be acquired: clouds still abate   280
The brightness of all human lustre. Were
No prickles on our roses, could we here
Hope to possess a good unmixed with ill,
We should pursue these low enjoyments still
And never raise up our desires on high
To th'only perfect pure felicity.
Therefore the wise dispenser who our good,
Which by ourselves is not well understood,
And our frail nature perfectly doth know,
In all conditions, either high or low,   290
So tempers good and ill that even the best
Of human state is not in all things blessed;
Nor are poor wretched mortals in the worst

[cdx] his

[401] rebuked

Of Fortune's plunges every way accursed.
And to relieve frail man, the Lord besides
Varies his fortunes with alternate tides,
Where floods of plenty now to vast heights rise,
Now the scant stream the dry shore scarce supplies.
  Of this Isaac a full example gives:
Grown poor with famine he at quiet lives,   300
In wants gains the protection of a king
Which did support in his low fortunes bring;
But when heaven's bounty gave him wealth again,
No more could he that fleeting grace retain.
Envy to foes converts his late kind friends,
And from the vulgar to the prince ascends.
With spite they look upon his prosperous state
Outgrowing theirs; envy engenders hate;
Which, burning in the king's envenomed breast,
All faith and generous temper dispossessed.   310
An unjust jealousy did then provoke
Him to ignoble actions. First he broke
His father's[402] league with Abraham,[cdxi] then sent
His guest to undeservèd banishment.[403]
'My realm,' said he, 'thy rising power distrust.
Leagues with the dead must not make us unjust
To those that live. Thou art too mighty grown
To be a sojourner: 'tis seldom known
That strangers suffered to acquire such power
Do not the natives at the last devour.   320
Thine and our safety to assure, thou art
Commanded from this city to depart,
Too dangerous to any state or throne.
It will become thee best to live alone.
Think it no injury to be exiled,

[cdxi] with Abraham *MS* with Abraham made *MSC*

[402] Genesis does not distinguish between the Abimelechs of chapters 20 and 26, but commentators tried to resolve the oddity of the same king's falling victim to the same deception twice by making them father and son. LH distinguishes this episode by a note of republican animus to courts not found in Genesis or the commentators at this point.

[403] A passage with contemporary resonance: reason of state makes monarchs expel religious exiles.

When 'tis a kindness that thou art not spoiled.'[404]
   Thus did Abimelech the patriarch chase.[405]
How changing are the tides of princes' grace,
Not ruled by justice or desert, but chance,
Which makes their high floods run back, or
   advance   330
Where partial interest lets them forth, and where
They find resistance from awakened fear.
Could mortals but with true discerning eyes
Behold the state of kings, they would despise
What now, regarding with unsteady view,
The general wishes of mankind pursue:
Not seeing that all who to the high throne climb
Must wade through blood and strife, check at no
   crime,
Tread on contemnèd piety and faith,
Quit every virtue in that horrid path,   340
Encounter sorrow, danger and affright,
With a guilt-stainèd conscience hourly fight,
With dreadful toil clamber steep barren rocks
And on the top of them abide the shocks
Of every raging passion, but ne'er know
Where the refreshing gales of pure love blow.
The gentle breaths[cdxii] of Joy and Friendship move
Not in the mountain's top but in the silent grove,
Where calm Peace, all the humble hermit's cells,
With Innocence her beauteous mother dwells.[406] 350
But they who in the region of the air
On cloud-wrapped hill[cdxiii] are placed know nothing
   there
But the conception of those storms whose birth
With hail and thunder plague the lower earth.
This is the sovereign's beatitude,
So much admired at a false distance viewed,

cdxii breath
cdxiii hie *MS* hill *MSC*

404 injured, destroyed
405 drive off
406 The text here seems defective.

Where, while men think the glorious tyrant
   reigns,
Insulting[407] Vice loads him with weighty chains.
Fear, sorrow, sad repentance, envy, hate,
Pride and revenge, not only do abate   360
But quite extinguish their lives' chiefest joy,
Their rest of soul, their peaceful sleep, destroy;
Cares and anxieties like furies still
Their wretched bosoms with sad torture fill;
Whipped by repentance, they may strive in vain
To recall virtue: vice must vice maintain.
Ambition carries with it[cdxiv] its own curse,
When th'ill[cdxv] are only safe by doing worse.
What bondage is it evermore to stand
In fear of subjects whom they should command!   370
Yet tyrants are exposèd to this fate,
Who, thinking none love them, do all men hate.
At all the glories others have they pine,
And think it treason mean men should outshine
Their prince though but in virtue and faire fame,
And all things eminent in subjects blame.
Is any liberal,[408] they say he parts
With those rich gifts to buy the people's hearts.
Do any thriftily their treasures hide,
They sinews for some future wars provide.   380
Do prudent men the public throng decline,
They're thought to have retired for close design.[409]
Are any strong, rich, valiant, learned, wise
Or pious, they're beheld with evil eyes,
Occasions sought to use them cruelly
If they do not those noble parts apply
Flattering the wicked to a servile use,
And lose their glory by that vile abuse.
   No wonder, then, if blessèd Isaac, who

---

cdxiv with *MS* with it *MSC*
cdxv the ill *MS* th'ill *MSC*

[407] scornfully triumphing
[408] generous
[409] secret intrigue

Had power and wealth with virtue joined, now
    grew   390
Hateful to Gerar's king and his vile host
Who could no excellence but in evil boast.
The peaceful holy man doth not oppose
His unjust banishment, but meekly goes
To the next valley out of Gerar's bounds.
Before had Abraham's cattle in those grounds
Been grazed, and Isaac's larger herds had fed
While he yet in the city sojournèd;
But the Philistines, even in the birth
Of their close[410] hatred, had dammed up with earth   400
Those wells which Abraham's slaves with toil had
    sunk,
Where all his bleating flocks and great herds drunk.
Isaac, before he from their city went,
Watered at other springs but, after sent
Out of their precincts, did no more refrain
To open the old springs, which he again
Called by those names they had in Abraham's days.
Philistian shepherds then did graze
Their thirsty flocks, and when his servants found
A crystal fountain, claimed the spring and ground: 410
Whom Isaac's herdmen for their malice beat,
And twice compelled them to a base retreat.
Then, unopposed, they sunk another well.
'Here,' Isaac said, 'God gives us room to dwell.'
Yet to avoid their troublesome offence,
Back to Beersheba he removed from thence.
    That night he pitched his tent upon the hill.
When sleep a general quiet did instil,
Jehovah now the second time appears,
Saying, 'I am Abraham's God: quit then thy fears,   420
For I do thy protection undertake.
To thee[cdxvi] I for my servant Abraham's sake
Perpetual grace and blessings have decreed,

[cdxvi] Thee will I *MS* To Thee I *MSC*

[410] secret

And numerous multitudes unto thy seed.'
Waking next morn, when Isaac's thought reflects
On God's new-promised grace, he then erects
An altar and invokes the Lord's great name,
Then pitched his tabernacle near the same
And, having worshipped God with thanks and
    prayers,^{cdxvii}
Again renews his honest household cares,   430
Employs his servants to search out new springs;
When to the patriarch busied in these things
A gallant troop from Gerar's plain ascends:
Abimelech with one of his chief friends
And the brave general of his martial men;
Whom Isaac gently greeting says, 'Why, when
You me so lately did with hatred chase,
Repair you now unto this distant place?'
Abimelech replies, 'We clearly see
The great Jehovah owns and blesseth thee: 440
Wherefore let us in mutual leagues be joined
And let an oath our friendly covenant bind.
Swear thou wilt not attempt our hurt, as we
Have rather done thee good than injury:
And though reasons of state[411] would not permit
Thee to continue in our cities, yet
In peace we thee on friendly terms dismissed.'
   The gentle Isaac would no more insist,
Nor urge on their reproach, but quit[412] the offence,
With kind did their harsh usage recompense,   450
Them to his tent in courteous words invite,
Then with a cheerful feast crowned the glad night.
Next day, when bright Aurora did disclose
Her purple rays, she with more splendour rose,
And all the radiant host of heaven smiled
To see the late-broke league now reconciled;
When now with mutual ceremonies both

---

^{cdxvii} prayse *MS* prayers *MSC*

[411] A striking anachronism: 'reasons of state' were associated with modern absolute monarchies.
[412] absolved

Confirmed their late-made union, take the oath,
And having finished those solemnities,
Part from each other in a friendly wise.   460
[Genesis 26.34–5,   Abimelech back to his court repairs,
36.2–5]   Isaac at peace intends[413] his own affairs:
Yet only must have truce, not perfect rest,
For griefs more sensible[414] will soon molest
His quiet soul. Esau, the child he loves,
Undutiful in his behaviour proves,
His father's and his grandsire's precepts slights,
Matching with the accursèd Canaanites.
He in the pleasant woods of fair Mount Seir
With nimble hounds oft chased the flying deer,   470
More wild than any beast he hunted there.
But at the last, entrapped with beauty's snare,
His fierce soul was subdued, and he who still
Had no design but pleasing his own will
Contended not for freedom but to have
The base ends which his flagrant lust did crave.
He was determined to be satisfied,
Though duty and religion both denied.
Bright Aholibamah with piercing rays
Ardour like lightning through his breast conveys,   480
Which working there begets a violent flame
That nothing but a savage heart became.
Nor did he check but flattered his desire.
'Can I,' said he, 'burn with a nobler fire?
If Nature in creation have designed
Man must be linked with womankind,
What should I seek in her that I must wed
But beauty wherewith pleasure may be fed?
Is't not a princess that inflames my love?
Can any other choice so happy prove?   490
My father tells me they're a cursèd brood,
But why should he appoint me my own food?
Shall as my grandsire's was, his steward be
Sent to strange lands, to fetch a wife for me

[413] attends to
[414] strongly felt

When I at home have made a nobler choice,
Wherein 'tis fit my father should rejoice.
But his^{cdxviii} froward zeal my marriage will oppose:
If then I finish it before he knows,
When things are past his power to prevent
He'll sooner give his^{cdxix} pardon than consent.'⁴¹⁵   500
   Rashly resolvèd thus, to Seir's great court
He comes, there doth himself so well deport,
So confidently utters his desire
As, winning on the princess and her sire,
To whom he seemed, though rough, yet bold and
   brave,
They free assent unto his wishes gave.
The princely kindred to the nuptials came.
Now had enjoyment quenched his first fierce
   flame,
For all things violent but short time last:
Eager desires die when fruition's past.   510
The beauteous Aholibamah may blaze,
But no more ardour to his soul conveys.
Adah,^{cdxx} Duke Eber's daughter, seems more bright
And with new^{cdxxi} violence did his dead flames light.
He who too roughly asks to be denied
Obtains this princess for a second bride,
And thus in triumph with his princely^{cdxxii} wives
He at his grievèd father's tent arrives.
Rebecca, godly, sober, modest, plain,
Did not with sinful riot entertain   520
Her daughters, but with pious kindness sought
(Since they unto her family were brought)
To instruct them in God's worship, and correct
Those vanities which graceless dames affect.

---

^{cdxviii} But his froward *MS* But froward *MSC*
^{cdxix} give pardon *MS* give his pardon *MSC*
^{cdxx} Adahs
^{cdxxi} more *MS* new *MSC*
^{cdxxii} reall wives *MS* princely wives *MSC*

---

⁴¹⁵ This extended narrative of Esau's courtships is developed at length from bare hints at a later point in the Genesis narrative, 36.2–5.

But they, proud of their princely families,
Her and her pious counsels much despise,
Practise their idol-worship in despite[416]
And even Isaac's admonitions slight,
Carrying themselves with such an insolent scorn
As could not be with any patience borne.   530
Nor yet had Esau any tender sense
Of what they suffered, or a penitence
For his own rash and disobedient fault
Which such affliction to his parents brought.
But inclination only guides our loves.
This just distaste a bitter sorrow proves
To Isaac's heart, yet thence it cannot chase
That kindness which gave Esau the first place
In his affection; but Rebecca's mind
More strongly to her second son inclined.   540
Confirmed with powerful reason, she professed
And justified her loving Jacob best.

Canto 18

[Genesis 27]   The mists of lasting night began to rise
And had already darkened Isaac's eyes
When, calling for his eldest son, he said:
'The powers of death my feeble soul invade,
Which cannot long resist his conquering might;
I have already lost the cheerful light.
Wherefore, before I go that path from whence
No traveller returns,[417] I would dispense
My blessings unto thee: then with thy bow
And rattling quiver to the forest go,   10
Hunt down some venison, the which slain there,
A savoury dish for thy old sire prepare
And bring it hither, that at thy hand I
May eat, and my soul bless thee ere I die.'
Esau forthwith departed to the chase.

[416] spite
[417] Cf. *Hamlet* 3.1.79–80.

Meanwhile, Rebecca being in the place
When Isaac gave the charge, she forms a plot
To have this blessing by her darling got.
She tells him what she heard his father say
And adds that if he would proceed the way   20
She had contrived, do what she could advise,
He might his brother's blessing thus surprise.
Jacob objects his hazard if descried
Rather t'incur a curse, but she replied,
'I will between thee and the danger stand:
Mine be the curse thou gain'st by my command.'
Then he himself did to her conduct[418] yield.
Two tender kids he brought her from the field.
Like venison she their savoury flesh prepares,
The skin of Jacob's smooth hands hides with theirs,   30
Puts him in a rich suit of Esau's clothes,
Who thus disguised unto his father goes,
Then says, 'Arise, my father!' Isaac cried,
'Who art thou, son?' To which Jacob replied,
'I am thy first-born, Esau; thy command
I have performed: accept it at my hand.
The hunted venison I for thee have caught
And, dressed according to thy palate, brought.
Then rise and feed upon this savoury mess
That eating it, thy soul thy son may bless.'   40
'How came't,' said Isaac, 'that thou found'st a prey
So soon?' 'God,' said he, 'sent it in my way.'
'Approach,' said Isaac, 'let me feel thy hand
That I thereby may surely understand
Thou art my eldest son'; then came he near.
''Tis Esau's hands', said Isaac, 'but I hear
The voice of Jacob: is there no deceit?
Art thou or dost thou Esau personate?'
He answered, 'I am Esau really.'
'Then,' said his father, 'my dear son, draw nigh.   50
Let me now of thy hunted dainties feed,
That I may bless thee as I have decreed.'
With that Jacob presents the meat and wine,

---

[418] leadership

When Isaac, fed, pursuing his design,
Thus speaks: 'Now let me kiss my son at last.'
As he received this kiss, the raiment cast
Forth Esau's smell. 'My son,' said he, 'doth yield
The fragrant smell of a well-prospering field.
Blessed be the Lord! Jehovah shower on thee
The dews of heaven, let the earth's fatness be   60
Thy wealthy portion, let thy fruitful ground
With thriving grain and floods of wine abound.
May various people all[cdxxiii] serve thee, and may
All nations unto thee a reverence pay.
Sovereign over thy brethren still be thou
And let thy mother's sons before thee bow.
Whoe'er wish thee accursed, themselves be so,
And blessings unto them that bless thee flow.'
    Jacob, thus blessed, forth from his father went;
Scarce gone, but Esau doth himself present,   70
Who, having hunted and dressed savoury meat,
'My father,' said he, 'Rise, my venison eat,
Then let thy soul to me a blessing give.'
Isaac too late doth now the fraud perceive;
But pious fraud whereby his zealous wife
Strove to correct the errors of his life
Who, governed by a partial blind affection,
Stuck to that choice which was not[cdxxiv] God's
    election,
Who in their birth, without a reason shown,
To make his boundless will and free grace known,   80
Declared love to the one, to th'other[cdxxv] hate;
Well pleased in this, makes that a reprobate;[419]
Before the children had done good or ill
Reveals the intent of his free-moving will,
And manifests his great prerogative

[cdxxiii] people serve *MS* people all serve *MSC*
[cdxxiv] was God's *MS* was not God's *MSC*
[cdxxv] one the other *MS* one to th'other *MSC*

[419] A strong assertion of double predestination, of the elect and the reprobate, drawing on Romans 9.10–16, cf. *R* 22. Milton denied that the reprobate were predestined and interpreted the Esau/Isaac story differently, *CPW* VI.168–202.

O'er all the creatures who their being derive
From his vast power which, bounded by no laws,
Acts freely without any second cause;
Though with their maker sinful men contend,
As if their narrow hearts could comprehend   90
His boundless power, forgetting they are dust,
According to their measures make him just,
Think men's deserts his recompenses guide,
His justice with an overweening pride
To their own balance bring: when on his breath
Alone depends all creatures' life and death,
And as merely of free grace life he gives,
So all the means by which his creature lives,
All sins that lead to death, are the effects
Of that free power which chooses or rejects.   100
Then happy he who on the Lord depends,
And without murmuring his decrees attends;
Who like the sacred prophet humbly says,
'Lord, though thou kill me, I thy name will
     praise.'[420]
    Isaac's corporal eyes were not more blind
Than the affections of his erring mind,
But, by the late events recovering sight,
His soul is struck with terrible affright
To find that he himself had given the doom
His darling should his brother's slave become.   110
As a stout man who with prevailing might
In civil war had slain his opposite,[421]
And, with glad haste run to despoil the dead,
Under the gilded helm had owned[422] the head
Of some dear friend whose dislodged soul had
     found
Unkind extrusion through his cruel wound,
Amazing horror all his senses fills;
From every limb cold clammy sweat distils;
The murderer like a marble statue stands

[420] Job 13.15.
[421] opponent
[422] recognized

By the pale corpse; his feeble knees and hands   120
By trembling only show he is alive.
So did it to the agèd man arrive
When now, the late occurrences revolved,
A trembling horror all his joints dissolved.
By God long since, by himself pronounced but
    late,
He sees his sons' irrevocable state,
And now acknowledges mortals in vain
Strive to prevent what God doth once ordain.
His wisdom human policy[423] befools,
And to his purpose man's powers ever rules,   130
Mocks at the silly worms whose brains work still
Fixing resolves, as if they could their will
Establish against what he hath decreed
Whose strong endeavours evermore succeed
Contrary to their own unfirm design,
Advancing that which they would most decline.
Old Isaac had not else so long delayed
The promised blessing to transfer, nor stayed
For venison now, whenas without it he
Might have his firstborn blessed (had he been free,   140
Not acted by a secret Providence
Whose workings were not obvious to his sense)
Then to the venison raised his appetite,
And framed th'occasion by which Jacob might
Surprise the promised blessing: this[424] withheld
Him when the different voice a doubt instilled
From giving credit to his ears: above
His more beguilèd touch, 'twas this did move
Him his own soul's misgiving to neglect,
That God's sure purpose might thus take effect.   150
    These things resolved in his disturbèd thoughts,
And he convinced thereby of his own faults
Who to the oracles of God so slight
Regard had given, nor having placed aright
His partial love, doted on him the Lord

---

[423] contrivance, statecraft
[424] i.e. Providence

As a profane wild reprobate abhorred;
Therefore at length he did his will submit
To God's; but could not altogether quit
His natural inclination. Yet he tries
His utmost and with strong faith fortifies   160
His frail heart, which, suppressing at the length
All human fondness,[425] gave his tongue the
   strength
To utter what was passed: 'Where is,' said he,
'Th'impostor that hath cheated thee and me,
Who before thine brought venison finely dressed
Of which I ate, and him my soul hath blessed?
Nor have I will or power to revoke
The promised blessing now already spoke.'
   A sad sense of his loss then Esau felt,
And did into a flood of sorrow melt,   170
But ah! too late: tears cannot now restore
The blessing he so much contemned before.
Chief of these native privileges he
For pottage sold, yet now he cries, 'Bless me,
Me also, O my dearest father bless!'
This prayer he made in his soul's bitterness.
Then Isaac said, 'The blessing I designed
For thee, but thee thy brother undermined.'
Esau replied, 'Makes he not good his name
Who by his subtle practice[426] twice became   180
Possessor of my rights? Hast thou let fall
Thy store[427] on him and left me none at all?'
Then answered Isaac: 'The supremacy
O'er all his brethren's his, and I have thee
His vassal made: him corn and wine I gave;
What now is left for thee, my son, to have?'
Then Esau, weeping, said, 'O search thy store:
Among thy blessings, hast thou not one more
Reservèd yet for me? pity my sad
Distress, and unto me one blessing add.'   190

---

[425] folly; affection
[426] deceit
[427] possessions

Then Isaac answered, 'Hear thy destinies.
Heaven thy land with fattening dew supplies.
Thy dwelling shall be in a fruitful ground,
With the earth's richest bounties ever crowned.
Thou by thy valour shalt thy life sustain,
But yet thy brother's vassal must remain
Till after a long tract of future time
Thy nephews shall to regal honour climb
And when they have their ancient fetters broke,
For evermore cast off his servile yoke.'   200
    Esau repined at this inferior fate
And, envying Jacob with a violent hate
For his large blessing, could not quite suppress
His deep resentment, but with bitterness
Against his fraud he privately inveighed
And secret bloody resolutions made
That whensoe'er his father Isaac died,
His thirst of vengeance should be satisfied
With Jacob's life. This by Rebecca's spies
Made known to her, she, prudent, doth advise   210
Jacob to make a politic retreat
Till length of time had cooled the violent heat
Of Esau's fury. He, persuaded, next
Pretends to Isaac that, her soul being vexed
With Esau's insolent wives, she to prevent
Jacob from marrying so would have him sent
To her own kindred, that no Hittite wife
Might add to the affliction of her life.
    What power like that of subtle women when
They exercise their skill to manage men,   220
Their weak force recompensed with wily arts!
While men rule kingdoms, women rule their hearts.
Her good persuasions happily succeed.
[Genesis 28]   Jacob's departure at that time decreed,
He, now approached to take his father's leave,
These blessings and instructions doth receive:
'My son,' said Isaac, 'this is my command,
That thou wed not a daughter of this land
But to thy mother's native country go
And woo her brother Laban to bestow   230

One of his daughters on thee for a wife;
And, having this a partner of thy life,
Let God Almighty thy chaste wedlock bless
With happy and abundant fruitfulness,
Thy pious nuptials crown, so prosper thee
That thou mayst multitude of people be.
Let Abraham's blessing upon thee descend
And unto all thy progeny extend.
The land which God to Abraham gave, where thou,
As he and I, art but a stranger now,   240
Let the inheritance of it be thine
And long continue in thy blessèd line.'
    This blessing only Isaac did provide
To furnish out his son, who had beside
No servants, horses, money, food, nor clothes.
Could tender parents thus their child expose
While they had flowing wealth to set him forth?
God's blessing is not of such little worth.
Whoever hath it carries with him more
Than all that's heaped in the vain worldling's store.   250
Full well the faithful patriarch understood
The Almighty's favourites want not any good.
As a small crystal stream which singly flows
From th'upper springs, augmenting as it goes,
At last becomes a great flood, and divides
Among the lower grounds his pleasant tides,
Such Jacob's fortunes were, who, well content
With the pure fountain of God's blessing, went
Unfurnished of all outward earthly things,
And, back returning, streams of plenty brings.   260
    Yet went he not thus unaccompanied
Because their trust on Providence relied,
For faith prohibits not that honest care
Wherewith the godly life's supplies prepare,
But contrary to this the sacred writ
Terms him an infidel who doth omit
The warranted provision for his own;[428]
But Jacob was dismissèd thus alone

---

[428] 1 Timothy 5.8.

T'avoid worse danger lest, his equipage
Making his journey known, his brother's rage   270
An opportunity might hereby gain
And he by treachery in the way be slain.
'Twas therefore thought convenient he should so
Depart as none might his departure know.
    The saddest circumstance was not yet past:
His dearest mother's farewell,[429] who at last,
Conquering her passions with a virtuous force,
Chased from her soul all womanish remorse,
Yet, shedding two full streams of pious tears,
With such kind words her banished darling cheers: 280
'My son, that I consent to thy remove
Is the effect of a triumphant love
Which parts with all the pleasure I enjoy
That my delights may not thy life destroy.
When thou art gone, I shall no comfort have
But that my griefs thee from thy brother's fury
    save.
I know by giving back his forfeit right
Perhaps he would be pleased, and so I might
Retain thee still: but Heaven forbid I should
For my own pleasure thus oppose thy good.   290
Fly to obtain the promises decreed,
Let steadfast hope thy fainting spirits feed;
In the distresses of thy wandering state,
Let God's sure word thy just soul recreate.
This land he doth for thee design
And will in time restore thee unto thine.
Give way unto thy brother's wrath a while,
And shun his sword by suffering an exile.
Too miserable should I be to have
Two sons at once go timeless[430] to their grave.   300
'Tis not love to the blessing doth incite
His furious wrath, but a malicious spite
Thou shouldst obtain the good he did despise.
Remove the hated object from his eyes

---

[429] The parting of Rebecca and Jacob is not described in Genesis.
[430] unseasonably

And that fire will consume itself at last.
Then, when the fervour of his rage is past,
I will recall thy banishment: now go.'
   Tears stopped her here. Alas, she did not know
This was the latest kiss she should receive;
Yet long her lips did to her darling's cleave,   310
Nor could poor Jacob with dry eyes depart.
A deathlike sadness did invade his heart
Which no free passage to his voice affords,
And when he heard her speak those loving words
Of calling him soon home, his grievèd mind
Did in itself an ill presaging find,
Which whispered him he should but^{cdxxvi} hope in
   vain
Ever to see those reverend looks again;
Nor was his augury false, for she deceased
Three years before his slavery was released,   320
And he at his return with sorrow found
His dear and prudent mother in the ground,
Who now, with a divided, doubtful heart,
'Twixt woe and joy sees her loved son depart,
Him to th'Almighty Guardian recommends
And on the promise patiently depends.
   Esau, now hearing how his brother went
By the strict order of his father sent
To fetch a wife from Syria and, departing thence,
Carried new blessings, he revolves[431] th'offence   330
Of his own matches and then, having weighed
How readily his brother had obeyed
Whose duty now this envious sinner thought
Would shine more bright by his opposèd fault,
He now designs his credit to redeem
And, though most impious, yet would pious seem;
Wherefore, to counterfeit obedience,
He goes to Ishmael's house, and brings from
   thence

cdxxvi not *MS* but *MSC*

[431] considers

Bashemath^{cdxxvii} whom Nebajoth's mother bore,
Ishmael's fair daughter, adding this wife more   340
To his unquiet Canaanitish dames.
Yet burns he still in their accursèd flames,
Nor doth those idol-worshippers remove
But still retains them in his guilty love.
True practice of dissembling hypocrites,
Who, cherishing within them sin's delights,
Outward obedience to God's will profess
And whate'er gives a fame of godliness
With violent and burning zeal they feign,
Yet closely[432] still their darling sins retain,   350
And, lying to God's holy spirit, add
A double guilt to what before they had.
'Tis probable that profane Esau might
The blessing with a fleshly appetite
Still covet only as it did include
Honour and wealth; for these, perhaps, pursued
With feignèd duty his lost father's love,
Striving his absent brother to remove
Or, at the least, endeavouring to prevent
That further loss his carriage[433] might augment.   360
But had not such a show to mend been forced,
He would those wicked women have divorced
And to his father's will his own resigned;
But he, alas, far otherwise inclined,
Only a plausible evasion sought
T'avoid the due reproaches of his fault.

Canto 19

[Genesis 28.10]   Poor Jacob, now exposed to banishment,
Forth from Beersheba towards Haran went,
But, overtaken with the hasty night
Whose spreading shades already veiled the light,

---

^{cdxxvii} Bathshemath

[432] secretly
[433] behaviour

He in the place a heap of rough stones found,
These for a pillow takes, and on the ground
His weary limbs distends,[434] nor long reposed
But gentle sleep his heavy eyelids closed.
   O how are mean men, if they know it, blessed![435]
They on the hard earth can find pleasant rest   10
When princes, rolling in their beds of plume,
With waking cares the tedious night consume.
Among the royal couches there are none
Afford such ease as this poor traveller's stone.
In his toiled brains no frightful dreams are bred
Nor starts he, wakened, with a guilty dread.
He who, unhoused, heaven's vast arch only covers
May sleep secure while restless care still hovers.
Where rich men lie their[cdxxviii] wealth requires a
   guard;
The poor man's sleeps are soft, though's bed be
   hard.   20
There are no terrors where the soul is pure,
But wicked greatness no watch can secure:
Still waking horror on the guilty waits,
With torturing conscience and her Hell-born mates
Despair, Suspicion, Dread, and dismal Woe,
Whence frightful melancholy visions flow
Whenever slumbers close the heavy eyes;
But where sweet Contemplation minds employs,
The dreams feed that pure soul with fresh delight,
Repeating the day's comforts in the night.   30
   Whate'er employs the busy force of thought
While mortals wake, by nimble Fancy brought
Back to their view in sleep again appears,
Mocking their charmèd touches, eyes and ears.
Thus the rough soldier who in war delights
Dreams of scaled forts, long marches, bloody fights;

[cdxxviii] where the rich man lies his *MS* Where rich men lie their *MSC*

[434] stretches out
[435] On rural sleep cf. LH's verses on retirement from a now-lost manuscript, *M* 339; on sleep as recreating daytime thoughts cf. *L* 4.1019–80.

The ploughman dreams of his new-springing grain,
The gripple[436] usurer[cdxxix] of his coming gain,
The labourer of his toil, the awful[437] slave
Of the last harsh commands his stern lord gave,   40
The scholar in his sleeps old authors reads,
At wrangling bars the glib-tongued lawyer pleads,
The wanton new young lovers entertains,
The knowledge of new fucuses[438] or fashions gains,
Invading foes and treasons kings affright,
Loose courtiers dream of bravery[439] and delight,
Seamen that the rough winds the seas deform
And all the billows crowd into a storm,
Of distant shores, strange islands, horrid rocks,
Deep gulfs, and all the ocean's monstrous flocks;   50
The planter grafts his pear-trees, prunes his vines,
Gathers his ripe fruits, tuns[440] his new-pressed
    wines;
These and a thousand waking actions more
The vigorous Fancy doth in sleep restore.
Other dreams from the temper rise, and some
From diabolical illusions come.
With natural dreams sometimes good spirits do
Mix warnings of those evils which ensue.
Sometimes when sleeps the fleshly senses bind,
God represents to the unbusied mind   60
In visions the events which he prepares,
For mortal men the ways of bliss declares,
Or else discovers hidden mysteries
Wherein his dear saints' consolation lies.
    Such in his desolate lodging Jacob found,
Who sees a ladder standing on the ground,
The top up to high Heaven advanced, from
    whence

[cdxxix] usurer *MS* us'rer *MSC*

[436] miserly
[437] fearful
[438] cosmetics
[439] finery
[440] stores in a barrel

The angels waiting on God's Providence
Perpetually in thick troops made descent
And back to heaven by the same steps went:^{cdxxx}   70
To heaven where his penetrating sight
Beholds the glorious uncreated light,
Where at the ladder's top Jehovah stood
And thus his lasting promises renewed:
'I am that God whom Abraham did before,
And since, thy father Isaac did adore.
The land on which thou liest, I have decreed
To give it unto thee and thy blessed seed,
Which I will make as numerous as the sands,
Dilate to th'east, west, north, and southern lands.   80
Blessings unto the whole earth's families
From thee and thy successors shall arise.
Lo, I am with thee and in every place
Where'er thou goest will be thy guard; my grace
Shall thee in all thy wanderings sustain
And to this land conduct thee back again.
Till all my promises accomplished be
I will in no distress abandon thee.'
    This said, himself again the Almighty shrouds,
The vision vanished with the shutting clouds,   90
And Jacob starts from sleep: then horror chilled
His blood, amazement his whole bosom filled
Till, recollecting his disturbèd sense,
Converting his wild dread to reverence,
His soul into a pious admiration breaks
And thus with trembling lips the patriarch speaks:
'Surely Jehovah is conversant here,
And it did not to my dull sense appear
How dreadful⁴⁴¹ is this place: sure 'tis God's court,
And heaven is entered by this sacred port.'⁴⁴²   100
    Night's chariot hasted on, by swift Hours drawn,
And the next day brought on his early dawn,

---

^{cdxxx} back to heaven by the same stepps went *MS* back to heav'n by the same stepps they went *MSC*

⁴⁴¹ awe-inspiring
⁴⁴² gate

When with like diligence as dames that feel
The spur of urging need rise to the wheel,
Rake by the cinders, and rush-candles light,
Calling their drowsy maids up while 'tis night,
Then ply their tasks and labour hard to gain
An honest maintenance for their small train,[443]
The son of Isaac from his hard bed rose,
The stone on which he did that night repose   110
Erects and consecrates unto the Lord,
And like a pillar sets it to record
The memorable vision; then adores,
And oil upon his rustic altar pours,
Calls the place Bethel and here makes a vow,
Saying, 'If God grant me his presence now,
If he protect me in the way I go,
If easy food and raiment he bestow,
Me to my father's house in peace restore,
Then will I for my God the Lord adore.   120
This stone which I a pillar make shall be
The house of God when he enricheth me.
Whate'er God gives me, tithe of everything
I here will to his holy altar bring.'
    Yet ere we part from Bethel once again,
We must review the vision and explain
What God did there to him, and us, intend,
For hereon many mysteries depend.
This ladder as to Jacob signifies
His mortal progress, which from th'earth doth rise   130
Till he Heaven's archèd palaces ascend.
The angels marching up and down defend
Him from the anxious danger of the way.
God stands above and doth his paths survey
Who, guarded by his providential care,
'Scapes the wild hunter Esau's murdering snare,
Now on the ground secured from wild beasts sleeps.
No killing serpent near his lodging creeps.
In spite of Laban's fraud, he largely thrives,
Wealthy and safe at home again arrives.   140

[443] followers, household

This as to him, but not to him alone:
By this the pilgrimage of all saints shown
Informs us that while Christians climb on high
By the harsh steps of crosses, poverty,
Scorn, persecution, self-denial, hate,
The austere progress of a Christian state,
God still is present, all their sufferings knows,
He watches over them, regards their woes,
Assures them of his never-failing aid
When Danger and the monster Death invade,   150
Over whose powers by him they shall prevail
And at the last Heaven's glorious palace scale,
There at their father's house sit down in peace
And share those perfect joys which never cease.
And all along till this sad journey's end
An host of angels on their steps attend,
Carrying their fervent prayers to God on high
And bringing down his liberal supply
By whom their labours never are forgot,
Who still is present though they see it not.   160
   Yet doth this ladder higher things display:
This ladder is the Christian's only way,
The blessed Messiah, Heaven's gate, by whom
The saints into his Father's glory come,
The mediator between Earth and Heaven
From the eternal Father's bosom given,
Whose Godhead, with the human nature joined
To the eternal comfort of mankind,
Remains the way to 'scape Hell's conquering
      powers
And climb up to the high celestial towers.   170
His merit and his intercession are alone
The stairs by which from God's eternal throne
His sacred ministers bring to mankind
The sweet refreshments they from his grace find,
And when death throws down this frail house of
      clay
Pious souls back to eternal[cdxxxi] rest convey.

[cdxxxi] to eternall *MS* t'eternall *MSC*

God stands at top still ready to receive
Those dear souls whom the holy angels heave.[444]

[Genesis 29]   Confident hope to Jacob's feet adds wings
And him to Nahor's land in short space brings.   180
Now the declining sun was hurried fast
Down the Hesperian[445] hill. The pilgrim passed
Then through a wild and untracked forest where
No sign of human dwellings did appear.
But he who in's first lodging on the ground
Visions of God and blessèd angels found
No solitary horror now can dread:
Each flowery bank a sweet perfumèd bed,
The starry sky a glorious roof esteems,
Soft air better than silken curtains seems.   190
Yet now under a tuft of agèd trees
Three shepherds resting with their flocks he sees,
Who while they there for their companions stayed
Invite him to their hospitable shade;
For courtesy then had not left the plains
But made her dwelling amongst gentle swains.
From these he learned that Providence had
    brought
His weary steps near to the place he sought,
That these belonged to Laban's city; he
Yet lived and flourished in prosperity.   200
Then Jacob asks the shepherds why they stay
There with their flocks, since the declining day
Had so much empire left as that they might
Well fill themselves before th'approaching night.
The men replied, 'There is an ample well
Hid with that mighty stone, where all that dwell
In Haran their dry flocks to water drive;
But until all the other flocks arrive
We are forced to stay because that weighty stone
Is more than a few men can move alone.   210
Nor long will they our expectation mock;
For lo, fair Rachel comes with Laban's flock,

---

[444] exalt (not necessarily in the modern physical sense)
[445] Western (Hesperus = the evening star)

And she's the only loadstone, the bright star
By whose light all our youth attracted are;
Yet she her thoughts pure as her looks doth keep,
Harbours no care but for her flock of sheep,
Who, of their guardian proud, before her play
Whilst all the amorous shepherds pine away,
Whose courtship she nor scorns nor entertains.
Of a successful rival none complains,   220
For her^{cdxxxii} lovers all the same indifference find,
And yet her coldness is of such a kind,
So managed, it a reverence begets,
And higher value on her beauties sets.
Now let your own eyes judge her wondrous face,
See how she moves on with becoming grace.'
   And then indeed the shepherdess drew nigh,
On whom as soon as Jacob fixed his eye,
Like one that suddenly out of dark rooms
Into the open glorious sunshine comes,   230
Awhile his dazzled eyes quite lost their sight,
Which was restored again even by that light
That troubled them before, and now doth find
Such winning sweetness with that splendour joined
That his delighted soul dwells in his eyes
And renders them so vigorous they surprise
The virgin's heart, whose youthful innocence
Made her yet think she needed no defence.
As when black clouds the face of heaven deform,
He who i'the open field would shun the storm   240
Runs to the shelter of a neighbouring oak,
Which, falling with the thunder's sudden stroke,
So his amazèd sense confounds that he
Long time remains in the uncertainty
Of his own life: so Jacob stood till, strength
Of virtue recollecting at the length
His scattered powers, he undisturbèd views
That beauty which with no less force subdues
His guarded heart than cannons which beat down
Before them all the ramparts of a town.   250

^{cdxxxii} For her *MS* her *MSC*

Finding himself then vanquished in the field,
That he the fort on generous terms might yield
To his fair foe he comes, whose kind rays melt
His gentle temper. Nature's force he felt
Contending with the late intruder, Love,
Which should more powerful in his bosom prove.
He tells her who he is, nor then forbears
To claim that dear relation with joy's tears.
To serve her then he bends his chief desires,
And Love a more than human force inspires.   260
His active limbs obey his eager mind,
Nor can he any difficulty find
In that he undertakes for her: the stone
Which all the shepherds did require, alone
He rolls from the well's mouth, with drink
   relieves
Her thirsty flock. She thankfully receives
His service, to her father tells these things.
Forth to his nephew Laban runs and brings
Him with glad welcome back. Jacob obeyed,
But with fair Rachel rather would have stayed   270
And put her tender lambs up in the fold.
   He cares no other object to behold,
Yet must he now a new one entertain:
Her elder sister, who becomes a pain
At first sight to his eyes, for hers were sore
And had that weakness no art could restore.
Unhappy maid! they only could let in
Love's arrows, but ne'er shot them back again.
She strove with studied courtesy and art
In time to circumvent the unyielding heart,   280
But 'twas too late t'attempt a fortress where
Her sister's conquering powers already were.
Who never had that tempting beauty seen
With her sweet carriage might perhaps have been
At length allured; but of that noble kind
Was Rachel's beauty that it showed a mind
Worthy of such a cabinet: Nature the mould
Formed to those gemlike virtues it should hold.
Vigour and courage in her bright eyes shone,

On the large[446] forehead wisdom had a throne.   290
A blushing modesty, accompanied
With tempting sweetness, did her motions guide.
The opening of her lips was eloquence,
They moved with such a taking innocence.
In every smile was gentleness and truth,
With that becoming joy that sets off youth.
Perfection was her shape, her gestures grace,
In every limb the beauty of a face.
Her voice was harmony, her radiant hair
Chaste Love's strong band, not lust's alluring
    snare.   300
Purity her complexion was, which no change felt:
Love's hot blasts never could that chaste snow
    melt.
Like steel that strikes the flint, she kindled fire,
But in herself ne'er harboured loose desire.
Yet was she not insensible of Love
That would a stain to all her beauties prove,
But when that fire into her bosom came
It burnt as purely as a martyr's flame.
Kindred and sympathy produced it at the first,
Which after virtuous conversation nursed;   310
Then Jacob's merit gave it stronger food,
Which she received, urged by just[cdxxxiii] gratitude.
    In vain poor Leah used her powerless charms.
Few are their conquests who want beauty's arms,
But where attractive grace and fair looks join,
Let single force its vain pretence[447] decline:
For easier may you the firm rocks remove
Than change the purpose of a well-fixed love,
Which, being once seated in a generous[cdxxxiv] mind,
No difficulty can[cdxxxv] in nature find   320
That it surmounts not, with delight t'acquire

[cdxxxiii] that *MS* just *MSC*
[cdxxxiv] being once seated in a generous *MS* being seated in a gen'rous *MSC*
[cdxxxv] No difficultie can *MS* Can no difficultie *MSC*

[446] wide
[447] claim

The dear enjoyment of that strong desire.
For this Jacob, the heir of promise, makes
Himself his uncle's hireling, undertakes
Seven years' harsh service, labouring without pain
Rachel, his dearest bargain, to obtain.
    He thought the long time short when once
      expired,
And as a cheap-bought treasure now required
His earnèd wife. The father yields; the guests
Are now invited to the nuptial feasts;   330
The joyful bridegroom, almost ecstasied,[448]
Attends the hour to meet his fairest bride;
Brought with due ceremony to her bed,
His joys with banquets of fruition fed.
The rosy morn her eastern gates displayed,
And sent forth beams with chaste night's
    treacherous shade;
Night which to Leah's lust, and Laban's fraud,
Had been a secret and pernicious bawd.
As some brave chief, scaling an enemy's town,
Whose valour from the battlements had tumbled
    down   340
The weak defendants and his standard placed
Upon the same walls where his foes were chased,
Thinking himself a conqueror while all
The wretched foes that come before him fall,
By's own false troops ill seconded behind,
The fort he thought his prize his prison finds:
So was poor Jacob lost in wild amaze
When, thinking on fair Rachel's unveiled[cdxxxvi]
    brows to gaze,
He meets her elder sister's blearèd eyes.
    What throng of passions did his soul surprise!   350
He starts from bed, conceiving such a hate
'Gainst Leah that he scorns t'expostulate
With her, now uglier by her impudence,

cdxxxvi Rachells vnveyld browes *MS* Rachells browes *MSC*

448 transported

But to his uncle urges home th'offence;
Which with pretexts h'endeavoured to excuse,
Told him they did not in^{cdxxxvii} that country use
Younger before the elder to bestow;
But if his discontents he would not show
Till Leah's seven days' feast should be expired,
And seven years more for Rachel would be hired   360
Before his work, his bargain should be paid
And Rachel's wedding too the next week made.
Jacob, whose deep offence could not remove
The fixed foundation of his ardent love,
Gives his assent to the harsh terms required,
And love conceals the rage which first it fired
Yet when he thought that Rachel gave consent
And that she had a power to prevent.
Unhappy she, whose designs only could
Do others mischief and herself no good,   370
For of all plagues women can share, the worst
Is with a loved husband's hatred to be cursed.
With smiling rays at last the wished day shined
Which the right bride unto her lover joined.
Her joys alone th'enamoured husband prized.
    This found insulting⁴⁴⁹ Rachel, and despised
Her hated sister. God, who humbles pride
And pities the afflicted, then denied
Children to beauteous Rachel, and her whom
He made not fair, blessed with a fruitful womb.   380
Thus the Almighty with wise Providence
Amongst his creatures doth his gifts dispense:
None can boast all, and none are left so poor
But they have some supply from that large store.
God doth good portions for each child provide,
Yet few with their own shares are satisfied,
But other lots prefer, as Rachel, blessed
With beauty and her husband's love, no rest
Of soul attained in these dear solid joys,

^{cdxxxvii} not that *MS* not in that *MSC*

⁴⁴⁹ triumphing

Which envy of her sister's fruit destroys.   390
Meanwhile despisèd Leah, a mother made,
In her child's name her husband doth upbraid:
'Behold, a son[450] from her who is not fair,
Behold, a son in answer of my prayer!
Though you my sister partially affect,[451]
God favours the distressed whom you neglect.
Fair sister, though you steal his heart away,
See, in this son his hate I better pay
Than you his love; but now my griefs the Lord
Hath seen, and I shall be no more abhorred,   400
Children shall me my husband's love procure,
Another son God's favour did assure.'
Him she called Simeon,[452] saying, 'In my sad state
God hears my sufferings by my husband's hate,
And with this son my fainting hope relieves.'
　　Now envious Rachel with impatience grieves;
Her swelling passions she no more contains
In reason's bounds; prudence no longer reigns
In her wild breast. 'Jacob', with a fiery[cdxxxviii] cry
She urges, 'give me children or I die!   410
What boots my beauty, your unfruitful love:
My hated sister can a mother prove,
And hopes, whatever fatal chance arrive,
In her succeeding issue to survive.
Time[cdxxxix] crops my fading beauties, every day
Some part of my frail glory bears away,
And man's love still declines at the same rate
As time doth women's loveliness abate;
But fruit in wedlock is a lasting tie:
Give me this blessing, then, or I shall die.'   420

cdxxxviii fiery *MS* fierce *MSC*
cdxxxix Times

[450] The contest of names between Leah and Rachel is overlaid with huge philological complexities; the episode splices together different narratives and was designed to offer genealogies of the tribes of Israel and Judah. Commentators still disagree on the exact wordplay in some cases; the commentary can only indicate some approximations in line with LH's own interpretation. 'Behold, a son' is a translation of 'Reuben'.
[451] love
[452] Simeon was linked with the Hebrew word for 'he heard'.

Her wild desire then Jacob reprehends:
'Am I,' said he, 'that God on whom depends
All human comforts? Is't not he by whom
Thou art denied the blessings of the womb?'
Calmed with this just reproof, she only prayed
Her husband to accept her waiting-maid,
Whose children, since the Lord had given her none,
She might adopt and breed up for her own.
Jacob assents, a son the handmaid bears,
When Rachel, saying, 'The Lord hath heard my
      prayers   430
And judged,^{cdxl} this blessing me from scorn
      redeems,'
Called his name Dan. Again her servant teems;
Him she calls Naphtali;⁴⁵³ 'For,' said she, 'sad
Contests long have I with my sister had,
And now prevailed'; though both the former year
And this Leah did also children bear,
Of whom the first she Levi⁴⁵⁴ called, to tell
She hoped her husband now with her would dwell;
Judah⁴⁵⁵ the fourth, t'express that praise
She owed the Lord; and now her thick births stays.   440
[Genesis 30]   Could her prophetic soul have known before
Who should descend of him that last she bore,
Well might she've been content to cease this birth,
Producing him whose son must bless the earth;
But then she wanted this foreseeing light,
And, jealous lest her sister's children might
In time as numerous as her issue grow,
She, too, on Jacob doth her maid bestow,
Whose pregnant womb in due time did^{cdxli} disclose
Another son. 'Fortune,' said Leah, 'flows   450

---

^{cdxl} judged] *ed.* leydg'd *MS; cf. Genesis* 30.6
^{cdxli} time disclose *MS* time did disclose *MSC*

⁴⁵³ Hebrew for 'my wrestling'.
⁴⁵⁴ Hebrew for 'he will become attached'. LH here departs from the order of the Genesis narrative, which records all Leah's children together.
⁴⁵⁵ Hebrew for 'I will give praise'. Commentators referred to the genealogy of Christ at Matthew 1.2.

In a full channel: Gad then be thy name,
By whom my single blessings troops became.'[456]
Another son her handmaid bears, and this
She Asher names, acknowledging her bliss.[457]
'Me,' said she, 'all the neighbouring daughters
　　shall
A happy and a fruitful mother call.'
Her eldest son then mandrakes finds and brings,
As children use to do all new gay things,
The purchase to his mother. Rachel spies
And longs for these, which she of Leah buys　　　　460
For Jacob's company that night, and then,
Her fallow womb conceiving fruit again,
She bore a son called Issachar,[458] and said,
'In this hath God mine and my maid's hire paid.'
Again she teems; 'Ah, surely now,' she cried,
'My husband now in my tents will abide';
Wherefore she calls him Zebulon.[459] One more,
Though of another sex, completes her store:
Dinah,[460] whose fatal beauty must in time
Cause Sechem's lustful, Simeon's barbarous crime.　470
Now childless Rachel, by affliction taught
A better temper, God humbly besought,
And he, at length regarding her distress,
Removed the causes of her barrenness.
Now with desirèd fruit she pregnant grows,
And Jacob's darling doth to light expose.
Joseph[461] she names him, saying, 'Since God hath
　　had
Pity on my long sufferings, he will add
More comforts yet, nor here his favours stay,
Since this hath taken my reproach away.'　　　　480

---

[456] Genesis 30.1: Hebrew for 'in luck'.
[457] Hebrew for 'good fortune'.
[458] Hebrew for 'my reward'.
[459] Hebrew for 'habitation'.
[460] Related by commentators to Greek for 'judgement'.
[461] A double etymology: J links the name with Hebrew for 'may he add', E with 'has taken away'.

Canto 20

[Genesis 30.25]   Twice seven years now Jacob[cdxlii] for Rachel hired;
The last of these at Joseph's birth expired,
When to his uncle Laban he addressed
And free dismission to his own home pressed
With all his wives and children, sole rewards
Of his long service. Laban, who regards
Not any man's convenience but his own,
By Jacob's faithful service wealthy grown,
Entreats his longer stay, bids him require
What terms he would: he might make his own hire.   10
At length they covenant to draw the flock,
That all the spotless should be Laban's stock
And Jacob's none but those whom Nature brands.
These, parted and put into several hands,
In distant pastures far asunder feed.
Jacob's in short time large increases[cdxliii] breed,
For, by an angel taught, he peeled rods throws
Into the watering-place, which on the ewes
Coming to drink such strong impressions wrought
That they speckled and ring-straked[462] young ones
    brought,   20
But only these before the strong ones laid,
Which from the weak removed,[463] by this means
    made
Jacob in short time goodly flocks possess,
For God did strangely all his labours bless.
Men, maids, goats, camels, sheep – which was alone
The riches of the world in those days known –
Jacob abundantly enjoyed; whose fame
Great as his riches grew till he became
[Genesis 31]   The envy of Laban's worthless sons, and they,

[cdxlii] yeares Jacob *MS* yeares now Jacob *MSC*
[cdxliii] encreaseth *MS* encreases *MSC*

[462] surrounded by coloured bands
[463] I.e. he laid them only before the strong ones and removed them when the weak came to drink.

Murmuring at his augmented fortunes, say: 30
'This wretch who, flying from his brother's hate,
Came hither a poor needy runagate,[464]
Himself hath with our ravished glories crowned,
While in our father's wealth his stores abound.'
Laban himself no more good looks allows
This envied nephew; with contracted brows
He, on the sudden growing cool and strange,
Betrays his ill intents by's outward change.
  This Jacob sees, suspects some bad design,
And prudently prepares a countermine.[465]   40
When in his soul his plots revolvèd deep,
Again God's angel visits him asleep,
Exhorts him to return without delay,
Assures him of his conduct in the way.
Wherewith confirmed, as soon as the next light
Gilded the east, preparing for his flight,
Laban now gone[cdxliv] to shear his sheep, he takes
This opportunity; and first he makes
His wives acquainted, tells them of the wrong
Their brethren did him, urges then the long   50
Harsh servitude he had for them sustained,
Th'advantage Laban by his travails[466] gained,
Who now beholds him with such altered eyes
As show some mischief in his bosom lies.
His injuries having oft been multiplied,
His wages changed and his return denied,
God by a vision did at last inspire
Him with a thought in secret to retire,
If they would give a kind and quick consent
And, while they might, their father's plots
    prevent.[467]   60
The sisters then replied: 'Long since were we
Thrown off and sold from Laban's family.

[cdxliv] Laban to *MS* Laban now gone to *MSC*

[464] runaway
[465] counter-plot
[466] labours
[467] forestall

Freeborn, he set us at a sordid price
Like slaves, not daughters; to his avarice
He gave us up, detained from us our dowers,
And now his sons, consuming what is ours,
Unthankfully at thy just gains repine;
Why should we not, then, in thy purpose join?
Can we in Laban's house pretend a share
Who never found but harsh unkindness there,   70
And are we not obliged to go with thee
Who at so dear a rate thy purchase be?'
This quick compliance cut off all delay,
Mounted on camels now they steal away.
Thorough Euphrates' fords their flocks they drive,
And at Mount Gilead undisturbed arrive.
    Three days ere Laban knew their flight were past,
But, hearing the unwelcome news, at last
He to his gods in furious passion went
T'inquire why they did not this chance prevent.   80
Vain, superstitious fool's hope, aid to have
Of senseless images that could not save
Themselves from Rachel's theft. For, yet her mind
Unto her youth's idolatry inclined,
Or to the idol-maker's art at best,
She had stolen, unknown to Jacob and the rest,
Her father's gods: which loss afflicts him more
Than his defeat and all their flight before.
Together then he all the kindred draws,
Tells them his loss for the religious cause.   90
Each man puts on his arms, mounts his swift steed,
And follows Jacob's track with furious speed.
As hounds laid on and trained[cdxlv] [468] by a fresh
    scent,
The whole troop with unanimous ardour went,
Boasting[cdxlvi] in their great zeal so to exact
A vengeance for the sacrilegious fact.[469]

[cdxlv] layd on on *MS* layd on and traind by *MSC*
[cdxlvi] Glorying *MS* Boasting *MSC*

[468] enticed
[469] crime

Under devotion's name thus do they hide
The rage of their own envy, hate, and pride,
Perhaps even from themselves: mistaken zeal
Hath made more wounds than Gilead's balm[470]
    can heal;   100
Engaged rash erring multitudes oft-times
Into rebellious parricidal crimes;
Made regal shepherds kill the gentle sheep
Which the Almighty gave them charge to keep;
Made subjects 'gainst their sovereigns to conspire,
With civil discord set the world on fire,
Made fathers sons and sons their fathers slay,
Brought flourishing kingdoms into sad decay;
For when the priests war's silver trumpets sound,
Cruelty rages without any bound,   110
And none more ardently pursue those fights
Than impious and dissembling hypocrites,
Ravished with joy to find that fair pretence
A cover for their native violence.[471]
    Thus Laban furiously his march pursues
Seven days, till he upon Mount Gilead views
The tents of Jacob now securely spread,
Who with fair Syria's plains forsook his dread.
But what success?[472] poor mortals can assure
Still no rest, perishing when most secure.   120
As Jacob cast about his fearless eyes,
Under the hill a glittering light he spies,
For Phoebus, hasting to the western streams,
Gilt Laban's armour with his setting beams.
The unlooked-for spectacle surprised his sight
And to his soul conveyed such dire affright
As merchants have who with swift sails and oars

---

[470] Jeremiah 8.22.
[471] Cf. *M* 58: 'We have spiritual weapons given us for spiritual combats, and those who go about to conquer subjects for Christ with swords of steel shall find the base metal break to shivers when it is used and hurtfully fly in their own faces ... the Roman prelate and his tyrannical clergy ... by degrees had so encroached upon all the secular princes that they were nothing but vassals and hangmen to the proud insolent Priest who, obtaining his empire by fraud, false doctrine, lies and hypocrisy, maintained it by blood and rapine'.
[472] result

From pirates fly till their own native shores
Appear in view, and, slackening then their haste
Where they the assurance of their safety placed,   130
By some more daring man-of-war pursued
And even in the harbour's mouth subdued,
On whom their chains fall with a sadder weight
Than if they'd in wide seas met the same fate.
But Jacob must abide it, now the night
And craggy mountain both oppose his flight.
His thoughts he then with noble courage arms,
Stands Envy's shocks, contemning Fortune's
   harms,
Sees Laban's harnessed troops climb the ascent
And in the midway pitched his spacious tent,   140
Where he, retired, doth with his friends advise;
But Jacob only on the Lord relies,
And well he might: for God at first did send
An unseen guard of angels to attend
His servant home, though yet he knew it not,
And Bethel's certain vision had forgot.
These Laban and his troops could have delayed
Or led them to wrong paths and while they strayed
Carried off Jacob safe.[473]

---

[473] Cf. Genesis 32.1–2. In fact Jacob conciliates Laban and reaches agreement with him; but soon afterwards he finds himself in new danger from Esau. 'Thus God is pleased to give his servants interchangeable causes of comforts and fears, that they may still be exercised for their spiritual proficiency' (*Westminster Annotations*, Genesis 32.9). Owen, *Works* XVIII.223, writes that Esau might have destroyed Jacob before he entered Canaan: 'In the promise about which their contest was, the blessed Seed, with the whole church-state and worship of the old testament, was included: so that it was the greatest controversy, and had the greatest weight depending on it, of any that ever was amongst the sons of men'. God will appear to Jacob as a wrestler and announce the change of his name to Israel. The poem thus breaks off at a point when very important matter was impending. LH compared her husband's enemies at the time of his arrest in 1663 to Laban and Esau, *M* 303.

Appendix
— Elegy 3: Another on — the Sunshine[i]

Heaven's glorious eye, which all the world surveys,
This morning through my window shot his rays,
Where with his hateful and unwelcome beams
He gilt the surface of affliction's streams.
In anger at their bold intrusion, I
Did yet into a darker covert fly;
But they, like impudent suitors brisk and rude,
Me even to my thickest shade pursued;
Whom when I saw that I could nowhere shun,
I thus began to chide th'immodest sun: 10
   'How, gaudy masker, darest thou look on me
Whose sable coverings thy reproaches be?
Thou to our murderers thy taper bear'st;
Th'oppressive race of men thou warm'st and
   cheer'st;
The blood which thou hast seen pollutes thy light
And renders it more hateful than the night
All good men loathe. You're grown a common bawd,
The brave that lead'st impieties abroad;
Who smiling dost on lust and rapine shine,
Nor shrinkst thy head in at disgorgèd wine   20
Which sinners durst not let thee see before;[1]

---

[i] Text: from Nottinghamshire Archives, DD/HU2, pp. 9—11, modernized (for original, see 'Elegies').

[1] Cf. the denunciation of wine in *Order and Disorder* 8.

Now thy conniving looks they dread no more,
Because thou mak'st their pleasant gardens grow
And cherishest the fruitful seeds they sow
In fields which unto them descended not,
By violence, bribery and oppression got.
Thou sawst the league of God himself dissolved,
Which a whole nation in one curse involved;[2]
Thou sawst a thankless people slaughtering those
Whose noble blood redeemed them from their foes;　　30
Thy stainèd beams into the prison came
But lost their boasts, outshined with virtue's flame;[3]
Thou saw'st the innocent to exile led;
And for all this veild'st not thy radiant head,
But com'st as a gay courtier to deride
Ruins we would in silent shadows hide.
　'Since, then, thou wilt thrust into this dark room,
By thine own light read thy most certain doom:
Darkness shall shortly quench thy impure light
And thou shalt set in everlasting night.　　　　　　40
Those whom thou flattered'st shall see thee expire
And have no light but their own funeral fire.
There shall they in a dreadful wild amaze
At once see all their glorious idols blaze.
Thy sister, the pale empress of the night,[4]
Shall nevermore reflect thy borrowed light.
Into black blood shall her dark body turn
While your polluted spheres about you burn,
And the elemental heaven like melting lead
Drops down upon the impious rebels' head.[5]　　　50
Then shall our king his shining host display,
At whose approach our mists shall fly away,
And we, illuminated by his sight,
No more shall need thy ever-quenchèd light.'

---

[2] Probably a reference to the Solemn League and Covenant (1643), in which England and Scotland united for religious reformation (*M* 154); Presbyterians and Independents each blamed the other for its eventual collapse.
[3] Several of the 'Elegies' discuss her husband's martyrdom in prison.
[4] Cf. *Order and Disorder* 2.158.
[5] Revelation 6.12–14.

Further Reading

Lucy Hutchinson

There is no full-length study of Lucy Hutchinson. Her own autobiography survives only in a fragment printed in 1806 from a manuscript now lost, and included in all editions of the *Memoirs*. The most accurate and up-to-date account of her life comes in de Quehen's introduction to his edition of Hutchinson's Lucretius. Keeble 1990 discusses Hutchinson's self-representation in the *Memoirs*. Sutherland's old-spelling edition of the *Memoirs* was the first to print (virtually) the entire manuscript; Keeble's modernized edition restores a further passage. Firth's edition, though textually incomplete, is still very useful for annotations and for reproducing passages from the manuscript drafts. MacGillivray gives an excellent account of the *Memoirs* in relation to contemporary historiography; see also Norbrook 2000b and forthcoming. Barbour, 1994, 1997, 1998, and de Quehen discuss the Lucretius translation. Narveson identified *T* as a translation from Owen.

Apart from the 1679 *Order and Disorder*, none of Hutchinson's works was printed in her lifetime. Most of her manuscripts descended through John Hutchinson's half-brother Charles to Julius Hutchinson, who published the *Memoirs* in 1806. This stimulated wide interest, leading to the publication in 1817 of two further manuscripts (*R*) and (*T*). There was then a long gap, during which many manuscripts were dispersed, until the Lucretius translation was published in 1996. A complete edition of her works, including *Order and Disorder*, is in progress under the general editorship of David Norbrook.

The Study of Genesis

Williams offers a useful survey of commentators on Genesis, less satis-
factory in its coverage of the later seventeenth century, where Bennett
and Mandelbrote provide an introduction. Hutchinson records that her
husband found the *Dutch Annotations* too short; it is not clear that she
drew particularly on any one commentary, though Calvin's would have
been important for her. Willet is a representative English commentary;
Ainsworth was popular in the mid-century; Whately offers character-
sketches of leading figures which often contrast interestingly with Hutchinson's. Norton provides an overview of English Bibles in the period.
Stimulating modern commentaries on Genesis include Alter and Bloom;
Schwartz offers a postmodern approach. Bach gives a useful overview
of feminist Biblical scholarship; with special reference to Genesis, see
Brenner and Jeansonne.

Milton and Biblical Epic

Paradise Lost has overshadowed the study of other Biblical poems in
the period, and Milton criticism offers much to illuminate *Order and
Disorder*. The only comparative discussions of the two poems to date
are by Moore and Wittreich. Lewalski 1985 discusses Biblical amongst
other genres; Ashton and Taylor discuss Du Bartas in relation to Milton.
Hardie explores Lucretian influence. Fowler's edition offers a comprehensive overview of *Paradise Lost* criticism and scholarship. Norbrook
1999a, ch. 10, gives a paradigm of the republican epic which applies to
Order and Disorder as well as *Paradise Lost*; Knoppers's discussion of
Paradise Lost and Restoration politics has much relevance for *Order
and Disorder*. The very large body of Biblical poetry by Dissenters in
the later seventeenth century – outside Milton – remains remarkably
underexplored, but will be discussed by Achinstein.

Seventeenth-century Women Writers

New scholarship continues to bring to light more and more work by
early modern women writers. The excellent annotated bibliography of
printed writings by Smith and Cardinale is by no means complete. Nor

does it include manuscript writings, which formed an important part of the period's literary culture for both men and women (Ezell 1987, 1993). For manuscript compilations by women see also the website of Nottingham Trent University's Perdita Project (http://human.ntu.ac.uk/ Perdita/PERDITA.htm). No doubt there are many more anonymous works which, like *Order and Disorder*, have been wrongly assumed without further examination to be by male authors. Greer et al. is a pioneering anthology of women's poetry. Lewalski 1993 discusses earlier seventeenth-century women writers; Hobby gives a wide-ranging survey of mid-century women writers with a special emphasis on religion; on women and religion see further Crawford, Hinds, Mack, and the anthologies by Wilcox and by Garman et al. On women in politics see especially Hughes, and Mendelson and Crawford, ch. 7, and on royalist women poets see Barash. Norbrook, forthcoming, offers some speculations about links between Hutchinson and Margaret Cavendish.

Theology

Hutchinson gives her own views in *R* and her summary of Owen in *T*. On the politics of the 'Arminian' reaction against Calvinist theology in the 1620s and 1630s see *M* 53–4 and Tyacke. Nuttall gives a lucid, condensed and subtle account of the widening role of the Holy Spirit in Puritanism. Wallace discusses the debates over predestination after the Restoration; on Owen see Toon and the extensive introductions in *Works*. *R* is briefly discussed by Braund. Danielson discusses Milton's criticisms of Calvinism, which are further reconsidered by Fallon.

Politics after the Restoration

The recovery of *Order and Disorder* falls in with a larger revision of the politics of this period. Lucy Hutchinson is normally assumed to have fallen silent in her later years, crushed by defeat, in keeping with a general view that the outward-looking, highly politicized Puritans of the 1640s and 1650s became the introverted Dissenters of the Restoration. When the view is from the mid-century the emphasis is likely to be negative, as in Hill 1984; for new perspectives see Ashcraft, De Krey, Greaves, Harris et al., and for an instructive study of how the Puritan enthusiasm and anger of the mid-century became rewritten for a later

Whig generation see Worden, 'Introduction'. Lacey offers a detailed narrative account of the Dissenters' relations with Parliament. Love explains the importance of circulation in manuscript rather than print in this period, often though by no means exclusively for political reasons. Keeble 1987 explores the writings of the Dissenters and their circulation.

Bibliography

Lucy Hutchinson

A Manuscripts

The main surviving manuscripts of Hutchinson's works are:

Nottinghamshire Archives, Nottingham:
DD/HU1: literary commonplace book with extracts in verse and prose, mainly in Hutchinson's hand, including passages from translations of Virgil by Sir John Denham and Sidney Godolphin, poetry by Thomas Carew, Edmund Waller and others.
DD/HU2: 'Elegies', in a scribal hand.
DD/HU3: religious commonplace book in Hutchinson's hand including notes on Calvin's *Institutes*, personal statements of belief dated 1667 and 1668, notes on sermons and some drafts of original verse.
DD/HU4: the life of Colonel Hutchinson, in Hutchinson's hand, followed by her transcription of his notes in his copy of the Bible.

James Marshall and Marie-Louise Osborn Collection, Beinecke Rare Book and Manuscript Library, Yale University:
Osborn Collection fb 100, the manuscript of *Order and Disorder*.

Northamptonshire Record Office:
MS Fitzwilliam Misc. vol. 793: treatise on religion addressed to her daughter (*R*): published 1817.

British Library
Additional MS 17018, fols. 213–17: reply to Waller, *A Panegyric of My Lord Protector*.

Additional MS 19333: Lucretius translation.
Additional MSS 25901, 39779, 46172N: account of John Hutchinson's services to Parliament, compiled in the mid-1640s and later used as a basis for the life.

Available in the early nineteenth century but currently unlocated are the manuscripts of the translation of John Owen (*T*) and a manuscript containing the autobiographical manuscript and some original poems.

B Printed Editions

Memoirs of the Life of Colonel Hutchinson, ed. Julius Hutchinson (London, 1806); ed. C. H. Firth (London, 1906); ed. James Sutherland (London, 1973); ed. N. H. Keeble (London, 1995).
On the Principles of the Christian Religion, Addressed to her Daughter; and On Theology (London, 1817).
Lucy Hutchinson's Translation of Lucretius: De rerum natura, ed. Hugh de Quehen (London, 1996).
'Elegies', in David Norbrook, 'Lucy Hutchinson's "Elegies" and the Situation of the Republican Woman Writer', *English Literary Renaissance*, 27 (1997), 468–521 (487–521).
'To M:ʳ Waller upon his Panegirique to the Lord Protector', in David Norbrook, 'Lucy Hutchinson versus Edmund Waller: An Unpublished Reply to Waller's *A Panegyrick to my Lord Protector*', *The Seventeenth Century*, 11 (1996), 61–86.

References and Further Reading

Achinstein	Sharon Achinstein, *Poetics of Dissent* (forthcoming).
Ainsworth	Henry Ainsworth, *Annotations upon the First Book of Moses* (n. pl., 1616).
Alter	Robert Alter, *Genesis: Translation and Commentary* (New York and London, 1996).
Ashcraft	Richard Ashcraft, *Revolutionary Politics and Locke's Two Treatises of Government* (Princeton, 1986).
Ashton	H. Ashton, *Du Bartas en Angleterre* (Paris, 1908).
Bach	Alice Bach (ed.), *Women in the Hebrew Bible: A Reader* (New York and London, 1999).
Barash	Carol Barash, *English Women's Poetry, 1649–1714: Politics, Community, and Linguistic Authority* (Oxford, 1996).
Barbour 1994	Reid Barbour, 'Between Atoms and the Spirit: Lucy Hutchinson's Translation of Lucretius', *Renaissance Papers* (1994), 1–16.

Barbour 1997	Reid Barbour, 'Lucy Hutchinson, Atomism, and the Atheist Dog', in Lynette Hunter and Sarah Hutton (eds), *Women, Science and Medicine 1500–1700* (Stroud, 1997), pp. 122–37.
Barbour 1998	Reid Barbour, *English Epicures and Stoics: Ancient Legacies in Early Stuart Culture* (Amherst, 1998).
Beaumont	*The Complete Poems of Dr. Joseph Beaumont*, ed. A. B. Grosart, 2 vols (Edinburgh, 1880).
Bennett and Mandelbrote	Jim Bennett and Scott Mandelbrote, *The Garden, the Ark, the Tower, the Temple: Biblical Metaphors of Knowledge in Early Modern Europe* (Oxford, 1998).
Bloom	*The Book of J*, translated by David Rosenberg, interpreted by Harold Bloom (New York, 1990).
Braund	Elizabeth Braund, 'Mrs Hutchinson and her Teaching', *Evangelical Quarterly*, 31 (1959), 72–81.
Brenner	Athalya Brenner (ed.), *A Feminist Companion to Genesis* (Sheffield, 1993).
Bunyan	John Bunyan, *An Exposition on the Ten First Chapters of Genesis*, in *The Miscellaneous Works of John Bunyan*, XI, ed. W. R. Owens (Oxford, 1994), pp. 95–277.
Burrows and Craig	John Burrows and Hugh Craig, '"Among the untrodden ways": Lucy Hutchinson and the Authorship of Two Seventeenth-century Poems', *The Seventeenth Century* (forthcoming).
Calvin	John Calvin, *Genesis*, trans. and ed. John King, 2 vols in 1 (Edinburgh, 1965).
Cavendish	Margaret Cavendish, Duchess of Newcastle, *The Description of a New World Called the Blazing World and Other Writings*, ed. Kate Lilley (London, 1992).
Chambers	A. B. Chambers, '"I was but an Inverted Tree"', *Studies in the Renaissance*, 8 (1961), 291–9.
CPW	*The Complete Prose Works of John Milton*, ed. Don M. Wolfe et al., 8 vols in 10 (New Haven, 1953–82).
Crawford	Patricia Crawford, *Women and Religion in England, 1500–1720* (London and New York, 1993).
Danielson	Dennis Danielson, *Milton's Good God: A Study in Literary Theodicy* (Cambridge, 1982).
De Krey	Gary De Krey, 'Rethinking the Restoration: Dissenting Cases for Conscience, 1667–1672', *Historical Journal*, 38 (1995), 53–83.
Dutch Annotations	Theodore Haak (trans.), *The Dutch Annotations upon the Whole Bible* (1637; London, 1657).
DWW	Guillaume de Saluste, Sieur du Bartas, *The Divine Weeks*

	and Works . . . translated by Josuah Sylvester, ed. Susan Snyder, 2 vols (Oxford, 1979).
'Elegies'	Lucy Hutchinson, 'Elegies', in David Norbrook, 'Lucy Hutchinson's "Elegies" and the Situation of the Republican Woman Writer', *English Literary Renaissance*, 27 (1997), 468–521 (487–521).
Ezell 1987	Margaret J. M. Ezell, *The Patriarch's Wife: Literary Evidence and the History of the Family* (Chapel Hill and London, 1987).
Ezell 1993	Margaret J. M. Ezell, *Writing Women's Literary History* (Baltimore and London, 1993).
Fallon	Stephen M. Fallon, '"Elect above the Rest": Theology as Self-Representation in Milton', in Stephen B. Dobranski and John P. Rumrich (eds), *Milton and Heresy* (Cambridge, 1998), pp. 93–116.
Farley-Hills	David Farley-Hills (ed.), *Rochester: The Critical Heritage* (London, 1972).
Fea	Allan Fea, *King Monmouth: Being a History of the Career of James Scott 'The Protestant Duke' 1649–1685* (London and New York, 1902).
Filmer	Sir Robert Filmer, *Patriarcha and Other Writings*, ed. Johann P. Sommerville (Cambridge, 1991).
Firth	Lucy Hutchinson, *Memoirs of the Life of Colonel Hutchinson*, ed. C. H. Firth (London, 1906).
Fokkelman	J. P. Fokkelman, 'Genesis', in Robert Alter and Frank Kermode (eds), *The Literary Guide to the Bible* (London, 1987), pp. 36–55.
Garman et al.	Mary Garman, Judith Applegate, Margaret Benefiel and Dortha Meredith (eds), *Hidden in Plain Sight: Quaker Women's Writings 1650–1700* (Wallingford, PA, 1996).
Gössman	Elisabeth Gössman, 'History of Biblical Interpretation by European Women', in Elisabeth Schüssler Fiorenza (ed.), *Searching the Scriptures, Vol. 1: A Feminist Introduction* (New York, 1993), pp. 27–40.
Graham	Elspeth Graham, Hilary Hinds, Elaine Hobby and Helen Wilcox (eds), *Her Own Life: Autobiographical Writings by Seventeenth-century Englishwomen* (London and New York, 1989).
Greaves	Richard L. Greaves, *Deliver us from Evil: The Radical Underground in Britain, 1660–1663* (New York and London, 1986).
Greer et al.	Germaine Greer, Jesyln Medoff, Melinda Sansone and Susan Hastings (eds), *Kissing the Rod: An Anthology of Seventeenth-century Women's Verse* (London, 1988).

Hardie Philip Hardie, 'The Presence of Lucretius in *Paradise Lost*', *Milton Quarterly*, 29 (1995), 13–24.

Harris et al. Tim Harris, Paul Seaward and Mark Goldie (eds), *The Politics of Religion in Restoration England* (Oxford, 1990).

Hill 1984 Christopher Hill, *The Experience of Defeat: Milton and Some Contemporaries* (London, 1984).

Hill 1993 Christopher Hill, *The English Bible and the Seventeenth-century Revolution* (London, 1993).

Hinds Hilary Hinds, *God's Englishwomen: Seventeenth-century Radical Sectarian Writing and Feminist Criticism* (Manchester and New York, 1996).

Hobby Elaine Hobby, *Virtue of Necessity: English Women's Writing, 1649–88* (London, 1988).

Hughes Ann Hughes, 'Gender and Politics in Leveller Literature', in S. Amussen and M. Kishlansky (eds), *Political Culture and Cultural Politics in Early Modern England* (Manchester, 1995).

Hutchinson, Waller 'To M.ʳ Waller upon his Panegirique to the Lord Protector', in David Norbrook, 'Lucy Hutchinson versus Edmund Waller: An Unpublished Reply to Waller's *A Panegyrick to my Lord Protector*', *The Seventeenth Century*, 11 (1996), 61–86.

Interpreter's George Arthur Buttrick et al. (eds), *The Interpreter's Bible*, 12 vols (New York and Nashville, 1952–7).

Jablonski Stephen K. Jablonski, 'Ham's Vicious Race: Slavery and John Milton', *Studies in English Literature, 1500–1900*, 27 (1997), 173–90.

Jeansonne Sharon Pace Jeansonne, *The Women of Genesis: From Sarah to Potiphar's Wife* (Minneapolis, 1990).

Keeble 1987 N. H. Keeble, *The Literary Culture of Nonconformity in Later Seventeenth-century England* (Leicester, 1987).

Keeble 1990 N. H. Keeble, '"But the Colonel's Shadow": Lucy Hutchinson, Women's Writing, and the Civil War', in Thomas Healy and Jonathan Sawday (eds), *Literature and the English Civil War* (Cambridge, 1990), pp. 227–47.

Knoppers Laura Lunger Knoppers, *Historicizing Milton: Spectacle, Power, and Poetry in Restoration England* (Athens, GA, and London, 1994).

Kugel James L. Kugel, *The Idea of Biblical Poetry: Parallelism and its History* (Baltimore and London, 1981).

L *Lucy Hutchinson's Translation of Lucretius: De rerum natura*, ed. Hugh de Quehen (London, 1996).

Lacey Douglas R. Lacey, *Dissent and Parliamentary Politics in England 1661–1689: A Study in the Perpetuation and Tem-*

	pering of Parliamentarianism (New Brunswick, 1969).
Leonard	John Leonard, *Naming in Paradise: Milton and the Language of Adam and Eve* (Oxford, 1990).
Lewalski 1985	Barbara Kiefer Lewalski, *'Paradise Lost' and the Rhetoric of Literary Forms* (Princeton, 1985).
Lewalski 1993	Barbara Kiefer Lewalski, *Writing Women in Jacobean England* (Cambridge, MA, 1993).
Locke	John Locke, *Two Treatises of Government*, ed. Peter Laslett (Cambridge, 1988).
Lods	Adolphe Lods, *Jean Astruc et la critique biblique au XVIIIe siècle* (Strasbourg and Paris, 1924).
Love	Harold Love, *Scribal Publication in Seventeenth-century England* (Oxford, 1993).
Ludlow	Edmund Ludlow, 'A Voyce from the Watch Tower', Bodleian Library, Oxford, MS Eng. hist. c. 487.
M	Lucy Hutchinson, *Memoirs of the Life of Colonel Hutchinson*, ed. Neil Keeble (London, 1995).
MacGillivray	Royce MacGillivray, *Restoration Historians and the English Civil War* (The Hague, 1974).
Mack	Phyllis Mack, *Visionary Women: Ecstatic Prophecy in Seventeenth-century England* (Berkeley, Los Angeles and Oxford, 1992).
McKeon	Michael McKeon, *Politics and Poetry in Restoration England: The Case of Dryden's 'Annus Mirabilis'* (Cambridge, MA, 1975).
Mendelson and Crawford	Sara Mendelson and Patricia Crawford, *Women in Early Modern England* (Oxford, 1998).
Moore	C. A. Moore, 'Miltoniana (1679–1741)', *Modern Philology*, 24 (1927), 321–39.
MS	'Genesis Chap. 1st. Canto 1st.' ['Order and Disorder']: Beinecke Rare Book and Manuscript Library, Yale University, Osborn Collection fb 100.
Narveson	Katherine Narveson, 'The Sources for Lucy Hutchinson's *On Theology*', *Notes and Queries*, N.S. 36 (1989), 40–1.
Norbrook 1996	David Norbrook, 'Lucy Hutchinson versus Edmund Waller: An Unpublished Reply to Waller's *A Panegyrick to my Lord Protector*', *The Seventeenth Century*, 11 (1996), 61–86.
Norbrook 1999a	David Norbrook, *Writing the English Republic: Poetry, Rhetoric and Politics 1627–1660* (Cambridge, 1999).
Norbrook 1999b	David Norbrook, '"A devine Originall": Lucy Hutchinson and the "woman's version"', *Times Literary Supplement*, 19 March 1999, 13–15.
Norbrook 2000a	David Norbrook, 'Lucy Hutchinson and *Order and*

	Disorder: The Manuscript Evidence', *English Manuscript Studies 1100–1700*, 9 (2000), 257–91.
Norbrook 2000b	David Norbrook, 'Historiography', in N. H. Keeble (ed.), *The Cambridge Companion to the Literature of the English Revolution* (Cambridge, 2000).
Norbrook 2000c	David Norbrook, 'Memoirs of the Life of Colonel Hutchinson', in David Womersley (ed.), *The Blackwell Companion to Literature from Milton to Blake* (Oxford, 2000).
Norbrook, forthcoming	David Norbrook, 'Margaret Cavendish and Lucy Hutchinson: Identity, Ideology and Politics', *In-Between* (forthcoming).
Norton	David Norton, *A History of the Bible as Literature*, 2 vols (Cambridge, 1993).
Nuttall	Geoffrey F. Nuttall, *The Holy Spirit in Human Faith and Experience*, 2nd edition, introduction by Peter Lake (Chicago and London, 1992).
Nyquist	Mary Nyquist, 'The Genesis of Gendered Subjectivity in the Divorce Tracts and in *Paradise Lost*', in Mary Nyquist and Margaret W. Ferguson (eds), *Re-membering Milton: Essays on the Texts and Traditions* (London and New York, 1987), pp. 99–127.
OED	*Oxford English Dictionary*.
Owen, *Works*	*The Works of John Owen*, ed. W. H. Goold, 24 vols (London and Edinburgh, 1850–3).
PL	John Milton, *Paradise Lost*, ed. Alastair Fowler, 2nd edition (London and New York, 1998).
R	Lucy Hutchinson, 'On the Principles of the Christian Religion', in *On the Principles of the Christian Religion, Addressed to her Daughter; and On Theology* (London, 1817).
Sandys	George Sandys, *A Paraphrase upon the Divine Poems* (London, 1638).
Schwartz	Regina M. Schwartz, *The Curse of Cain: The Violent Legacy of Monotheism* (Chicago and London, 1997).
Scott	Jonathan Scott, *Algernon Sidney and the Restoration Crisis, 1677–1683* (Cambridge, 1991).
Shawcross	John T. Shawcross, *Milton: A Bibliography for the Years 1624–1700* (Binghamton, 1984).
Sidney	Algernon Sidney, *Discourses Concerning Government*, ed. Thomas G. West (Indianapolis, 1990).
Smith and Cardinale	Hilda L. Smith and Susan Cardinale, *Women and the Literature of the Seventeenth Century: An Annotated Bibliography* (New York, Westport and London, 1990).

Sutherland   Lucy Hutchinson, *Memoirs of the Life of Colonel Hutchinson*, ed. James Sutherland (London, 1973).

T   Lucy Hutchinson, 'On Theology' (translation from John Owen, *Theologoumena Pantodapa*), in *On the Principles of the Christian Religion, Addressed to her Daughter; and On Theology* (London, 1817).

Taylor   George Coffin Taylor, *Milton's Use of Du Bartas* (Cambridge, MA, 1934).

Thomas   Keith Thomas, *Man and the Natural World: Changing Attitudes in England 1500–1800* (London, 1983).

Toon   Peter Toon, *God's Statesman: The Life and Work of John Owen* (Exeter, 1971).

Tyacke   Nicholas R. Tyacke, 'Puritanism, Arminianism, and Counter-Revolution', in Conrad Russell (ed.), *The Origins of the English Civil War* (London, 1973), pp. 119–43.

von Maltzahn   Nicholas von Maltzahn, 'The First Reception of *Paradise Lost* (1667)', *Review of English Studies*, 47 (1996), 479–99.

Wallace   Dewey D. Wallace, Jr, *Puritans and Predestination: Grace in English Protestant Theology, 1525–1695* (Chapel Hill, 1982).

West   Robert H. West, *Milton and the Angels* (Athens, GA, 1955).

*Westminster   Annotations upon all the Books of the Old and New Testa-
Annotations*   ment* (London, 1657).

Wharton   *The Surviving Works of Anne Wharton*, ed. G. Greer and S. Hastings (Stump Cross, 1997).

Whately   William Whately, *Prototypes, or, The Primarie Precedents out of the Book Of Genesis* (London, 1640).

Wilcox   Helen Wilcox (ed.), *Women and Literature in Britain 1500–1700* (Cambridge, 1996).

Willet   Andrew Willet, *Hexapla in Genesin* (London, 1605).

Williams   Arnold Williams, *The Common Expositor: An Account of the Commentaries on Genesis 1527–1633* (Chapel Hill, 1948).

Wittreich   Joseph Wittreich, 'Milton's Transgressive Maneuvers: Receptions (Then and Now) and the Sexual Politics of *Paradise Lost*', in Stephen Dobranski and John Rumrich (eds), *Milton and Heresy* (Cambridge, 1998), pp. 244–66.

Worden   Edmund Ludlow, *A Voyce from the Watch Tower. Part Five: 1660–1662*, ed. A. B. Worden, Camden Fourth Series 21 (London, 1978).